INDIA
BRIEFING

Asia
Society

The Asia Society is a nonprofit, nonpartisan public education organization dedicated to increasing American understanding of Asia and broadening the dialogue between Americans and Asians. Through its programs in policy and business, the fine and performing arts, and elementary and secondary education, the Society reaches audiences across the United States and works closely with colleagues in Asia.

The views expressed in this publication are those of the individual contributors.

INDIA BRIEFING

A Transformative Fifty Years

Marshall Bouton
Philip Oldenburg
Editors

Published in Cooperation with the Asia Society
Mai Shaikhanuar-Cota, Series Editor

An East Gate Book

M.E.Sharpe
Armonk, New York
London, England

An East Gate Book

Copyright © 1999 by the Asia Society

Library of Congress ISSN: 0894-5136
ISBN 0-7656-0338-1 (hardcover)
ISBN 0-7656-0339-X (paperback)

Printed in the United States of America

The paper used in this publication meets the minimum requirements of
American National Standard for Information Sciences—
Permanence of Paper for Printed Library Materials,
ANSI Z 39.48-1984.

BM (c) 10   9   8   7   6   5   4   3   2   1
BM (p) 10   9   8   7   6   5   4   3   2   1

Contents

Preface

This edition of *India Briefing* was conceived during the fiftieth anniversary year of India's independence. Like previous editions, it attempts a wide-ranging assessment of Indian affairs. But unlike any previous *India Briefing*, this volume has as its timeframe not just the recent past, but the entire period of India's independent nationhood. The chapter authors were asked to trace and interpret India's politics, society, economy, foreign relations, and culture over the last fifty years. At this historical juncture, the editors also thought it appropriate to commission a special essay on the uses of history in Indian public life. The contributors were not asked necessarily to be comprehensive in their accounts but to focus on those trends and issues that they believe to have been most salient in each of these arenas. They were also invited to draw from their assessment implications for India's future course.

The editors are fortunate to have enlisted six highly qualified individuals to take on such ambitious assignments. They have produced authoritative and insightful essays that help us to think afresh about India's accomplishments and unfinished agenda after a half century of national experimentation. It is neither desirable nor possible in this preface for the editors to summarize such varied and complex analyses. But we would briefly outline four broad views that we believe emerge from the chapters.

First, in contrast to prevailing impressions outside of India, the dominant view in the essays is the pervasiveness of change in India since independence. The chapters on politics, society, and culture outline the highly adaptive transformations in these spheres: progress in extending democracy, reinventing caste, and creating new cultural forms and institutions. The chapters on the economy and foreign policy present a record of far less change, showing that despite significant industrialization, the improvement in the material well-being of the Indian people has fallen far short of the goals set fifty years ago, and India's position in the international community has not improved at all.

Second, the engine of India's transformation has been indigenous

values and social dynamics interacting with new institutions and seeking new outlets. Yogendra Yadav traces the evolution of India's democracy away from elite, Western values and toward an ethos rooted
in India's lower social groups and vernacular idiom. D.L. Sheth argues
that caste is being transformed by political competition and urbanization from a vertical, ritually based hierarchy into a horizontal structure
for social and political mobilization. Kapila Vatsyayan shows us that
Indian cultural expression has traversed the social space created by
industrialization, resulting in new and hybrid forms.

Third, the pace of change is accelerating. India's politics is in the
midst of several historic shifts—the participation of lower groups, coalition politics at the Center, and decentralization—with uncertain outcomes. The political mobilization of backward castes and *dalits* (the
"untouchables") has reached the north Indian heartland with almost
revolutionary force. The spread of mass media is threatening the homogenization and commercialization of cultural forms. Only in the
past decade has India's economy begun to liberalize and be open to the
world, but globalization will force more rapid change in the years
ahead. The end of the Cold War has forced India to embark on a new
foreign policy course, including an overt nuclear weapons capability.

Fourth, the rapidity and breadth of change is posing fresh challenges
even to India's core national principles and institutions. Can India's
existing federal structure accommodate the rising political participation
and demands from below? Will national unity be maintained if the
political process fragments along multiple ethnic, linguistic, and caste
lines? Does the "creolization" of politics threaten effective governance? Is India's democracy capable of delivering the economic
growth and distribution necessary to its ensuring its legitimacy and
stability over time? Can India's public and private economic actors
deal effectively with the economic globalization? How can India best
attain its long-sought place among the world's leading nations in a
fast-changing international system?

It was the editors' wish that this volume raise these and other questions for readers as India enters a second half century of independent
nationhood and the new millennium. We are very grateful to the chapter authors for their insights, hard work, and patience with the extended
process of assembling this special edition of *India Briefing*. We wish
also to thank two Asia Society staff members for their central contributions to the enterprise. Karen Fein helped get the project underway.

Mai Shaikhanuar-Cota deserves special acknowledgment for picking up the project in the middle and gently but persistently shepherding it to completion. Thanks are also due to Patricia Farr for her efforts in shaping the manuscript. Finally, the editors and Asia Society are pleased to continue with this volume their collaboration with Douglas Merwin and his colleagues, Angela Piliouras and Patricia Loo, at M.E. Sharpe.

Marshall M. Bouton
Philip Oldenburg
June 1999

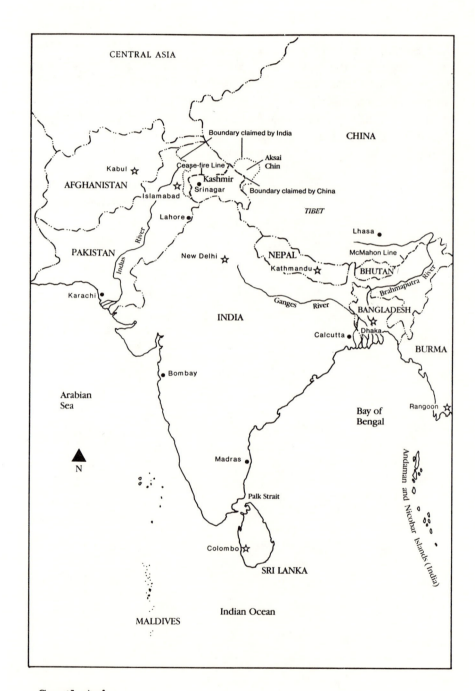

South Asia

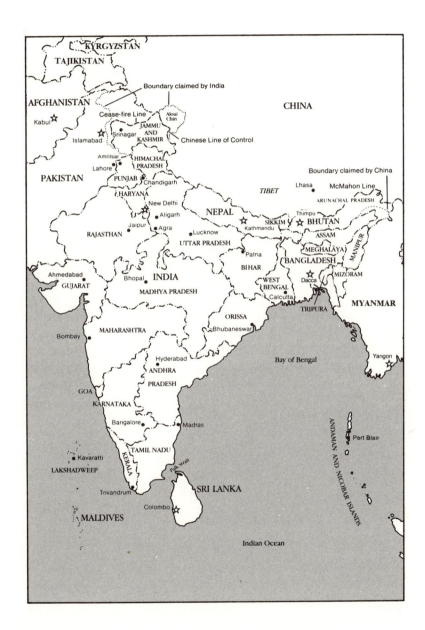

India

INDIA
BRIEFING

Politics

Yogendra Yadav

Two events drew international attention to Indian politics in the year when India officially celebrated the fiftieth anniversary of its independence from the British empire. The first was the outcome of the twelfth general election to the Lok Sabha, the popular chamber of the Indian Parliament, held in March 1998. For the fourth time in succession, it was a "hung" parliament with no single party having a majority. But it was clear that the Bharatiya Janata Party (BJP)—usually described to the foreign audience as a party of right-wing Hindu fundamentalists— and its numerous recently acquired regional allies had done better than others. After years of inching toward it, the BJP had finally come to power at the center. The event was noted even outside India with concern, for it aroused fear that some of the achievements of plural democracy in India would be rolled back. To many, India appeared to be yet another Third World state on the slippery slope of ethnic majoritarian politics.

The second event came soon thereafter. The new and rather shaky BJP government decided to end India's 24-year-old nuclear ambiguity by conducting five nuclear tests in May 1998, declaring that India was a nuclear weapon state, and demanding an entry to the exclusive nu-

Acknowledgments: An early version of this paper was presented at a workshop, *India at Fifty,* organized by the Institute of Commonwealth Studies, London, in May 1997. I would like to thank Professor James Manor for inviting me to this workshop and to thank all the participants for their comments. The libraries of Queen Elizabeth House, the Social Sciences Faculty, and Nuffield College, all at Oxford, provided congenial settings and useful references. Rita and Donald Cruise O'Brien's "Gift to Indian Democracy" was an invaluable asset. Some fragments of this paper were carried in the *Hindu* and in *Seminar.* I owe special thanks to Rajni Kothari and Alfred Stepan for reading an earlier draft, Sudipta Kaviraj and Sunil Khilnani for their valuable comments on its presentation, and Philip Oldenburg for being amazingly meticulous, patient, generous, and demanding, all at the same time.

clear club. The club was not amused, and a spate of economic sanctions and abuses followed. "Just when you thought the world was safe ... India's Nukes," proclaimed the cover story of *Time* magazine, depicting India as a rogue state. Friends of India bemoaned the fact that India had decided to go against the current of history. The fact that the tests enjoyed considerable popular support in the country strengthened doubts about the future of India as a moderate liberal democracy.

These two events probably were not the two most significant landmarks in the history of Indian politics. They were certainly not the events most representative of the larger trends of democratic transition in the 1990s. Yet the logic of short attention spans reserved for countries like India ensures that, for a long time to come, the "global" image of Indian democracy will be formed by the television footage associated with these two events. In the current international information (dis)order, democracies outside the first world are routinely judged by norms drawn from the history and the present contingencies of democracies in the West. From its inception, Indian democracy has had to respond to an agenda that bears only a tangential relationship to its inner trajectory and has had to account for its life in a register kept to write someone else's history. A fair assessment of India's democratic experience must, therefore, be anchored in an understanding of the Indian model of democratization in its specificity. I begin by describing that model. I then map how it fared in what I see as the three phases of India's democratic politics. Finally, I come back to a synoptic assessment of its success, its distortions, its inherent weaknesses, and the challenges that confront it.

The Indian Model

Fifty years ago when India began its journey, it was easier to describe the destination and the route, for the privilege of describing these lay without much contestation with a small section of India's westernized elite. All of them did not think alike, but their differences were not unbounded. There was significant overlap of the various ideologies and social contexts. The model of Indian democracy was founded on that consensus. Since then, the number of those who wish to participate in the process of defining the Indian model has increased phenomenally, thanks, no doubt, to the success of the processes initiated by the original inheritors of the legacy of the British Raj. Moreover, our awareness of the complexities of mass ideologies and the crooked logic of collective action has rendered the question of the meaning of the Indian model less amenable to a confident answer.

At first sight, the initial design of the Indian democratic enterprise might not look original at all. Many of the attempts to articulate the vision of democracy in an independent India appear to result from a desire to imitate the experience of liberal democracy in the West. The speeches and the writings of the nationalist leadership and the debates of the Constituent Assembly are full of fond references to democracies in the West. Indeed, the basic design of the Indian Constitution was consciously borrowed from the European and the American traditions. The parliamentary system governing the relationship between the executive and the legislature; the federal structure for governing the interaction between the center and the states; the idea of fundamental rights; an independent judiciary to safeguard those rights; and the constitution itself—all would sound familiar to students of the constitutional history of the West. A large number of the provisions of the constitution retained verbatim the corresponding provisions in the Government of India Act of 1935, the political design set by the colonial masters.

Yet, the Indian Constitution was not a simple imitation of the British model or of any existing constitution, for no attempt at copying can be free of some modification. Elements picked up from various Western models—such as the parliamentary system from Britain, the judicial system and the Bill of Rights from the United States, the Directive Principles from Ireland—were combined in a unique mix. Besides, various specifically Indian elements were introduced by way of "redefinition" of some of the familiar Western ideas and institutions. Community as much as the individual was acknowledged as a basis of citizenship in the affirmative action policies of the state. Secularism was redefined in a specifically Indian manner. These and many other examples demonstrate that creativity in the garb of imitation has been the preferred mode of political innovation in modern India. Right from the beginning, the Indian model of democracy involved selective usage and subtle adaptation of the language of modern liberal democracy.

The constitution, however, was not the main aspect of India's innovative path to democratization. The essence of that path lies in the unwritten political model that has informed the practice of democracy over the last five decades. The Indian model, as its most shrewd interpreter Rajni Kothari argued in his magnum opus, *Politics in India*, involved the *primacy* of the political and a redefinition of the *boundaries* of the political. Politics was not just one of the areas that the Indian elite sought to transform; it was at the heart of India's tryst with modernity. In a bold move that broke from the political models available at that time, the Indian elite chose to pursue multiple goals simultaneously: to make democracy work, to create a single political community in a large and diverse society, to pursue Western-style economic development, and to bring about fundamental changes in society.

They opted for political democracy, more specifically the constitutional-representative-democratic-republican form of government, in a society that lacked any historic precedent of such governance at the scale they confronted. By opting for democracy, they also made themselves subject to radical egalitarian expectations of a political community of equals, a community in which the people were self-ruling. Some of them realized that this was a distant ideal from the form of government they had established.

The second goal was built into the first: the survival of democracy in the face of the amazing diversities that defined India required the creation of a single political community across the recently acquired political boundaries of the Indian state. The lessons of the partition of territory between India and Pakistan were too painful a reminder of the need for what was then called "national integration" and later "nation building." The creation of a modern public sphere required bringing together a huge number of communities that have had little to do with each other. The modern public sphere also provided the resources for meeting this requirement.

In the realm of the economy, the Indian elite opted for Western-style development in the hope that the path to development would be open to anyone who cared to step in. They may not have hoped for a miraculous entry to the world of consumer goods for everyone, but they did expect substantial and speedy economic growth in aggregate terms. Their economic goals included a reduction in the historical gap between India and the developed world and a substantial trickle down of the gains of economic growth to the worst-off.

Finally, the Indian elite aimed at bringing about fundamental changes in the structure of the society they had inherited. Even those who did not share the radical desire for the abolition of the traditional social hierarchy and its inequities looked forward to mitigating the worst effects of the caste system. At any rate, the goal of social modernization that would transform the traditional, "parochial" beliefs of the masses into modern, "cosmopolitan" values was widely shared.

Democracy was not just one of the goals; it was also the principal instrument of realizing all the goals simultaneously. The power of a modern state, the mobilizing capacity of universal adult franchise, the dynamics of competitive politics, the firm grip of a system of political institutions, and the vision of an enlightened elite were the main elements in the politics-centered approach to modernization adopted by India. The colonial state had expanded considerably the boundaries of the political and had annexed for politics the crucial privilege of deciding the boundaries of the political. The nationalist movement expanded the political domain further by including within it various social and economic issues that the colonial power had avoided. The modern Indian state was to exercise power over this wide arena and bring about the social transformation necessary to the realization of the fourfold goal mentioned above. Its reach was to be made effective by a wide range of bureaucratic apparatuses, while the constitutional institutions would ensure that the game was played according to the rules. The introduction of the universal adult franchise was meant to draw a hitherto unprecedented number of participants into the game of governance as well as to secure their acceptance of its outcome. Open electoral competition was the dynamo expected to harness the energy of the political actors, while political parties were to channel this energy toward creative political change. The enlightened political elite was supposed to steer the way, keeping its gaze fixed on the larger, if distant, goals.

All this was not spelled out anywhere, at least not in the formal text of the constitution. When we look back from a distance of fifty years, it is easy to read a clear design in what must have been a mix of prudent judgments, half-examined convictions, and sheer hope. The above formulation of the "Indian model" draws heavily upon Rajni Kothari's subtle interpretation of the working of democratic politics in the first two decades of independence. Kothari insisted that the historical trajectory of Indian politics must be assessed against this "model." In arguing that the Indian model should be the starting point of the discussion, he had already parted company with the then-dominant mode of thinking about democracy in non-Western societies. Cast in a somewhat simplistic universal framework of modernization, the dominant approach measured political development by the extent to which a traditional society had come to resemble the political system of the advanced societies of the West. Western democratic theory has changed considerably since then, but the checklist approach to democracy that expects non-European societies to take the same route as the West still persists. To that extent, the approach implicit in Kothari's work still provides a useful starting point for any attempt to assess the experience of the last fifty years.

At least some of the designers of this Indian model were acutely conscious of the fact that they were stepping into uncharted territory, that they were attempting something for which there was no precedent. The Indian elite had already done to the received Western models of democracy what the Indian masses were to do to the elite's own model. By selective adoption and adaptation, they had already begun the creolization of the idea of democracy, a process that was to have profound historical implications.

The Story of India's Democracy

Establishment of democracy was an invitation by the Indian elite to ordinary Indians to join them in playing a new game. It is true that the invitation must not have come as a surprise to keen observers of nationalist politics in the decades prior to independence. In opposing British rule, the nationalist leaders drew upon the most progressive strands of modern European thinking. It is no wonder that democracy was an article of faith for them. Besides, the last two decades before independence were marked by intensification of popular movements that gave rise to expectations of self-rule among the lower orders of society. All this left a very narrow range of options for the Indian elite when it came to choosing the form of government. Yet those options were more than is realized now. Pakistan's choice of what in effect was a viceroy system illustrates the range of options open then. The establishment of democracy in India was undoubtedly a bold invitation, for the rules and the possible consequences of this game were not entirely clear to the elite, and more important, they did not know the players they had invited to join very well.

The history of Indian politics since independence is the story of how the Indians accepted the invitation and discovered this new game, at first with hesitation and amusement and then with a fierce obsession. It is a history of what this encounter did to them and to the game itself. What happened afterward is not difficult to understand. After the initial unease, the guests felt at home in their new setting and then changed the rules to suit their taste. For the first few years, everyone felt guilty about demanding that language be the basis of political reorganization of the federal map of India, but very soon it became an indisputable principle. The invited players now turned their backs on the hosts and started enjoying themselves. The game was different now. It took on a life of its own and was played for purposes substantially at variance with the intentions of the original hosts. Devi Lal, the farmer leader from Haryana and the deputy prime minister during 1989–90, was frank enough to admit in a press conference that he had not read the election manifesto of his party. Although not everyone had read, or even cared about, their party manifesto in the past, decades ago this admission would have been a major political scandal. That this news appeared as no more than a small diary item indicated the sea change in India's political culture. It indicated that the consequences of the game of democracy were turning out to be radically different from what anyone had intended or anticipated, presenting a new set of opportunities and constraints for which there were no well-known precedents in the history of democracy in the West.

It is a comment on the imaginative charms of the original model that Indian politics is still understood as a series of deviations from it and that every deviation is seen as a sign of decline and disorder. This tendency contributes to the predominant way of telling the story of Indian politics. It goes something like this: The first decade and a half were a golden period when a charming prince called Jawaharlal Nehru ruled this country. His rule saw economic growth, rule of law, political institutionalization, secular policy, and a farsighted foreign policy. His death in 1964 was followed by a steady and then rapid decline during the reign of his progeny, real and otherwise. The reign of his daughter, Indira Gandhi, was characterized by institutional decay, a growing authoritarian streak, intolerance toward ethnic minorities, and the beginning of an aggressive and narrow foreign policy. Finally, in the third phase, local chieftains and thugs took over, leading to complete chaos and continuous crises. The democratic institutions are in tumult, regional powers have gained at the expense of the national parties, and sectional demands and exclusivist politics dominate the political agenda. The rise of the BJP to power, in tandem with the latest series of nuclear explosions, in a sense completes the story of an impending political crisis, of a dream lost.

The storyline is simple but powerful. Like all stories of its kind, it has the power to give meaning to any event, big or small, and to serve as a yardstick that distinguishes normalcy from deviation. Like all stories, it looks at things from one vantage point and whispers a moral in our ears. Thanks to its charms and the English-speaking upper-caste origins of those who publicly articulate ideas about Indian democracy, this narrative continues to dominate the imagination of all the political analysts, academic or otherwise. Implicit in this dominant story of Indian democracy, or for that matter in contemporary democratic theory, is what may be called a "hardware" approach to democracy: democracy is above all an institutional mechanism that can be made to work properly in any setting, given the right conditions of installation.

I think the story of Indian democracy can be told differently. In fact, the challenge of understanding India at fifty requires that we tell this story differently. It requires that we treat democracy like a language or a software that cannot even begin to work without the establishment of a firm protocol of shared symbols with its users. If it is to have a life, democracy must exist in and through the minds of ordinary people; it must learn to work its way through the beliefs and values they happen to have. We must change our approach, for the "palace-eye-view" of politics has hidden from us for far too long the story of popular opposition to designs imposed from above, of the participatory upsurge of the lower orders of society, and of the less-known attempts to weave dreams of social emancipation in the language of modern democracy. It is crucial to contest the dominant story, for its moral is deeply, if subtly, antipolitical.

India's Democratic Politics

The First Phase: The Congress System

The first phase, the famous "Congress system" of the 1950s and 1960s, was characterized by a wide gulf that separated the assumptions of all-powerful westernized elite from popular beliefs. In this period, the Indian National Congress, the party that led the national movement, dominated the political scene: it won all the national and practically all the state-level elections. India was undoubtedly a democracy, for the rulers were being elected by the people in a system of open and fair competition among different political parties. But in the realm of ideas, it hardly respected the democratic principle of equal respect. "Guided Democracy" was a euphemism used by leaders like Mohammed Ayyub of Pakistan and Sukarno of Indonesia to describe their versions of semiauthoritarian regimes in the postcolonial setting. That, of course, did not apply to the decision-making structure of Indian democracy. But in terms of ideas, Indian democracy was firmly guided in the first phase.

The democratic invitation, which meant an invitation to participate in the new spectacle of elections, was accepted by an ever-growing number. The turnout jumped from 46 percent in the first general election, in 1952, to 55 percent in the third election, in 1962, and to 61 percent in the fourth one, in 1967. The new entrants had begun to defeat the English-speaking inhabitants of the Indian state with serious political consequences. The idea of "linguistic states" was forced down Nehru's throat in the mid-1950s. Charan Singh, the farmer leader from Uttar Pradesh, successfully defied Nehru's proposal for Soviet-style cooperative farming.

Yet the structure of the game basically followed the rules set by the hosts. There were deviations and distortions. The inquiry against Pratap Singh Kairon, Nehru's favorite chieftain in the Punjab, revealed the extent to which corruption had already been institutionalized. But on balance the game was manageable, or at least recognizable. The first Backward Classes Commission recommended reservations on caste basis, but its chairman Kaka Kalelkar bent over backward to ensure that its recommendations were not implemented. The matter could be silently buried in the parliamentary records. There was no dearth of political opposition to the Congress rule. There were the Socialists and the Communists as well as the right-wing opposition parties. The Communists actually managed to come to power in 1957 in the state of Kerala, which was the first time a Communist party anywhere in the world won a democratic mandate and the first time the central government of India shamelessly dismissed a legitimately elected government in a state. But, barring some followers of Gandhi and of the indigenous socialism advocated by Ram Manohar Lohia, there was little challenge to the vision of democracy shared by India's English-speaking elite.

Nehru's schoolteacher-like mannerisms symbolized the didactic relationship between the political elite and ordinary people in this first phase. If we focus on the flow of ideas, it was clearly a one-way traffic. Ordinary citizens were autonomous in this realm only to the extent to which they misunderstood, deliberately or otherwise, the ideas they received from above—a dubious privilege that lower orders of society have enjoyed throughout history. From a certain vantage point, it was a fairly satisfactory state of affairs. If you were born in the right kind of family, took care to keep away from the heat and dust of this country, and took a telescopic view of things, Indian democracy could appear very much like an authentic or at least a "developing" liberal democracy.

The insulation of democracy from popular beliefs gave it a certain breathing space, an initial settling-in period for the new set of institutions. The legacy of nationalism meant that the new regime enjoyed a high level of popular legitimacy even if the people did not quite understand what they were supporting. Thanks to these favorable conditions, the modern Indian state not only inherited the powers of the colonial state but could also expand considerably the scope of its activities to cover what was regarded earlier as the private or the societal domain. Rather than being dictated by the relations of production, politics was very much in a position to fundamentally alter property relations. In the first decade after independence, the Indian government passed a series of land reform laws aimed at changing the pattern of land ownership. There already was, to be sure, microlevel collusion of the politically powerful with the dominant economic interests, but there were very few overt macro- or structural-economic limits to politics. Thus the smooth transfer of power in 1947 brought into existence something that appears as an astonishing accomplishment in retrospect. Without much fuss, it signaled the beginning of an era of centrality of politics in the public sphere. It is amazing to see the extraordinary power modern political agencies have come to occupy in a society that was characterized by the absence of a political center, where politics was heretofore a limited and self-limiting activity. A future historian might remember these fifty years not for the more noticeable political events but for the creation of the space in which these events took place.

Behind this appearance, however, the content had already begun to change. If one takes cognizance of what the actors thought they were doing, rather than going by an external description of their behavior, it is clear that a new and unfamiliar life was being infused into the formal structures of liberal democracy. The few field studies of local politics and the fictional accounts available through contemporary literature in the Indian languages provide sufficient proof that patron-client networks and systems of reward distribution were already in place in the first decade after independence. And what is worse, most of these were based on criteria other than those of which liberal democracy could approve. Competitive politics had already formed linkages with the preexisting social divisions. Caste acquired a new salience in political mobilization. This development, initially condemned as casteism in politics but later theorized as the politicization of caste, was to have enduring effects both on democracy and on the institution of caste.

The fact that the basic building blocks of competitive politics in India are not individuals or groups based on ideas and interests but communities based on birth has been something of a scandal in the eyes of commentators, analysts, and some elite practitioners of Indian politics, irrespective of their ideological preferences. It has been interpreted as the Indian corruption of the ideal of liberal democracy. This sense of shame informs the dominant story of Indian politics. It may not be out of place here to remember that this gap between the self-image and the reality of liberal democracy is not specific to India. A comparison, for example, with the history of democracy in the United States in the nineteenth century shows that this gap lies at the very heart of the practice of liberal democracy. The problem is not that real life has failed to live up to theoretical ideals, but that theory has failed to take into account the nuances of real life. A more sensitive theory would have noticed that this gap may have actually helped the growth of democracy, for its articulation through the preexisting social divisions helped competitive politics take firm root in the society and assume something like an organic growth. A closer look at the interaction between caste and politics would have shown that the basic building blocks were never really the product of "primordial loyalties." Before becoming the basis of politics, units such as caste or community underwent a secular process of packaging in which interest, and to some extent ideology, mattered as much as they did anywhere else.

The workings of the famous "Congress system" in the first phase should be viewed in this context. The one-party-dominance system, in which both the governmental and the effective oppositional roles were performed by the different factions of the Congress, served as a nursery of the multiparty system. There was very little ideological polarization, except on the very extremes of the political spectrum, as the Congress occupied a wide range of middle positions through which different interests could be articulated. At the macro level the diverse character of the Congress ensured that its support was evenly spread across different sections of society, a feature mirrored by its major opponents. The composition of the political elite was heavily biased in favor of the upper caste, the upper class, and the English-educated.

Occasionally the game threatened to break down, for popular beliefs refused to be tamed, at least on some questions. One such question proved to be that of the "linguistic states." The British division of the country into administrative subunits has not respected the natural cultural divisions. At the time of independence, the Indian rulers kept those divisions more or less intact, despite the fact that more than two decades earlier, Gandhi had already reorganized the Congress Party on the principle of the linguistic state. The resultant resentment formed the basis of the first organized political movement in a large number of states for redrawing the federal units on the basis of language. After initial reluctance based on the typical secular suspicion of such "primordial" sentiments, Nehru conceded the demand by setting up the States Reorganization Commission and accepting its recommendations in most cases. Skillful political handling routinized and thus rendered harmless the legitimate political expression of regional diversity. As has already been observed, popular self-identities in terms of local communities were also granted backdoor entry by all the parties through a process of politicization of castes.

A combination of good design, skillful execution, and fortune thus ensured that the new democracy did not create alienation or face deep-seated hostility from those sections of the population whose beliefs did not find much play in the system. It is true that these sections were not very active in the first phase of electoral politics. Consequently, the first two—in some cases the first three—elections witnessed a relatively low level of popular participation and competitiveness. But this actually helped the structure of competitive politics take root and thus contributed to early institutionalization. The electoral system, party organizations, legislatures, the judiciary, and the bureaucracy got a grace period in which their capacities were not subjected to the strenuous test of popular democracy.

The Nehruvian phase of Indian democracy is widely seen, and

rightly so, as a period of consolidation. The achievements of this phase, and of Nehru in giving a long-term institutional base to democracy in a fragile moment, must not be undervalued. But it must be remembered that these achievements were made possible by a discursive chasm between the elite and the masses. Such a reminder is necessary, for a loudly proclaimed nostalgia for Nehruvian democracy is a common refrain in Indian politics. Often this desire to re-create Nehru's India reflects a longing for an infinite extension of the time when politics was not spoiled by the entry of commoners. It barely conceals a desire to save democracy from the people.

The Second Phase: The Coming of Age

The second phase of Indian democracy can be said to have begun with the fourth general election held in the year 1967. In this election, the monopoly of the Congress Party's power was broken for the first time. In an election marked by higher turnout and intense participation of the "backward" communities, the Congress was voted out in many states, although it managed to retain a thin majority at the center. Congress stalwarts like Kamraj and S.K. Patil lost elections. The Congress Party was not finished—its reincarnation was to win an unprecedented majority in the next election—but the Congress system came to an end. It was also the culmination of a series of political developments—the Kamraj plan to shift some of the Congress heavyweights to organizational work, the rise of the "syndicate" of regional bosses and the beginnings of "backward class" politics in the south—that brought about a qualitative change in the chemistry of power.

A weaker candidate for the beginning of the second phase is 1969, the year in which the Congress faced its first major split. The legislative wing, under the leadership of then prime minister Indira Gandhi, broke from the organizational wing that was led by many regional stalwarts. It was also the year of the beginning of the Naxalite movement, the extreme left-wing protest movement that was to attract a new generation of radical youth and address itself to the question of inequality of land ownership. Alternatively, the break was in the year 1971, when Indira Gandhi scored a decisive electoral victory on the plank of poverty removal. It was the first of the four "wave" elections, in which one party swept through the polls with the help of a massive swing of votes cutting across various states, that changed the electoral geography of India. But none of this created the kind of world-turned-upside-down feeling that was generated by the results of the 1967 elections.

Whatever the exact cutoff point, it is clear that after about two decades of the initial phase of installation and incubation, the nature and the character of Indian democracy changed significantly. This second phase of Indian democracy is recalled as signaling the failure of the system, as the beginning of its regrettable decline. Yet, it is at least equally plausible to read this phase as the natural outcome of the first phase of successful installation and consolidation. It marked the coming of age of Indian democracy. The infant was now taken out of the incubator and placed into the more natural though also more risky environment. Far from being a result of the failure of the system, it was a direct consequence of the extraordinary success of democratic politics in drawing new sections of the population into the political arena.

As more and more participants came to see the game as their own, they brought their own expectations, demands, and beliefs. At least some of the sections hitherto excluded from centers of power thought it was time they had a say in framing the rules of the game. The most notable group among these were the peasant-proprietors belonging to the middle castes, well below the "twice-born" (*dwija*) castes but distinctly above the ex-untouchables. Traditionally involved in agriculture and handicrafts, this group of castes had lagged behind the upper castes in education and other dimensions of the modern public sphere. They were, however, the first ones to take advantage of the opening offered by democratic politics. Benefiting from their relatively secure economic background, these castes staked their claim to political power. This phenomenon took the form of new political parties like the Bharatiya Kranti Dal (BKD) in Uttar Pradesh, the Dravida Munnetra Kazhagam (DMK) in Tamil Nadu, and the Vishal Haryana Party in Haryana. In most cases, their rise was facilitated by the major parties. The Congress itself acted as the agent of mobility of the "backward castes" in southern states like Karnataka and Kerala, while the reluctance of the Congress to play that role in the north meant that the Socialist parties, especially the Samyukata Socialist Party (SSP) led the entry of the "backward" into mainstream politics.

This second phase was marked by the beginning of an interaction between elite ideologies and popular belief systems. As political competition grew more intense, political actors were forced to pay attention to the tastes and preferences of ordinary voters. Charan Singh blew a hole in the ideology of industrialized development by exposing the neglect of the agrarian sector in particular and rural India in general. The Socialists in the north and parties like the DMK in the south made the empowerment of "backward castes" the leading plank in their critique of the Congress. The Naxalites, and then the youth movements in Gujarat and Bihar, gave expression to the frustration of the new generation. The grace period was over, and generalized pleas for hope in an incomprehensible ideological language were simply insufficient.

The first casualty of the new compulsions of the political market was the edifice of borrowed high ideologies for both the government and the opposition. These had to be quietly and quickly replaced by homespun, or rather homemade patchwork, ideologies. Mrs. Gandhi replaced Nehruvian socialism with the more attractive if vacuous slogan of "*garibi hatao*" or "get rid of poverty." Highly visible policy initiatives like the nationalization of all the major private banks as well as of the coal industry, and the abolition of the "privy purse" of the ex-princely families accompanied the new rhetoric. The Socialist parties translated their ideology in terms of social justice to the lower castes. The Jana Sangh, the parent party of the present-day BJP, moved toward the middle position and formally adopted "Gandhian socialism" as its ideological self-description by the time of its reincarnation in 1980. The Communists stuck to a pure ideology but paid the price in terms of their political containment. The Swatantra Party, the party of the political right in the pure sense, also failed to innovate and simply disappeared.

The overall impact on the ideological map was admittedly shabby: stitched in haste by tailors of varying skills, the new clothes did not quite fit the customer. English-speaking analysts and pure ideologues interpreted these developments as the decline or demise of ideology in politics. Yet a paradigmatic change had taken place. Everyone, save the die-hard ideological purists, came to recognize that the clothes must fit the customer, and not the other way round. Indeed, much of the political innovation was taking place through the back door, in response to the "regrettable compulsions of practical politics." None of the innovators had the audacity to call the innovation by name; usually the tendency was to dissimulate, to deny that these changes were at all significant.

The immediate result of this paradigmatic shift was the rise of populism as the dominant political ideology. The label needs to be understood carefully, for it has become an abused word in the commentaries on Indian politics. Populism is equated with political irresponsibility, with shortsighted measures meant to appease the people without really helping them. As such, it has come to be seen as pure evil and a sign of ideological corruption. Such a reading fails to understand the role of these nonstandard ideological packages in the process of democratization. Populist ideologies bridged the gap between popular aspirations and the language of high ideology without formally displacing the latter from its dominant position. Mrs. Gandhi's ideology of *garibi hatao*, the Janata Party's redistributive policies, Charan Singh's demand for remunerative prices for agricultural products, N.T. Ramarao's policy of supplying cheap rice and saris to the poor, and Devi Lal's decision to waive the farmers' outstanding loans all illustrate various versions of populism. Not many of these schemes proved successful, and indeed the motives behind them were far from noble. Yet these "corrupt" versions made the language of democracy accessible to the newly enfranchised and reduced the yawning gap between the theory and the practice of politics. At the same time, populist ideology did not necessarily reflect popular beliefs, let alone rework high ideology in light of popular aspirations and needs. At this stage, it was not easy for ideas to travel from the bottom upward.

The Indian version of populism involved a selective appropriation of the language of socialism, which had been incorporated in the political mainstream following the official adoption in 1956 by the Congress of the "socialist pattern of society" as its goal. Socialist symbols and rhetoric served to package substantive policies that had little to do with either pure socialist doctrine or an egalitarian agenda. If anything, mainstream politics grew less sensitive to the real needs of the people, at least to those needs that did not lend themselves to easy aggregation. Yet, insofar as rhetoric tends to restrict the actors, the language of socialism set limits to what could be defended and legitimately argued in the political arena. First used to reap electoral harvest in 1971, populism continued to be the reigning ideology of Indian politics until the end of the 1980s. Different political brands were worked out by recombining familiar elements under the socialist label.

Elections were now about whose claim to offer the same menu was found more credible by a nationwide electorate. This changed the character of elections. In the first phase, elections had been about electing a representative. The sum total of the local verdicts constituted the national verdict. But beginning with 1971, elections became something like plebiscites. The entire country was addressed as a single audience and was asked to give its verdict on a single issue. And they responded in the same spirit by voting for their members of Parliament (MPs) as if they were directly electing the prime minister. A regionally fragmented electorate gave way to a national electorate, whose swinging moods could cause a more or less uniform swing of votes across the country (or at least across the "Hindi heartland"), resulting in massive electoral waves from 1971 to 1984. It was not impossible to defeat the Congress, yet it continued to be the reference point around which other parties compete.

The picture at the state level looked somewhat different: the Congress was displaced from the ruling position in 1967 in most of the northern Indian states. The party or, as in most cases, the coalition of parties that replaced it, varied in their social base and ideological persuasion as well as in the duration for which they could replace the Congress. In most states the Congress came back to power by 1972, and its local fortunes fluctuated with the national fate of the Congress. But in the south Indian state of Tamil Nadu, the Congress had been reduced to a third force in the 1970s. In Bihar, the second most populous Hindi-speaking state, the Congress returned to power but never regained the social base it had lost in the late 1960s. In West Bengal, it lost power to the Communist parties in 1977 and has yet to reclaim it. The defeat of the Congress in the 1983 state assembly elections in Andhra Pradesh and Karnataka, its two remaining bastions in the south, completed the circle. By then, Maharashtra was the sole major state of the Indian union where the Congress had not been ousted from power at least once. The rise of regional political parties like the Asom Gana Parishad and the Telugu Desham foreshadowed the political developments of the 1990s.

If the party system in the first phase was called the "Congress system," the second phase should be described as the Congress-Opposition system. Congress was still the only political party with a truly all-India spread. Yet it could not take electoral victories for granted. Ranged against it were a number of political parties with different ideologies and varying levels of political support: the ever splitting and reuniting versions of the Janata family of parties, mainly in the north; the right-wing BJP, the reincarnation of the Jana Sangh, moving from its traditional base in the north to the west; the two Communist parties, which were effectively contained by then to the three states of West Bengal, Kerala, and Tripura; and the regional parties. Political competition was organized along Congress versus non-Congress lines. Occasionally, all the non-Congress parties—routinely referred to as "the opposition" even when in power—would come together to defeat the Congress, as they did in 1977 and 1989. The system of one-party dominance in the first phase had by then given way to a system of one-party salience.

The Congress itself had been reinvented by Mrs. Gandhi following its split. The coalition of social forces that formed its support base was also reconstituted. It retained its capacity for cross-sectional mobilization, but its support was no longer randomly scattered across all social groups: its core was now constituted by a rainbow coalition. It was a rainbow with thick edges: groups on the margins of society tended to vote for Congress much more than anyone else. These included the *dalits*, or the 15–16 percent of the population made up of ex-untouchables at the bottom of the Hindu social hierarchy; the *adivasis*, or tribals, who lived outside the pale of Hindu social order and made up 8 percent of the population; and the minorities, mainly the 12 percent of the population who were Muslim. The reinvention of the Congress and the occasional electoral success of the opposition resulted in a rapid turnover of the political elite and some enduring changes in the social composition of the political elite. Leaders from non–upper caste background had their first taste of power, especially in the south and the west. Their entry into the centers of political power accelerated the process of cultural encounter set in motion by the introduction of universal adult franchise.

This first encounter of Indian democracy with popular beliefs left it simultaneously deeper and weaker. It helped Indian democracy take root. Greater participation and more intense politicization showed that the process of democratization was continuing and that the system of representative democracy had greater acceptance among the people than was imagined at the beginning of India's democratic career. Repeated, almost ritual, alteration of government gave the people a sense of control and contributed to their sense of political efficacy. The social constituency of politics was considerably widened in the south as political power passed from the hands of the "twice-born" to the peasant-proprietors. The rise of the dominant Other Backward Classes

(OBCs) in the south had some impact in the northern states of Uttar Pradesh and Bihar and in the western state of Gujarat. Although the tide was yet to turn in these states, an inexorable process of downward percolation of power had been set in motion.

This period also showed the weakness of political institutions exemplified in the Emergency. In some ways, it was a part of the larger crisis of political institutions. In this phase, the logic of imported liberal democratic institutions clashed with the cultural codes embedded in the everyday practice of Indian public life. Consequently, there began a process of erosion of political institutions, especially those that required functional autonomy. The Emergency was by no means the necessary outcome of this erosion, but it was surely one of the possible outcomes.

June 1975 was politically the most insecure moment for an inherently insecure person like Mrs. Gandhi, then prime minister. She used the internal emergency provisions of the Indian Constitution to turn her personal crisis into a national emergency and suspended basic human and political rights of citizens. The following nineteen months showed how fragile the institutional edifice was. Political opposition was silenced more easily than Mrs. Gandhi may have thought. There were unmistakable elements of fascism as Mrs. Gandhi's son became an unconstitutional center of power, leading illegal demolitions of slums and campaigns of forced sterilization. Civil services and the judiciary caved in even more willingly as there was considerable talk of the "committed" bureaucracy and judiciary. The record of the press and the intelligentsia was far from heroic, notwithstanding later reconstructions. There were, of course, honorable exceptions in each of these categories. And yet, what brought India out of that phase was not heroism but something that must be described as the spirit of democracy. Something of that spirit continued to give Mrs. Gandhi a bad conscience and ultimately forced her to call for general elections in 1977. It was the same spirit that translated into the loss of popular legitimacy of her regime, at least in the north, the epicenter of authoritarian excess.

The results of the Lok Sabha elections of March 1977 were astonishing, even for those who had hoped and worked for Mrs. Gandhi's defeat. Her party was defeated in all but 2 out of the 226 parliamentary seats in the north Indian "Hindi heartland." The first non-Congress government came to power at the center led by the Janata Party, a hastily put-together combination of all the major non-Congress parties. In a limited respect, the Emergency demonstrated that Indian democracy had developed self-corrective mechanisms and could invent new anchors for itself in times of crisis.

Two decades of plebiscitary politics had considerably weakened the local character of democracy, encouraging the need to articulate issues that did not and could not find expression in mainstream politics. Since the fate of the representative did not depend on what he did or did not do, there was very little incentive to raise local demands at the center. Besides, the organizational capacity of political parties shrank as leaders like Mrs. Gandhi established direct relationships with the people, sometimes deliberately undermining their own parties. Governance became more remote than ever. Although the governments came to power with hitherto unprecedented majorities, they soon lost popular confidence. The failure of socialist rhetoric to deliver the goods also contributed to a deeply felt popular frustration. The gap between the people and the centers of power was filled by protest movements such as the Marxist-Leninist Naxalbari movement and the agitation by students in Gujarat and Bihar for corruption-free public life. A large number of nonparty political formations and some parties with a movement character like the Janata Party in 1977 or V.P. Singh's Janata Dal in 1989 filled a crucial gap in influencing the political agenda of the mainstream at a time when it was growing insensitive to popular demands.

If this phase led to the creation of a national political community, it also squeezed out some of the claims to power based on regional and ethnic diversity. The insensitive handling of two such claims in the states of Assam and the Punjab led to prolonged political crises. In Assam, a student movement protested against massive illegal migration into the state that threatened their culture and livelihood. In the Punjab, a movement for a part-regional, part-religious charter of demands nearly turned into a civil war in response to Operation Bluestar, an attack by the armed forces on the Golden Temple, the highest religious shrine of the Sikhs, in 1983. This was followed by the large-scale massacre of the minority Sikh population in 1984 in which the culprits were believed to have been shielded by the central government The rise of regional parties restored something of the voice of diversity as well as faith in the self-correcting mechanisms of democracy.

By the mid-1980s, the stage was set for another political transition. However, Indira Gandhi's assassination in 1984 and the following general election blocked the natural flow of political events and postponed the arrival of the next phase by five years. For all its problems and weaknesses, the second phase had established that the people could not be kept out of the democratic process.

The Third Phase: Mandal, Mandir, and Market

The third and ongoing phase of democratic politics began somewhere around the turn of the decade with the almost simultaneous arrival of the three Ms on the domestic horizon and the collapse of the Soviet Union, which silently but very effectively signaled the demise of the hegemony of the language of socialism in Indian politics.

The three Ms stood for Mandal, Mandir, and Market. Mandal was the chairman of the governmental commission formed in 1980 that recommended reservation of government jobs for the OBCs to improve their social and educational conditions. In 1990 when the recommendations of the commission were suddenly implemented by the Janata Dal government, Mandal came to refer to the entire phenomenon of OBC self-assertion movement. Mandir (temple) refers to the Hindu fundamentalist movement supported by the BJP in favor of the claim that the Babri mosque situated in the holy city of Ayodhya was actually occupying the site of a temple of Lord Rama. The movement culminated in the demolition of the Babri mosque by Hindu fundamentalists in December 1992. The third M, Market, stands for the policy of economic liberalization and integration into the global economic regime. Now controlled by the World Trade Organization, that policy was sprung on the unsuspecting Indians in 1991 by Manmohan Singh, then finance minister of a minority Congress government. After four decades of following a "socialist" path, admittedly with rapidly diminishing enthusiasm and almost no conviction, policymakers decided to make a U-turn without even forewarning the electors, let alone seeking popular mandate on this question.

It can be argued that these changes were not as sudden as they appear. The first two years of Rajiv Gandhi's premiership signaled some of the changes. The first two budgets—presented, ironically, by V.P. Singh—gave the first indications of the economic "reforms" of the 1990s. It is also true that the beginnings of the three Ms had been present since the first phase: the assertion of the OBCs began in the southern states in the 1960s; the Hindu fundamentalist campaign against cow slaughter took place in 1966; and, in 1974, the government had to reverse its decision to nationalize the wholesale trade in wheat. Yet it was only in the 1990s that these tendencies came to dominate the political agenda nationwide.

What followed was a fundamental change in the terms of political discourse. Some of the changes in the ideology of the Communist parties, indisputably the purist practitioners of high ideology, illustrate the extent to which the terms of discourse had changed. Following the Mandal agitation, after decades of holding on to a doctrinaire belief in class, the Communist Party of India accepted the reality of caste as a marker of social inequality in Indian society. Both of the Communist parties thought it necessary to turn to progressive elements within the Hindu religion to counter the BJP's position on the Mandir issue. Like all other state governments, irrespective of their stated ideology, the Left Front government in West Bengal actively pursued the policy of attracting foreign investment to promote industrial growth in the state. Other parties also made quick, if silent, amendments to their ideological postures. Notwithstanding its loud proclamations about nationalist economic policy, the BJP stuck faithfully to the economic agenda of the Congress. Despite fanning agitation against it, the BJP also officially accepted the Mandal report and has since made all possible efforts to accommodate the OBC upsurge within its organization. Belatedly, the Congress also accepted Mandal; even the all-mighty Sonia Gandhi was forced to concede to the demands of the party's OBC MPs on the Women's Reservation Bill. The silence and the inaction of the Congress government following the demolition of the Babri mosque also illustrated the attempt by the party to slip away from its established secular position. Within less than a decade, what are considered as the norms of acceptable behavior in the public arena have undergone a basic change.

These dramatic changes do not, however, rupture our story of the encounter of the language of democracy with popular imagination. The third phase takes this encounter a step further. The sudden ideological unsettling has created a context in which, for the first time, ideas from the lower orders can leave their imprint on high ideology. The removal of the token supremacy of socialism had both a liberating and a debilitating effect on democratic debate. Some of the new beliefs that have come into play in this phase are from the lower orders of society and articulate interests that could not be articulated under the previous ideological hegemony. This development liberated those like Kanshi Ram, the supremo of the Bahujan Samaj Party (BSP), a party mainly of the *dalits*, or Laloo Yadav, a charismatic and controversial OBC leader from Bihar, from having to pack their sectional demands in the language of high ideology that had hitherto weighed against them. It also made possible a reconfiguration of the "third force" to allow for a coalition of regional parties with the Left, something their fundamental ideological differences would not have allowed in the past.

This rising of ideas from the lower orders does not apply across the ideological dimensions. The New Economic Policy, with its ideology of privatization and free trade, is by no means an influence from below. The price paid for the influence of the lower orders on the political discourse was the shrinking of the agenda itself. Economic policy no longer figures on the menu of political choices. Major economic decisions are now in the technical domain for the experts to settle. Something of the extraordinary autonomy that politics had enjoyed since independence has already been eroded in the current phase.

If the second phase had turned the ordinary voter into a customer whose tastes had to be taken into account by political entrepreneurs, the third phase has turned them into demanding and often discerning customers. In that sense, there is, for the first time, two-way traffic in ideas. It is not surprising that a democratic upsurge is also taking place among the hitherto disempowered sections. In this context, it is worth noting some of the findings of the two wide-ranging and representative national surveys of the Indian electorate conducted by the Centre for the Study of Developing Societies during the 1996 and 1998 general elections. The surveys report a dramatic upsurge in all forms in political participation, from voting to membership, in political parties among the *dalits*. There is the beginning of change among the *adivasis,* too, for their turnout recorded a sudden jump in the 1996 election, although a similar change is not evident in their other activities. For women, the increase in participation has affected all levels except voter turnout, which recorded only a marginal improvement in 1998. These are meaningful statistics. Also significant is that India is perhaps the only major democracy in the world where turnout and political activism are higher among the very poor than among the upper middle class. These are surely instances of participatory upsurge associated with the journey of the idea of democracy.

This radicalization of the encounter of ideas does not, by itself, produce a radical agenda of politics. The erosion of the established language of high ideology and the inability to replace it with a home-spun alternative have deprived political formations of the lower orders of any aggregating or screening ideological device. The beliefs brought to the center of politics by the rise of the lower orders (especially the *dalits* and the OBCs) are often fragmentary in character, concerned with only one section and with a single issue. The Samajwadi Party (SP) and the Rashtriya Janata Dal, the two political expressions of the OBC upsurge, have not been able to evolve an agenda or an identity that speaks for all the OBCs. More often than not, these are seen as parties that look after the interests only of the Yadavs (agrarian caste). No wonder the SP reserves its fury not for the Congress or any other party of the upper caste but for the BSP, the party of the *dalits*.

The BSP's slogan, *"Vote hamara raj tumhara nahin chalega"* (Our Vote and Your Rule: No More), captures the evocative power and the narrow vision of these ideologies. On the one hand, it holds out the promise of liberation by asserting the democratic right to self-rule. At the same time, the "our" and "your" in this equation are defined in strictly sectional terms. "My rule" in this context means no more than the rule of those born in my community. Thinly wrapped in the language of liberal democracy, these sectional claims do not even attempt the task of ideological mediation of competing sectional claims, let alone provide an integrated vision for the polity. Although the BSP seeks to establish the rule of the *bahujan*, the majority, it has never attempted to reconcile the claims of the *dalits* with those of other victims of the caste system, the OBCs, or other oppressed groups such as the *adivasis*. What was achieved in the previous phases through mediation and accommodation within various parties is now attempted through political coalition among different parties by stapling together the different ideological fragments belonging to each. Thus, the mediation of the *dalit* and OBC claims takes place through the temporary and inherently fragile alliance between the BSP and the SP.

Politics in this phase represents the fuller working-out of the logic of universal adult franchise. Electoral politics has now become the central arena of democratization. It is marked by greater politicization and higher participation, especially in the state- and local-level elections, of the lower orders of society. The urban upper middle classes have obviously not shared the participatory enthusiasm. While the political system continues to enjoy fairly high legitimacy, the legitimacy of the political agencies and actors has suffered a decline. If the second phase was accompanied by the first democratic upsurge, what we have seen in the last few years is best described as the second democratic upsurge.

The most noticed political development in this period has been the dramatic rise of the BJP to power. Facing the first general election after its rebirth, the party had managed to send only two MPs to the Lok Sabha in 1984. The number rose to 80 in the next election, in 1989, as the BJP rode piggyback on the success of the newly formed Janata Dal (JD). The breakup with the JD only helped it further as the figure rose to 121 in 1991 in the wake of Mandal and Mandir. In the next election, in 1996, the BJP emerged as the single-largest party in a fractured parliament, with 160 MPs. It accepted the presidential invitation to form the government but could not sustain the experiment beyond thirteen days; the United Front formed a new government that lasted eighteen months with outside support from the Congress. The BJP's long wait came to an end in the 1998 midterm poll, when it raised its strength to 180 MPs and surpassed 250 MPs, if one included its regional allies.

Although the BJP has come to power, it has yet to win a popular mandate. With 25 percent of the popular vote, it is technically the second-largest party just behind the Congress in the 1998 election. More importantly, it has yet to fully overcome the three barriers that have historically blocked the BJP's bid for power. It is beginning to surmount the geographical barrier: it is unable to go beyond the north and the west, but much of its newly acquired vote in the south and the east is on loan from its allies, including the AIADMK (All-India Anna Dravida Munnetra Kazhagam) in Tamil Nadu, the Biju Janata Dal in Orissa, and the Trinamool Congress in West Bengal. The ideological barrier—its isolation from the mainstream—has also been partially overcome, thanks to its allies such as the Samata Party and the fact that the middle position itself has shifted toward the BJP in the last decade. The most important barrier that it still needs to cross is the social barrier—its inability to change its profile as a party of the socially privileged. The findings of the National Election Study in 1998 show that although support for the BJP has become broader than before, it is far from acquiring the kind of widespread support the Congress enjoyed in the past. The BJP continues to be the darling of the upper-caste Hindus and the urban "middle classes," although it has also succeeded in getting a substantial vote from the OBCs. It still lags behind among the *dalits* and the *adivasis*. Despite marginal improvement in this respect, it has not even begun to win the confidence of the Muslims.

While the BJP has made a difference to the character of Indian politics, no less significant is the effect Indian politics has had on the BJP. The competition for power between the "forward" and the "backward" castes is as intense in the BJP as in any other party. While it succeeded in carrying out its hawkish line on the nuclear tests, it should be remembered that its enthusiasm for the tests was shared by every major political party in the last two decades. The bomb should not draw our attention away from the fact that in framing the National Agenda for Governance, the BJP had to give up various items of its aggressive agenda of cultural homogenization in deference to the wishes of its regional allies. The party relinquished its demands for construction of a Ram temple at Ayodhya, withdrawal of the special status of Kashmir, and introduction of a uniform Civil Code.

The BJP's rise should be viewed as a part of the larger reconfiguration of the party political space. Although it may not be correct to speak of a realigning election in the Indian context—for there was no stable alignment to begin with—the changes brought about by elections from 1989 to 1998 show many similar features. Step by step, these elections have brought to an end the salience of one-party rule. At the national level, India seems to be moving toward a multiparty system. The Congress has been losing popular votes in every election since 1984 and is now just one among many parties. The decline of the Congress, or the move toward a post-Congress polity, is accompanied by a fresh outlining of the relationship between social divisions and political loyalties. If the Congress dominance in the first two phases was characterized by a rainbow coalition of social communities, its decline in the third phase has meant that the various stripes of the rainbow are coming apart. While the Congress has held onto a shrinking but more or less evenly spread rainbow, its major competitors are rather skewed in their social support. It is as if everyone is running away with a piece of the old rainbow. Even the Congress does not have the same social profile in all regions of the country. Wherever it faces the BJP, the Congress is a party of the lower segments of society. But in states like West Bengal and Kerala where it is pitted against the Communists, it is a party of the privileged. For the first time since independence, political parties are developing macrolevel identification with various communities. This is accompanied by a widening of the social base of political elites. The much-delayed transfer of political power to the OBCs has started taking place in northern India.

This national picture does not tell very much about perhaps the most salient aspect of the emerging political reality of the 1990s, namely the decoupling of the national political arena from that of state politics. Throughout the 1970s and 1980s, state politics was often no more than a reflection of developments at the national level. Citizens voted in the state assembly elections as if they were electing their prime minister. Now the logic has almost reversed. Not only is the state arena largely free of the influence of national developments, but people now vote in the national election as if they are electing their chief minister. The emergence of state or region as the effective level of political decision making has changed the party system. While the national picture appears as if there is a multiparty system, a look at the state level shows the effective emergence of a two-party system. The emerging party system is best described as a system of multiple bipolarities. Practically every state is moving toward a bipolar political competition, but the pairs differ from state to state, thus creating the impression of a multiparty system.

It will take more time—yet another election, or perhaps even more than one—for the emerging picture of this latest phase of democratic politics to clarify. If the current coalition woes of the BJP continue unabated, the party may be forced to go for the next election very soon. However, one of the trends is already fairly significant and might, in retrospect, appear to be the defining characteristic of this phase. This is the erosion of the autonomy of politics, driven by economic globalization and by the sharpening of ethnic divisions. This process is most evident in the case of economic liberalization. It has now been seven years since the economic policy took a U-turn, without any mention of such a change in the election manifesto or the campaign or any evidence of popular support for it either before or after its introduction. Since then India has seen two general elections and three new prime ministers. But there has been no serious political debate about these new policies. The same set of bureaucrats, all trained with the World Bank, continue to take all the important economic decisions with only cosmetic changes or occasional intervention by the political rulers. In the long run, however, this is bound to affect the quality of democracy.

As the second democratic upsurge brings the hitherto disempowered into positions of state power, they might discover that history has cheated them once again, that there is little they can do with state power. This is perhaps the deepest irony in the story of the journey of the idea of democracy.

India's Established Democracy

Let me now leave this story and turn to an audit of the working of democratic politics in the last fifty years. Here one needs to distinguish between two different questions: Has India succeeded in establishing a democracy? And, has the Indian democracy succeeded in achieving its goals? While the first is a question about what democracy is, the second is about what democracy does, or can be expected to do.

The first question allows a more cheerful answer, if only because of the sad record of most other postcolonial polities of which this question reminds us. Going by the baseline definitions of procedural democracy, India is, and is likely to remain so in the foreseeable future, a democracy. In other words, democracy has come to be "the only game in town." And that, as students of comparative democratization never forget to remind us, is no mean achievement. This is recognized across the political spectrum in India, even by the system's harshest critics. A few years ago, when the Communist Party of India (Marxist-Leninist) came aboveground after years of underground violent antisystem politics and decided to contest elections, they were unwittingly paying a big compliment to Indian democracy.

To say that India is a democracy is not merely to make a statement about the formal constitutional structures of democratic governance that India has retained. More important, it is a statement about the presence of the language of democracy in India. India has, to use Shiv Vishwanathan's memorable phrase, "by-hearted" democracy: this characteristically Indian English expression captures well how Indians have creolized the idea of democracy. They have accepted the Western idea of democracy as their own and then proceeded to take liberties with it as one does with one's own possessions. As a result, the idea of democracy has been localized and routinized. Note, for example, the frequency with which the virtually unlimited franchise election is used in settings that do not require it: from academic councils of the universities, to managing committees of colleges, to the chairmanship of the cooperative banks, to sports selection committees. Election has come to be the principal mode of settling competing claims to power in the entire public arena. Or witness the ubiquity of protest culture, from matters significant to trivial: collective public protest is an ever-present reminder of the belief in democratic rights. In its Indian version, the idea has come to shape ordinary Indians' beliefs about citizenship, their political rights, and the virtues of political participation. The idea of democracy has, above all, come to supply the only valid criterion for claims to legitimate rule and, correspondingly, the moral basis of political obligation.

The idea is embodied in political processes, which have on balance retained a certain dynamism, at least up to this point. The fundamental trend toward greater participation and more intense politicization has continued to spread the idea of democracy both vertically and horizontally (except in the state of Jammu and Kashmir and some parts of the northeast). Competitive politics has retained its dynamic capacity to attract hitherto nonpolitical segments, articulate cleavages, and build bridges. Thanks to its capacity to connect itself to the preexisting social cleavages and to transform them, democracy has taken root in Indian society.

The idea of democracy also has powerful and reliable carriers by now. India has a wider pool for recruitment of political elite than do most postcolonial polities. A rough estimate suggests that the number of elected political representatives, from the national to the village level, is no less than three million. Consequently, there is a large contingent of political actors (at least ten million including representatives, rivals, hopefuls, and "also-rans") whose instinct for self-preservation can be relied upon in defense of democracy. The logic of competitive politics has ensured that these active participants do not come only from within the traditional social elite, although this elite continues to enjoy a larger than proportionate share. Indeed, the number of registered political parties—166 contested in the 1998 general election—is large, although their dynamic capacity and legitimacy has weakened somewhat over the last two decades. The idea of party is no longer a Western import; it has merged into the landscape of every village and has found its way into practically every Indian language. Last but not least, there are the movement groups, nonparty political formations, and various other organizations of civil society including many NGOs that have done much to deepen the idea of democracy in

India. They have taken up causes that do not lend themselves to easy aggregation, demands of groups that are electorally nonviable, and issues that have yet to make their mark on the national political agenda. They have kept the spirit of democracy alive when the machinery of competitive politics has failed to nourish it.

Lest this description make democracy look more secure a possession than it actually is, let me also recall the aspects that cause concern for the future of democracy in the procedural sense, even if there is no immediate or imminent danger of its collapse. The formal institutional apparatus of Indian democracy has never been very strong; the institutions of liberal democracy did not undergo the kind of "by-hearting" that the idea of democracy did. It is true that these institutions are still stronger than their counterparts in other postcolonial polities, but they are not the strongest links in the democratic chain, and the very process of democratization is weakening them further. Claims that cannot be processed in the electoral arena have not found anything close to adequate attention. The judicial apparatus has never been ready to take on the load of litigation thrust upon it. Notwithstanding the recent activism of upper levels of the judiciary, the judicial apparatus has become less effective over the years. The civil service has been politicized since colonial times. Democratization has made it more politicized without the corresponding benefits of accountability, for the bureaucracy has still to outgrow its colonial legacy. The combined effect of these maladies is the denial of an effective rule of law to ordinary citizens.

Intermediary political institutions that were to act as a link between the people and the centers of power have declined considerably. The near collapse of democratic procedures within political parties has left a major void that, of late, has been filled by managerial-style politics and criminalization. The very autonomy of the political process, which lies at the heart of India's path to democratization, faces encroachment as a result of the instrumental linkage of political power with the dominant economic interests and as a result of the structural limits created by the recent globalization of the Indian economy. All these are not signs of the impending demise of democracy, as many radical democrats would have us believe. But if these trends continue to grow without adequate counter from within the political process, we could be moving slowly toward a "low-intensity democracy."

Successes and Failures of India's Democracy

As we move from a procedural to a more substantive definition of democracy, from a definition focused on a set of institutional inputs to one that demands a desired set of outcomes, the distinction between the two questions suggested above, between what democracy is and what democracy does, disappears. At this level, it also becomes difficult to sustain a "universal checklist" definition: democracy cannot be defined without reference to the historically specific dreams and ideals that were articulated through the label. This brings us back to the four goals implicit in the Indian model with reference to which the achievements and failures of democratic polity can be discussed.

The very achievement and sustenance of procedural democracy partly realizes the first goal of political democracy. A democracy provides dignity and liberty simply by being there. In the Indian model, democracy was also the key instrument, the necessary condition, for the realization of all its other goals. In that sense, taking into account the growing limitations mentioned above, Indian polity has achieved something worth defending. It has also met, at least until now in most parts of the territories that fall within its boundaries, the minimal substantive expectations of any regime, democratic or otherwise: protecting its own form and protecting its citizens from complete anarchy. The fact that India has kept at bay even the remote possibility of a military takeover; that it has successfully defended (at times through brutal and undemocratic means in the states of Nagaland and Mizoram in the northeast) the territorial borders it inherited; and that most of its citizens have been spared the experience of complete anarchy, is unlikely to enthuse a radical democrat. But it is useful to remember that democratic regimes usually collapse not because they fail to realize the higher ideals associated with democracy, but because they cannot be relied upon to meet the bare minimum expectations.

The achievements of democracy as a set of institutions or as a regime do not, of course, satisfy the deeper ethical impulse associated with the idea of democracy. As a political ideal, democracy gives rise to the promise of a community of equals, where the ordinary citizens enjoy true liberty and are governed by none except themselves. The nationalist movement in India had translated this ideal as the goal of *swaraj*, of self-rule in a deeper sense. It would indeed make impossible demands on one's credulity to suggest that Indian democracy has come anywhere close to meeting this ideal. Perhaps no democracy has, but this constitutes a poor consolation to those who accepted the ideal for its ethical appeal. Ever since the famous "tryst with destiny" speech given at midnight of August 14, 1947, the promise of a community of equals has been a false one. What has come about as a result of the working of democracy is neither a community nor equality. The political community, or rather politicized social communities, it brings into existence is no community, for its shared life is shallow, if not perverse. The liberty it offers, at least formally, is distributed in extremely unequal measure. The power it brings to the people as an abstraction is rarely, if ever, exercised by the real people. And there are still many people—full citizens of the republic of India—who feel as powerless under this democracy as they did under British rule.

The performance of Indian democracy in achieving national integration has left much to be desired. But, as the examples of India's neighbors show, we could have done worse. There are areas (Kashmir and the hill states in the northeast) and periods (Mrs. Gandhi's second regime, for example) that constitute exceptions, but on balance the Indian elite has stuck to the "salad bowl" rather than the "melting pot" model of integration of diversities. That is to say, various communities and aspiring nationalities have not been forced to give up their identity as a precondition of joining the Indian enterprise. They have been accepted as distinct and different ingredients in the Indian mix of multiculturalism. And, again on balance, it has worked: legitimate political articulation of social and regional diversities and the mediation of competing claims through mechanisms of political accommodation have achieved what consociational arrangements for power sharing among different social groups do in other societies. There has been more than one instance of majoritarian excess (the anti-Sikh riots in 1984 and the demolition of Babri mosque in 1992, to take two examples from recent history), but democratic politics seems to have evolved mechanisms of self-correction in this respect (as illustrated by the 1997 elections in the Punjab and the politics of Uttar Pradesh). In retrospect, effective political accommodation of visible diversities looks like one of the outstanding achievements of Indian democracy in the last fifty years.

By its very nature, however, this is an inherently fragile achievement, ever contingent on the skills of the political actors in working out the power-sharing arrangements or in allowing the mechanisms of self-correction to work themselves out. This is a lesson well worth remembering as India confronts the most organized challenge to the politics of diversity in the form of the BJP government at the center. The most serious challenge to the survival of diversity comes from forces that are less organized, less visible, and not even considered political in the ordinary sense: forces of cultural homogenization, the monoculture of modernity, and the ideology of nation-state. While there is something to be said for the capacity of democratic politics to deal with the more obvious political challenges to diversity, it has proved a weak ally in the struggle against these deeper threats from within.

The promise of social revolution that the democratic invitation has always contained has been realized only in parts and in fragments. It is not that democratic politics have left society unaffected. In fact, these fifty years may be recorded in the history of Indian society as years of fundamental transformation triggered, above all, by the mechanism of competitive politics. At least in one respect, it did bring about something of a revolution: the role of ritual Hindu hierarchy as a predictor of secular power has diminished dramatically over the last fifty years. While this is a fundamental change, it does not in itself guarantee equality. Unsurprisingly, the functioning of democratic politics has contributed more to a vigorous circulation of the elite and to an expansion of the circle itself than to the establishment of social equality. Its contribution to social equality is mainly by way of the politicization of castes and communities, which then struggle in the secular domain for equality of self-respect.

Since the gender divide does not lend itself to easy aggregation along party political lines, competitive politics has failed to bring about the kind of change in this aspect that it has on caste inequality. The representation of women in the parliament and the state assemblies has stagnated at the abysmally low levels of 8 and 4 percent, respectively, over the last fifty years. The national movement may not have had a greater proportion of women's participation, but it ensured that women have a stronger voice in public life. If women's issues are discussed much more in the political arena than their presence in legislatures or their voice in political parties would warrant, the principal reason is the politics of ideas to which the growing women's movement has contributed a great deal. Consequently, India has had fairly "progressive" legislation on gender justice, including the provision for reservation of one-third of the seats for women in the election of local democratic bodies. The resolute opposition to a similar bill for the Lok Sabha and state assemblies shows the lack of political will that underlies the symbolic progressivism on women's issues.

The single biggest failure of democratic politics lies in the nonfulfillment of the promise of material well-being. Far from ensuring a life of equal and reasonable comfort for everyone, it has not succeeded even in providing the minimum needs of the people, or in removing the worst indignities or the ugliest disparities in the material conditions of life experienced by its citizens. It is true that the conditions of life for most of the people have not deteriorated substantially, that India has achieved some reduction in the proportion of the poor in its population, and that the Indian economy is not caught in an impossible spiral of inflation or in a debt-trap. That is perhaps an achievement, at least in comparative perspective. It is also true that a majority of the population feels that its economic condition has improved in the recent past and that an overwhelming majority of people think that their children have better opportunities in life than they did. But there is a significant minority—mainly artisan communities and Scheduled Tribes—that disagrees and has experienced an overall deterioration in quality-of-life. For others, too, there has been a visible decline in some of the crucial resources such as the availability of public health and the quality of public education.

Democratic politics only provides a potential formal mechanism for conversion of the majority of the poor into a political majority that can then take charge of state power to redistribute material resources and to augment them in such a way as to meet the needs of the most disadvantaged. The functioning of democracy in itself does nothing to ensure that the mechanism is actually used to this end. The other condition, that of the availability of a political agency that can transform the potential majority into a political majority by winning their political trust, has proved to be highly contingent. The Indian model expected politics to provide three crucial elements of what was then called economic development: politics was to provide the blueprint for economic development; it was to confer the political will to implement the design in the face of structures of economic interests; and it was to create popular support for egalitarian politics. In practice, it succeeded in providing only the third component—and that only in part. The most recent phase of globalization and liberalization marks a decisive retreat from what remained of the politics of egalitarianism. Not only is there no effective political will to do something, but there is very little by way of a coherent intellectual design as to what needs to be done in the first place. This combination of political amnesia and cognitive paralysis poses the most important challenge to the ethical impulse underlying the Indian enterprise today.

Conclusion

Let me round off this story by asking a general question implicit in it: What happens when the idea of democracy travels downward? Fifty years ago, no one felt it necessary to ask this question. Fifty years ago, the decision to establish democracy in a poor, unequal, postcolonial society did not look as courageous as it does now in retrospect. The spirit of the time helped everyone overlook the fact that no other society had successfully taken this path before. Nor has anyone done so since then. India has failed to remove poverty or inequality or to shake off the cultural burden of colonialism, yet it has succeeded in remaining a democracy. Fifty years ago, hardly anyone had thought about this possibility: of democracy being the lone survivor in the family of ideals we set out with. Neither the historians nor the political theorists of democracy had prepared us for this possibility, nor have they done so since.

There was another reason for not thinking about this question. The founding fathers of our democracy, the original hosts of this game, entertained the illusion that the democratic idea would remain intact as it traveled downward. The Indian model assumed a pure diffusion of ideas; it was assumed that the grafted institutions and ideas of Western democracy would travel down in their pure form to the masses. The model was unspoiled by the suspicion that the recipients of these ideas were themselves thinking minds, that they could transform the received ideas just as the elite had done to the doctrine of liberalism. What this model did not have, to use the recent vocabulary of social science, was a theory of reception. This was a crucial blind spot, for the success of democracy depended in large measure on re-creating the democratic dream in the popular imagination, in anchoring the universal ideal in the specifically Indian context. Some of the founding fathers may have entertained a different kind of illusion: that the idea of democracy would be automatically transformed by the people when it traveled downward. In this romantic version, the people would make democracy speak their language and would devise the system best suited to their needs.

The experience of the last five decades confirms neither of these versions. The journey of the idea of democracy in India has not only changed the lives of the millions it has touched, but it has also changed the idea of democracy itself in more ways than one. Call it "creolization" or "vernacularization" of democracy, this transformation is at the heart of whatever success democracy has achieved in India. The serious attempt to marry the democratic idea to popular beliefs, to develop shared protocols with the preexisting language of the people, is what has distinguished India from other countries where the democratic enterprise never took off. And that is also what can continue to maintain this distinction in the future.

Creolization in itself is no magic remedy. Indigenization of democracy is a necessary condition of the working out of this idea, but it is not a sufficient condition. A large historical process like this one follows no one script and does not produce neat outcomes. It leaves gaps, it produces contradictions. And there is no hidden hand at work here that might straighten every wrinkle. There is, in other words, no shortcut to creating and sustaining the language of radical democracy beyond weaving every strand and tying every thread.

Economy

Kirit S. Parikh

Fifty years ago, at the dawn of independence, India started on a journey of economic development. It did this with clarity of purpose: It wanted to eliminate poverty over a period of fifteen years. To accomplish this goal, it chose a path of central planning in which it would define the contours of development through five-year plans. The economy was to be a mixed one in which both public and private sectors would coexist. However, the public sector was expected to reach the "commanding heights" of the economy over the years and help in the establishment of a "socialistic pattern of society": an economy in which all would have equality of opportunity.

The broad strategy of development adopted by India seemed logical given its own historical experience and the empirical evidence provided by the experiences of other countries. Over the two decades preceding the end of World War II, world trade had stagnated. Without growing global trade, export-led development for India seemed difficult if not infeasible, and import substitution seemed a more attractive strategy. As for the experiences of other countries: in less than thirty years, the Soviet Union had used central planning to become a major global power; even the United States and Britain had successfully used price and production controls. Planned economic development based on an import-substitution strategy seemed logical. However, India did not choose to fully follow the Soviet path because a democratic framework based on adult franchise was held to be a more important objective than rapid economic development. A mixed economy seemed to be the sensible middle way. The Indian elite at the time looked up to Western, particularly European, nations as modern and progressive. So, an obvious choice was to follow examples such as Britain and France, where a strong state with a mixed economy existed in a democratic framework. One may also note that there was broad agreement on this strategy among academic economists at the time, not only in India but also around the world.

However, as the global economy evolved in the post–World War II period of the 1950s and 1960s, some of the assumptions behind India's development strategy proved to be wrong. World trade expanded dramatically over that period and import substitution proved to be more expensive than anticipated. What is now called "government failure" became apparent. Plans were not implemented in time. Corruption became apparent. As politicians, businesspeople, bureaucrats, and trade unions seemed to manipulate the system to enrich themselves, the original purposes of policies were defeated.

All these factors were perceived in the late 1960s, and India should have changed its course. But it did not; in fact, it continued down the same path until the middle of 1991. Why didn't it change course in the late 1960s? The answer lies partly in the compulsion that pushed Indira Gandhi, who was fighting for her political survival in 1969, toward a pronounced radical leftist stance, and partly in the political economy of the situation. A set of vested interests had been created by the policy regime. They resisted attempts to change. In fact, they recruited more and more people into a vicious circle in which bad policies created opportunities for large illegal, easy gains. These offered an incentive to further distort the policies to create new opportunities for making money in unproductive activities. Mrs. Gandhi may have been further confirmed in her leftist stance by the experience of the Bangladesh crisis of 1971, when India was saddled with the burden of caring for 10 million refugees and the world refused to help. On top of this, when India offered military help to Bangladesh's Mukti Bahini, it had to do so in the face of the threat of possible U.S. military intervention. The success of India's actions in Bangladesh may have strengthened the prime minister's belief in self-reliance and in choosing a path independent of outside help.

This situation continued until the middle of 1991, when an economic crisis forced the government to dramatically change direction. A process of economic reform was begun, and India embarked on a new journey. In the short period since the reforms began, the Indian economy has made dramatic progress. What is more important is that there is a political consensus on the broad thrust of the reforms. Even among academic economists, a large majority supports this process. The "closet liberalizers" seem to have "come out."

The future of the Indian economy is bright indeed. Even the dark clouds of political instability that seem to hover over the economy have a silver lining, and I remain optimistic about the coming decades.

This is, in brief, the story I wish to tell in the following pages. We begin with the Indian economic scene at independence, which helped provide a context within which India's approach to economic development was formulated. The next section elaborates on the maturation of the approach, after which we look at how planning paradigms and models evolved over time. The performance of the Indian economy until 1990 is then reviewed, followed by a discussion of what went wrong. We then move on to a description of the crisis of 1991 and the reforms, followed by a review of their accomplishments. A discussion of the future of the Indian economy is followed by a conclusion.

The Economic Scene at Independence

To understand what motivated India's choice of development strategy, we should look at the economic scene at independence. India in 1947 was a very poor country. Per capita income had been stagnating over the long period of colonial rule, and the standard of living was abysmally low. The bulk of India's population depended on agriculture that was largely at the mercy of the vagaries of monsoon and that made little use of modern technology or inputs.

Chandra[1] has summarized the economic backwardness and under-development of India graphically:

> In 1950, the per capita availability of cereals and pulses was 394.9 grams per day; of cloth 10 meters a year. The death rate was 27.4 per 1,000 persons and the infant mortality rate was between 175–190 per 1,000 live births. An average Indian could expect to have a life span of barely thirty-two years. Epidemics like smallpox, plague and cholera and diseases like dysentery and diarrhea, malaria and other fevers carried away millions. Malaria affected nearly one-fourth of the population. In 1943, there were 10 medical colleges turning out about 700 graduates and 27 medical schools turning out nearly 1,000 licentiates (Gujral 1965).[2] In 1951, there were only 18,000 graduate doctors in

---

1. Bipan Chandra, "The Colonial Legacy," in *The Indian Economy: Problems and Prospects,* ed. Bimal Jalan (New York: Viking Penguin, 1995), pp. 12–13.

2. M.L. Gujral, "Health Organization and Medical Relief," in *Economic History of India 1857–1956,* ed. V.B. Singh (Delhi: Allied Publishers, 1965).

independent India. The vast majority of towns had no sanitation and large parts of those cities which had, were kept out of the modern system, sanitation being confined to civil lines and other areas where Europeans and rich Indians lived. For example, the area of old Delhi, from Chandni Chowk to Sadar Bazar, was not covered by the modern system of sanitation. A modern water supply system was unknown in villages and absent in a large number of towns. A vast majority of towns were without electricity and for rural areas was unthinkable. The vast majority of Indians had no access to education and in 1947, nearly 88 percent were illiterate.[3]

Under British colonial rule, India had lost many decades of growth. Both agricultural and industrial growth were minuscule, making over-all growth very small. Estimates of the annual growth rate of national income over the period from 1914 to 1946 vary from 1.22 percent to 0.73 percent. In per capita terms these correspond to 0.26 percent to −0.22 percent.[4]

Blyn estimates that per capita agricultural output declined by 0.72 percent per year over 1911–41, and the food-grain output declined at the rate of 1.14 percent per year.[5] The low level of agricultural technology is reflected in the decline in food-grain yield at a rate of 0.44 percent per year.[6] Blyn also underlines the meager effort made to improve agricultural technology in India and observes that "as of the late 1930s, about 32 million ploughs were being used in India and agricultural development agencies were selling 7 or 8 thousand (im-proved ploughs) per year."

This neglect of agriculture and its resulting decline were reflected in frequent famines that ravaged all parts of India. In the second half of the nineteenth century, nearly 30 million people died of starvation in famines. Partly as a consequence, India's population grew only 0.4 percent per year between 1871 and 1921.[7]

3. A. Maddison, *Class Structure and Economic Growth: India and Pakistan since the Moghuls* (London: George Allen and Unwin Limited, 1971).

4. R.W. Goldsmith, *The Financial Development of India: 1860–1977* (Delhi: Oxford University Press, 1983).

5. George Blyn, *Agricultural Trends in India, 1891–1947: Output, Availability, and Productivity* (Philadelphia: University of Pennsylvania Press, 1966).

6. A.K. Bagchi, *Private Investment in India 1900–1939* (Cambridge: Cambridge University Press, 1972).

7. J.N. Sinha, "Demographic Trends," in *Economic History of India 1857–1956,* ed. V.B. Singh (Delhi: Allied Publishers, 1965).

Similarly, the level of industrialization was low. In 1939, year-round employment in factories was only 1.5 million.[8] India's population per the 1941 census was 389 million. Even though Indian industries got a boost during the war years, by 1951, employment in modern industries was only 2.3 percent of the labor force.[9]

Although the level of industrialization was low, Indian industries had some vigor, unlike agriculture. Indian entrepreneurs had established factories in a diversified set of industries. They had done this on their own and in spite of the colonial government's policies. Thus, in many consumer goods industries, such as in the manufacture of textiles, sugar, soap, matches, and paper, India was more or less self-sufficient. Moreover, some intermediate and capital goods industries had also begun to develop, including the production of iron and steel, cement, basic chemicals, metallurgy, and engineering goods. The independence movement, with its boycott of imported goods, put an emphasis on *swadeshi* (self-rule). The two world wars also provided opportunities for Indian industries to grow as the wars reduced the supply of foreign goods and demanded manufactured goods to support military efforts. Although it was self-sufficient in consumer goods industries, India depended mainly on imports of machinery and machine tools for capital goods. In 1950, almost 90 percent of these were imported.[10]

By 1950–51, India had settled down somewhat from the aftermath of the upheaval of partition, and embarked on its journey of economic development. At that stage, its population was 361 million, with a life expectancy at birth of 32.4 years for men and 31.7 years for women and literacy rates of 27.2 percent for men and 8.9 percent for women. Its per capita net national product was Rs.240 ($50); it produced 50.8 million tonnes of food grain, or 140 kilograms per person of food grain per year; it made 1.04 million tonnes of steel, 2.7 million tonnes of cement, and 0.3 million tonnes of crude oil; and it generated 14 kilowatt-hours of electricity per person per year. From this low level of development, India started off with hope and, what is most remarkable, with faith in democratic universal adult franchise.

---

8. See Bagchi, *Investment in India 1900–1939*.

9. Bipan Chandra, *Nationalism and Colonialism in Modern India* (Delhi: Orient Longman, 1979).

10. P. Chaudhuri, *The Indian Economy: Poverty and Development* (Delhi: Vikas Publishing House, 1979).

The Genesis of India's Development Strategy

Long before independence, Indian nationalists had started thinking about the objectives and strategy of economic development that independent India should pursue. Thus, we have four documents representing four different perspectives: the report of the National Planning Committee (NPC) set up by the Indian National Congress in 1938; the Bombay Plan published in 1944–45 by some of India's leading industrialists; the plan published by the doyen of Indian engineers, M. Vishveshwariayya;[11] and the People's Plan published in 1944 by the Federation of Labor, B.N. Banerjee, et al.[12] These four different perspectives of politicians, industrialists, technologists, and labor leaders all agreed on the central objective of poverty removal and on the importance of the role of government in economic development. They all desired a doubling of per capita income in ten to fifteen years, elimination of poverty, minimum calorie intake targets, eradication of illiteracy, and provision of medical care. Incidentally, none of these goals have been met even now, fifty years after independence. While the NPC and Vishveshwariayya strongly stressed industrialization—with particular emphasis on heavy and capital goods industries—and equated development with industrialization, the People's Plan called for an emphasis on agriculture. The Bombay Plan asked for more balanced development, recognizing the importance of heavy and basic industries but also cautioning against excessive emphasis on them. Import substitution, self-reliance, and dominant roles for the state and the public sector were clearly articulated in most of these plans. Accordingly, the eradication of poverty and the satisfaction of basic needs are reflected in the directive principles of the constitution adopted in 1950. All of India's plans have reiterated these objectives over the period of the next fifteen years.

The NPC was headed by Jawaharlal Nehru, the future prime minister and chairman of the commission. The committee included "well-known industrialists, financiers, economists, professors, scientists, as well as representatives from the Trade Union Congress and the Village Industries Association."[13]

---

11. Sir M. Vishveshwariayya, *Planned Economy for India* (Bangalore City: Bangalore Press, 1934).

12. B.N. Banerjee, et al., *People's Plan for Economic Development of India* (Bombay: The Indian Federation of Labor, 1944).

13. J. Nehru, *The Discovery of India* (New York: The John Day Company, 1946), p. 399.

The NPC recognized that the first task was to set an objective, a goal.

> Obviously we could not consider any problem, much less plan, without some definite aim and social objective. That aim was declared to be to insure an adequate standard of living for the masses. In other words, to get rid of the appalling poverty of the people. . . . There was lack of food, of clothing, of housing and of every other essential requirement of human existence. To remove this lack and insure an irreducible minimum standard for everybody, the national income had to be greatly increased, and, in addition to this increased production there had to be a more equitable distribution of wealth.[14]

The Bombay Plan was prepared by Purshotamdas Thakurdas, J.R.D. Tata, G.D. Birla, Shri Ram, Kasturbhai Lalbhai, A.D. Shroff, Ardeshir Dalal, and John Mathai—top industrialists in the country.[15] They also identified elimination of poverty as the central objective of development.

This consensus on the central objective was easy to understand, given the widespread and deep poverty in the country. Not so obvious was the consensus on the need for government planning and activism. Back in 1931, at the session in Karachi of the Indian National Congress presided over by Sardar Patel, Gandhiji (Mahatma Gandhi) moved the Resolution on Fundamental Rights and Economic Programme that was drafted by Jawaharlal Nehru. With the support of the three most influential leaders of the Congress, it stated that, in independent India, "the state shall own or control key industries and services, mineral resources, railways, waterways, shipping and other means of public transport."[16]

Gandhiji was skeptical of too much state power. Yet he also recognized the potential ill effects of private monopolies. His solution was "trusteeship," under which private individuals would operate large enterprises as trustees of society's capital.[17]

While the authors of the Bombay Plan wanted an active role for

---

14. Ibid., p. 402.

15. Purshotamdas Thakurdas, et al., *A Plan for Economic Development for India* (London: Penguin), 1945.

16. K.T. Shah, ed., *Report—National Planning Committee* (Bombay: Vora and Co., 1949), p. 27.

17. M.L. Dantawala, "Trusteeship: An Alternative Ideology," *IASSI Quarterly,* Vol. 10, no. 1, July–September, 1991, pp. 179–210.

government in development, they preferred to have state control rather than state ownership, except in special cases. They recognized the need to regulate private industries and to have some limitation on the rights attached to private property. The Bombay Plan accepted a large role for state control in a variety of forms including the fixation of prices; limitation of dividends; prescription of work conditions and wages for labor; nomination of government directors on boards of management; control of production through licensing of new enterprises and expansion of existing ones; control of allocation and distribution of consumer goods, raw materials, semifinished goods, and capital goods; control of new capital issues; and control of trade and foreign exchange.

There was also a consensus that rapid economic development required accelerated investment and optimal allocation of the scarce resources of investable surplus and foreign exchange. In short, government planning was needed to accelerate savings and investment as well as to ensure optimal allocation. The free market was not expected to accomplish this by itself because the country was very poor and had a low savings rate, and because critical infrastructure projects required large investments beyond the capability of Indian private entrepreneurs. Having experience with the East India Company—which came to India to trade, gradually established control over part of the country, and finally led to the takeover of India by the British government—the option to invite foreign investors to set up such projects was not even discussed.

The need for a concerted effort and balanced development of different sectors of the economy was generally accepted. A large country such as India was not expected to have the scope for expanding exports without a fall in the price of its exports in a world where trade had remained stagnant. Thus, markets for domestic products had to be found domestically. This, along with many other externalities, required a big push by the state, according to Rosenstein-Rodan,[18] whose thoughts were quite influential. He argued that "the whole of the industry to be created is to be treated and planned like one huge firm or trust." Maintaining that the "first task of industrialization is to provide training and 'skilling' of labor" and that "it is not profitable for a

---

18. P. Rosenstein-Rodan, "Problems of Industrialization of Eastern and Southeastern Europe," *Economic Journal,* 1943, pp. 202–211.

private entrepreneur to invest in training labor" because "an entrepreneur who invests in training workers may lose capital if these workers contract with another firm" he concluded that "although not a good investment for a private firm, it is the best investment for the state. It is also a good investment for the bulk of industries to be created when taken as a whole, although it may represent irrecoverable costs for a smaller unit." However, complementarity of different industries provides the most important set of arguments in the form of a large-scale planned industrialization.[19]

Rosenstein-Rodan illustrated this by an example. Suppose a shoe factory is set up that employs 20,000 workers who were earlier unemployed. The workers would want to spend their income on a variety of goods but only a small fraction of the income would be spent on shoes. The shoe factory, in the absence of exports, would find that there is not adequate demand for the shoes it produces. Now, instead of one shoe factory, a whole range of factories are set up, each producing a different consumer good; then the workers employed in all the factories would create a demand for all the goods produced by the factories. Thus, the industries that produce the bulk of the goods demanded by wage earners can be said to be complementary. Because of this, it was argued, industries have to be developed in a balanced and somewhat simultaneous way. This argument was valid for an economy that had little opportunity to trade with others, and, due to the export pessimism of Indian planners, it was seen as an important justification for government activism.

To the nationalists, economic development meant industrialization based on modern science and technology. Because land was scarce in India, there was limited scope to provide increasing incomes to growing populations engaged in agriculture. The long-term solution to increasing incomes was to employ workers in more productive activities for which wages could be higher. Only industrialization provided such an opportunity. This was clear in Jawaharlal Nehru's statements,

> No country can be politically and economically independent, even within the framework of international interdependence, unless it is highly industrialized and has developed its power resources to the ut-

---

19. T.N. Srinivasan, "Development Thought, Strategy and Policy: Then and Now," background paper for *World Development Report 1991* (Washington, DC: The World Bank, 1990).

most. Nor can it achieve or maintain high standards of living and liquidate poverty without the aid of modern technology in almost every
sphere of life.[20]

To pursue a policy of industrialization, it was argued, heavy industries must get priority. All industries need capital goods, and many
require the input of capital goods such as steel. With poor resources
for export, India must produce capital goods domestically in order
to industrialize rapidly. Absence of capital goods and heavy industries would make India dependent on others. Thus, both the NPC
report and the Bombay Plan argued for the development on a priority basis of electrical power and basic capital goods industries as a
necessary condition for rapid industrialization. In fact, the Bombay
Plan allocated nearly 35 percent of its total plan outlay to basic
industries.

Gandhiji's emphasis on *khadi* (hand-spun cotton) and *swadeshi* during the independence movement had its own economic logic. This was
reflected in India's approach to industrialization. While heavy and
basic capital goods industries were to be given high priority, the small-
scale sector was to be promoted at the same time. This sector was to
provide consumer goods as well as components for engineering industries. Thus, medium-scale, small-scale, and cottage industries were to
provide employment and reduce the need for capital, as they were
presumed to be more labor-intensive than large-scale industries. These
industries had to be protected by product reservations. This was also
perceived as a way to promote widespread entrepreneurship and to
spread industrial activities geographically. Both the NPC report and
the Bombay Plan argued for emphasis on and protection of medium-
scale, small-scale, and cottage industries.

Entry of foreign capital was resisted by Indian nationalists. As mentioned above, the East India Company experience made them see foreign capital as the beginning of economic dependence and domination.
Although the need for inflow of capital, modern machinery, and advanced technology was recognized, the nationalists argued for obtaining them by borrowing capital rather than by accepting direct foreign
investment. The Bombay Plan proposed to ensure that investment
funds should not be accompanied by political influence or interference.

---

20. J. Nehru, *The Discovery of India* (New York: The John Day Company, 1946),
p. 356.

The plan also suggested that the government should borrow loan capital internationally and should, in turn, provide it to domestic entrepreneurs through domestic financial institutions. It was also seen as necessary for the state to prohibit foreign ownership, management, or control of key areas of the economy.

Finally, Indian thinkers had realized the need for agricultural development as a complement to industrialization. Modernization of agriculture was important because the bulk of India's population depended on agriculture, and because increasing agricultural income was needed for consumer demand of goods produced by industries.

Thus, the strategy of economic development that India followed had the following elements:

- The central objective was to eliminate poverty.
- Planning had a critical role in mobilizing savings, in allocating scarce resources, and in coordinating balanced development.
- Public ownership and control of critical sectors was necessary. The public sector had to take the initiative in the early phase of development, as the private sector was not capable of mobilizing required resources and unable to take the needed risks.
- The scarce resources of savings and foreign exchange had to be allocated through import licensing and domestic production permits.
- Economic development meant industrialization through self-reliance and was to be based on science and technology.
- Primary emphasis was to be on heavy and basic capital goods industries.
- Medium-scale, small-scale, and cottage industries had to be promoted and protected in order to generate employment and lower capital needs.
- Agricultural development was to proceed side by side with industrialization, as it is complementary to industrial development.
- Foreign capital had to be mainly in the form of loan capital. Borrowing was to be done by the government and distributed to domestic entrepreneurs through financial institutions.
- Direct foreign investment was to be permitted only if it did not involve political influence or interference by foreign vested interests. Foreign ownership or control over key sectors had to be prohibited.

One should reiterate that this was not something that was imposed by a Fabian Jawaharlal Nehru, who was too much of a democrat to do that, but that there was a national consensus on these objectives. Even when he would have liked India to adopt socialist principles of economic organization, Nehru wanted this to happen democratically: "So long as a big step in the right direction was taken, I felt that the very dynamics involved in the process of change would facilitate further adaptation and practice." He also hoped that democracy, based on adult franchise, would push the government in a socialist direction.[21]

The Evolution of Planning Paradigms and Models

In the first two years after independence, the government was preoccupied with the aftermath of partition, with its bloodshed, millions of refugees, and their rehabilitation. At the same time, the problem of some 500 princely states also needed resolution. It is a tribute to the spirit of democracy and the mass base of the independence movement that, despite these problems, the Constituent Assembly drafted a constitution and India declared itself a republic on January 26, 1950. The first general elections were held between October 1951 and February 1952. Even before the election the government got down to the business of economic development. The NPC was constituted in March 1950, and the first five-year plan was launched in July 1951.

The First Five-Year Plan

The First Five-Year Plan covered the period from 1951–52 to 1955–56. More or less a collection of projects, the basic notion behind the plan was a conviction that government must undertake a large number of development projects, and the plan was intended to tell the people of India that a new era had begun. Operating from the assumption that the most pressing problem of India was its uncertain agriculture, the plan initiated a number of major multipurpose schemes to provide irrigation, generate power, and help in flood control. One of these schemes was the Bhakra Dam in the Punjab, which later proved to be the cornerstone of the Punjab's agricultural development. The First Plan was considered to be a success as most of its projects were initiated and made considerable and timely progress. The investment rate in-

---

21. Ibid., pp. 346, 349.

creased over the plan period from 5 percent of GDP to 7 percent of GDP. The target of private investment of Rs.16,000 million was realized, but the public sector investment target of Rs.240,000 million was not fully achieved.

The First Five-Year Plan did not have a formal planning model but, instead, stressed investment for capital accumulation in the spirit of the one-sector Harrod-Domar model. This model argued that production requires capital, and capital can be accumulated through investment; the faster the accumulation, the higher the growth rate. Investment in large infrastructure and heavy industries, "the temples of modern India," as Nehru called them while inaugurating the Bhakra Dam in July 1954, required initiative by the public sector. The role of the public sector began to crystallize and became formalized in the Industrial Policy Resolution.

The Second Five-Year Plan

Planning for economic development generated much excitement and attracted some of the leading intellectuals in the country. Consequently, the Second Five-Year Plan (1956–57 to 1960–61) was based on a theoretical model developed by P.C. Mahalanobis, a member of the NPC and a noted statistician who had earlier founded the Indian Statistical Institute (ISI). Mahalanobis's model was similar to the model of the Soviet economist Feldman, whom Mahalanobis may have known, as the ISI collaborated with Soviet academicians. The Mahalanobis model suggested that if a country wants to reach a high level of consumption rapidly, the best strategy is to invest first in building the capacity to produce capital goods for some years. After accumulating enough of such capacity, the country can use the capital goods to augment its capacity to produce consumer goods. Thus, the emphasis on heavy industries and capital goods was theoretically justified and formed the basis of the Second Plan. This Second Plan raised the investment rate to 8 percent of GDP.

The Mahalanobis model on which the Second Five-Year Plan was based provided the real intellectual articulation of India's development strategy. Subsequent plan models, in a sense, only further elaborated that philosophy. The basic insights of the Mahalanobis model are the following: (1) The one-sector Harrod-Domar model assumes that all savings can be converted into investment. However, to convert savings into investment, one needs investment goods. Thus, one must look at sectoral details; (2) An emphasis on basic capital and heavy industries (machines to build machines to build machines ... to build fertilizer plants) in the early years would give much higher consumption in the future.

The distrust of international trade was not confined to Indian planners alone. Raul Prebish in Latin America had argued that trade between the Center (developed countries) and the Periphery (developing countries) is unequal and that it leads to dependence of the Periphery upon the Center. The newly independent countries, keen to avoid any dependence whatsoever, naturally remained skeptical of trade.

It should, however, be noted that the Second Five-Year Plan did argue that India has a comparative advantage in heavy and basic industries and that an emphasis on these was justified. With its large deposits of high-grade iron ore (of which India is a substantial exporter), manganese, and coal, all relatively close to each other, India had all the natural resources to produce steel at a low cost. All it needed was technology and know-how, which others were willing to provide. Thus, four steel plants were established in India, one each with the help of Soviet, West German, British, and U.S. collaborators. If, in the end, the Indian steel industry has not always been globally competitive, it has more to do with its being under the public sector and less with Indian's comparative advantage. However, the Mahalanobis model was a closed-economy model reflecting the export pessimism that was widespread in the post–World War II years.

Toward the end of the Second Plan, questions were raised in Parliament by the socialist leader Dr. Ram Manohar Lohia about the beneficiary to this development. Nehru, ever sensitive, responded:

It is said that the national income over the First and Second Plans has gone up by 42 percent and the per capita income by 20 percent. A legitimate query is made where has this gone? It is a very legitimate query; to some extent of course, you can see where it has gone. I sometimes do address large gatherings in the villages and I can see that they are better-fed and better-clothed, they build brick houses. . . . Nevertheless, this does not apply to everybody in India. Some people probably have hardly benefited. Some people may even be facing various difficulties. The fact remains, however, that this advance in our national income, in our per capita income has taken place, and I think it is desirable that we should enquire more deeply as to where this has gone and appoint some expert committee to enquire into how exactly this additional income that has come to the country or per capita has spread.[22]

Subsequently, a committee was appointed under the chairmanship of P.C. Mahalanobis. A working group was also constituted around this time to define a poverty line. This working group defined it in terms of aggregate per capita expenditure per person that would provide 2,100 calories per person per day in urban areas (and 2,400 in rural areas) along with minimal clothing. Accordingly, the NPC prepared a fifteen-year perspective plan to provide these basic needs to the entire population.[23]

The Third Five-Year Plan

The theoretical construct behind the Third Five-Year Plan (1961–62 to 1965–66) was more sophisticated than that behind the Second Plan. The perception that planning required sectoral allocations of investment was further refined in subsequent plan models. Multisectoral input-output models were used to determine intersectorally consistent investment allocations. This consistency ensured that the development of all sectors would be such that there would be neither shortage nor excess capacity in any one sector. The demands for and supplies of output of all the sectors would balance. Academic economists developed even more elaborate intertemporal models for optimal allocations.[24]

The Fourth Five-Year Plan

The Fourth Plan approach was essentially the same as that of the Third Plan. However, the Fourth Five-Year Plan recognized that it was not enough to ensure consistency of demand and supply for the target year alone. The balances had to be ensured for intermediate years as well in order to ensure that in a technical, physical sense it was possible to go

22. Planning Commission, *Report of the Committee on Distribution of Income and Levels of Living*, vol. 1 (New Delhi: Planning Commission, 1964), p. 1.

23. P. Pant, "Perspective of Development 1961–76," in *Poverty and Income Distribution in India*, T.N. Srinivasan and P.K. Bardhan (Calcutta: Statistical Publishing Society, 1962).

24. R. Eckaus and K.S. Parikh, *Planning for Growth—Multisectoral Intertemporal Models Applied to India* (Cambridge, MA: MIT Press, 1968).

"from here to there," or from the initial starting state to the state envisaged by the plan targets. This was done for the Fourth Plan period. In addition, the Fourth Plan approach paid much greater attention to the structure of imports, which were exogenously projected in the Third Plan model. In a sense, the Fourth Plan endogenized imports in the model to make them consistent with the sectoral demand-supply balances.

The Fifth Five-Year Plan

The Fifth Five-Year Plan recognized that aggregate private consumption projections must be consistent with the development of the economy and that aggregate income, savings, and consumption must balance. However, the methodology of the Fifth Plan reverted to the target-year model of the Third Plan variety and did not explicitly account for the material balances over the individual years of the plan. The Fifth Plan methodology also paid attention to financial resource mobilization, and a detailed scheme for financing the plan was worked out.

This basic theoretical construct of a multisectoral model to determine a set of balanced sectoral capital allocation and target output levels has continued, albeit with refinements of various kinds, for subsequent plans. An important assumption behind this approach is that government will be capable of realizing plan targets with appropriate policies. These policies, however, have not been adequately articulated so that one could not say whether the policies would have led to the desired outcome. This has been a major weakness of Indian planning. The formal connection between the financing scheme and the planning model was weak, and it was not possible to see the connections between the physical targets and the financial resource flows.

The Fifth Five-Year Plan was the first to bring poverty alleviation explicitly into the plan model. It generated variants in which significant redistribution of income were stipulated. However, the assumption of an all-powerful government persisted, and the policies required to achieve such redistribution were not spelled out, let alone integrated into the plans.

Subsequent Plans

The Sixth Five-Year Plan modeling system integrated the various features of the methodology of the Third, Fourth, and Fifth Plans. In the earlier plans the investments over the plan period were not formally made consistent with a long-term perspective plan. This was done in the Sixth Plan. Submodels of important individual sectors were used to work out material balances, as in the Fourth Plan. The financial-resource-mobilization calculus elaborated in the Fifth Plan model was more formally linked to the main model. Similarly, private final consumption was also incorporated into the model, as in the Fifth Plan. And, although the Sixth Plan model was a target-year model, by assuming that all sectors would grow smoothly over the plan period, it implicitly introduced investment gestation lags. This, however, does not account for the adjustment difficulties due to bottlenecks arising from the initial composition of capacities in the different sectors of the economy. Yet, while the methodology of the Sixth Plan was technically superior to that of earlier plans, it did not introduce new conceptual evolution in planning methodology, and it still exhibited a number of fundamental difficulties.

The modeling sytem of the Seventh Plan was in spirit essentially the same as that for the Sixth Plan. No new methodological innovations were made in the Eighth Five-Year Plan, either.

This is a very brief description of the planning models behind India's five-year plans. Of course, planning involved many technical working groups of experts as well as integration of the experience, wisdom, and knowledge of many people. Yet, in a sense, the models reflect the perception of the problem and the premises behind the strategy of development that India followed:

1. Efficient allocation of investment is the most critical problem of development. In its attempt to realize planned allocations, the Indian government created an elaborate system of quantitative restrictions based on licensing and control.
2. The government was perceived to be all-powerful and, despite India's mixed economy, able to attain the plan targets through the system of licensing and control.
3. The input-output model implied that the inputs required in a production process would be needed in fixed proportions (Leontief technology). The implication was that possibilities of substitutions either did not exist or were not considered important. This also minimized the importance of prices.
4. Plan targets were a matter of faith in that they implied that

planners could know all that was needed and that information availability was no constraint.

5. Development was equated with industrialization.

6. Self-reliance was equated with self-sufficiency. Coupled with export pessimism, this encouraged an import-substitution strategy.

7. The public sector was to be given primacy over the economy not only because the emphasis on heavy industry required public sector initiatives but also because private entrepreneurs could not be trusted to act in the national interest.

8. There was an implicit distrust of markets and the private sector, with its profit-maximizing behavior. In spite of the elaborate mechanism of controls, the government could not control the profit-maximizing behavior of traders, but could only alter their modes of operation. Instead of providing socially beneficial services, the government was engaged energetically in unproductive rent seeking, resulting in politicians and bureaucrats too willing to be corrupted.

9. The distrust of markets and the faith in quantitative controls implied a belief that everyone but politicians and bureaucrats is selfish. We now know better.

10. With an all-powerful government, incentives and policies did not seem important. Many of the plan documents contained chapters on framing policies. They also recognized the limitations of available policy instruments to the government. Yet the plans contained very little evidence of the necessary economic analysis to show that the available policy instruments could indeed lead to their realization. Although stability of prices and noninflationary development was desired in the plans, prices were not acknowledged in the construction of the models, nor was the relationship between prices and policy instruments elaborated or explored.

The plan documents usually stated that appropriate policies would be devised to reach the targets. But individuals, whether consumers, producers, traders, bureaucrats, or politicians, all adapt their behavior to protect their own interests in response to government policy. Whether any kind of policy could have led to the realization of the targets was not obvious. For example, plan documents set targets for the production of wheat and rice. But food is grown by more than 70 million farmers in the country. What policies could induce the farmers to *want* to grow food and make them able to grow food as per the targets is a question never addressed in the Indian plans.[25] Moreover, if there were policies that could have led to the realization of the targets, it was often not clear whether these policies were likely to be followed.

Let us return to how the plans performed. The Third Plan ran into trouble caused by two consecutive severe droughts (with a probability of occurring once in 200 years) and by the India-Pakistan war in 1965, which interrupted the process of economic development.

Prime Minister Nehru died in 1964, and his successor, Lal Bahadur Shastri, passed away in January 1966. Indira Gandhi was put into place as prime minister by the party bosses of the Indian National Congress, the majority party. They had hoped to control her, but she had different ideas. Without a dominating charismatic leader, in-fighting in the Congress became more active. In the election of 1967, the Congress Party lost a number of states to the opposition, who had formed anti-Congress coalitions. Mrs. Gandhi decided to revitalize the party and capture the public imagination. In 1969, she split the Congress Party, took a radical stance, and nationalized major banks.

The economic consequences of this nationalization were far-reaching. It led to a vast expansion of bank branches and spread banking services to smaller towns and rural areas. It also led to a large expansion of employment in the banking industry. Today, the bank employees' union exercises significant political clout and constitutes a major obstacle to financial sector reforms. The government's populist policies and frequent interference unsettled the banking industry. Banks were directed to give loans to public sector enterprises irrespective of their viability. The public sector units, assured of loans from nationalized banks, operated with soft budget constraints. Even the little pressure for efficiency that a hard budget constraint would have imposed was removed. Banks were also directed to give loans on concessional terms to agriculturists. While that should have been welcome to many poor farmers who needed credit to increase yields, these

---

25. N.S.S. Narayana and K.S. Parikh, "Agricultural Planning and Policy in Draft Sixth Plan: Will Farmers Fulfill Planners' Expectations?" *Economic and Political Weekly,* vol. 14, nos. 30, 31, and 32, August 1979, pp. 1295–1306.

loans were often written off through political fiat. This created a climate in which farmers who repaid their loans felt foolish.

In the general election of 1971, Indira Gandhi presented a new slogan "*garibi hatao*" (remove poverty), in response to the opposition's slogan "*Indira hatao*" (remove Indira). Her radical stance led to a massive election victory, and the Congress Party captured two-thirds of the seats in Parliament.

Indira Gandhi's finest hour was the liberation of Bangladesh in 1971. In the following state election, the Congress captured many states. Unfortunately, the more than two-thirds majority in Parliament and control over most of the states that she had gained were frittered away, and no new significant economic measures were initiated. More visible "socialistic" measures were carried out. In spite of contrary advice given to Indira Gandhi by some of her advisors—such as Bagicha Singh Minhas who was then a member of the NPC—the wholesale trade in wheat was nationalized. Fortunately, the potentially disastrous consequences of that nationalization quickly became evident, and the decision was reversed. The 1973 oil shock put the Indian economy under great stress and led to high inflation, which was further aggravated by the drought of 1974. Thus, the wholesale price index increased by 49.7 percent between January 1973 and January 1975. This was unprecedented, as the inflation rate had seldom exceeded 10 percent prior to 1973.

In June 1975, the Allahabad high court set aside Mrs. Gandhi's election and disqualified her from contesting election for three years. She considered resigning when, at the urging of her son Sanjay Gandhi, an internal Emergency was declared that lasted until 1977. Sanjay was a believer in private enterprise and did not support socialistic policies. Meanwhile, Mohan Kumaramangalam, an influential leftist adviser of Mrs. Gandhi, had died. These events ended the tide of nationalist takeovers in 1973–74 and initiated the end of the influence of the Soviet-inspired Left. In fact, during the emergency the government broke a railway strike with a toughness against workers that had never been seen before. Many other excesses were committed during the Emergency; the corruption of absolute power spread rapidly. As a result, in the national elections of 1977, Mrs. Gandhi and her party were humiliated by an angry electorate. However, two years of rule by the Janata Dal between 1977 and 1979 did not produce any new initiatives on the economic front. The earlier policy regime more or less continued.

Indira Gandhi returned to power in the general election of early 1980 with the slogan "government that works" and initiated some measures of economic liberalization. She borrowed from "the IMF to relieve resource constraints due to the impact of the second 'oil shock'—itself a major departure for a Nehruvian."[26] That brought about some positive results. Following her assassination in 1984, Rajiv Gandhi succeeded her in office. In the general election of 1984, Rajiv Gandhi won the largest majority ever: 76 percent of seats and 48 percent of the popular vote, surpassing even those counts obtained by Nehru. Rajiv Gandhi carried the process of economic liberalization a bit further, as described by Desai in an earlier *India Briefing*:

> Rajiv Gandhi accelerated both the borrowing and the opening up of the economy, instituting a policy of import liberalization and industry deregulation. The exchange rate was actively manipulated to depreciate the rupee and thereby encourage exports. Incentives were given to exporters: half of export profits were deductible for income tax purposes: for example, the interest rate on export trade was reduced from 12 percent to 9 percent, and duty-free input of capital goods was allowed in selected export industries. This policy did not touch the public sector, nor was the public sector given priority for new industrial products and processes. Rajiv's was a policy of accelerating growth by borrowing, but without any drastic restructuring of the economy.[27]

Rajiv Gandhi wanted to move much faster down the road of economic reforms, but perhaps the very large majority took the sense of urgency from him. He said (to this author in a meeting of the Economic Advisory Council just before the election in 1989) that he would keenly pursue the reform agenda in his second term after the election, but he never returned to power. The seeds of the macroeconomic crisis of 1991 were sown during the 1980s by general policy inaction. India's national account was nearly balanced in its external trade in 1978, but the oil crisis of 1979–81 pushed the current account deficit to 2 percent of GDP (30 percent of exports) by 1981. No particular measures to correct the situation were taken, and the deficit increased. It averaged 25 percent of exports over 1982–84 and 40 percent of exports over

26. Meghnad Desai, "Economic Reform: Stalled by Politics?" in *India Briefing: Staying the Course,* ed. Philip Oldenburg (New York: The Asia Society, and Armonk, NY: M.E. Sharpe, 1995).

27. Ibid., p. 82.

1984–90. Although the deficits were covered by IMF loans disbursed over 1982 to 1984 and by commercial borrowings, the debt burden was such that even the export boom of the second half of 1980s, stimulated by a flexible exchange-rate policy, was inadequate to meet rising interest payments on external debt.

In addition, the large fiscal deficit of the government increased from 4.5 percent of GDP in 1980 to 8.5 percent by 1985–86 and stayed at that level over the second half of the 1980s. The coalition government of V.P. Singh followed by that of Chandrashekar only accelerated the buildup to the economic crisis of 1991.

The Performance of the Indian Economy (1947–91)

After this thumbnail sketch of political history, we look at the performance of the Indian economy in the planning era from 1947 to 1991.

If one were to look back from the vantage point of 1990, on the eve of the economic crisis of 1991, one would have noticed many changes over the previous four decades. But the achievements were disappointing compared with India's hopes and aspirations. What were India's achievements and what had been the disappointments?

Poverty had not increased. In fact, it had been reduced even though the population had increased. Yet more than 200 million people remained below the poverty line.

"Abundant" food was produced: price support for food-grain production brought what appeared to be ever-increasing stocks of food-grain. Still, the more than 200 million people below the poverty line did not get enough to eat.

Life expectancy at birth had increased from thirty-two to fifty-five years, and yet fifty-five was still below that of other countries. Although in most countries the life expectancy for women is higher than that for men, in India it remained lower for many years. The gap has been narrowing slowly, and only recently did life expectancy for women become higher than that for men.[28] The "nonchild" literacy rate, expressed as the percentage of the population above 7 years who could read, had increased from 20 percent in 1951 to 55

---

28. Pravin Visaria, "The Demographic Dimension of Indian Economic Development Since 1947," in *The Development Process of the Indian Economy,* eds. P.R. Brahmananda and V.R. Panchamukhi (New Delhi: Himalaya Publishing House, 1987).

percent for 1991, but that still left approximately 200 million adult illiterates in 1991. The 3.6 percent per year growth rate of the Indian economy over 1951–85 was higher than the 2.2 percent per year growth rate of the population, but was still much less than the planned growth rates over these years.

A diversified industrial base had been created. Yet, many of the industries were not internationally competitive and produced substandard goods at high prices using considerable physical and financial resources. India had pursued a policy of self-reliance that permitted only selective imports of technology and in which import content was reduced in a planned way. However, many of these industries seemed to need to import technology all over again. The public sector was developed in order to reach the "commanding heights" of the economy and to generate investable surplus. Instead, it absorbed large amounts of resources without producing commensurate returns. Rather than leading the economy to commanding heights, the public sector crippled it with infrastructural bottlenecks and inefficiency. The emphasis on the public sector may have helped contain the expansion of large private monopolies but the cost of inefficient public monopolies may have been a lower growth rate and a larger incidence of poverty.

In summary, growth had been inadequate; poverty, hunger, and illiteracy persisted amid abundant food stocks; much of industry remained internationally noncompetitive and required import of technology; and the public sector did not generate significant surplus and remained inefficient.

We can look at this in some detail. To take care of fluctuations in GDP due to transient shocks such as from the weather, growth rates have been worked out over different periods based on a trend line. Between 1951 and 1981, the growth rate of GDP averaged only 3.6 percent per year and that of per capita GDP only 1.4 percent per year. The growth rate over the 1980s was 5.4 percent but was not sustainable, as became evident in the macroeconomic crisis of 1991.

A major element of India's development strategy was industrialization. The structure of the Indian economy had changed significantly over the years. Agriculture contributed only 30.9 percent to GDP in 1990–91 compared with 55.4 percent in 1950–51. The share of industry had gone up from 11.4 percent in 1950–51 to 21.1 percent in 1990–91. Although the public sector had absorbed a large part of planned investment, in 1990–91 the public sector contributed only 2.78 percent to GDP.[29]

While the structure of the economy changed significantly, the structure of employment did not show a commensurate change. In 1961, 75.6 percent of workers were engaged in primary sectors (agriculture, fishery, and mining). By 1993–94 this was reduced to only 64.7 percent. Employment in the secondary (industry) sector increased from 11.2 percent in 1961 to only 14.8 percent in 1993–94.[30]

The most disappointing aspect of India's performance relates to its main objective of poverty removal. Almost every plan has had a target of removing poverty within fifteen years. And yet, poverty persisted and still persists in abundant measure. Over the years a large number of antipoverty programs have been initiated, and sizeable resources have been allocated to these measures. To a great extent, these programs had not reached the poor and the money spent had largely leaked out to the not-so-poor. One gets the feeling that perhaps faster economic growth would have helped the poor more than this government intervention.

Progress in some other measures of well-being and human development was also disappointing. Goals expected to be achieved in fifteen years were not achieved even after forty years. Thus, infant mortality lowered from 165 per 1,000 births in 1960 but was still as high as 90 per 1,000 births in 1990. The combined enrollment ratio for primary and secondary school was only 69 percent in 1990. The ratio was much lower for girls than for boys. This means that illiteracy will persist for years to come. India has increased its spending on education from 0.8 percent of GNP in 1950–51 to 3.2 percent of GNP in 1993–94. However, in 1990, India's expenditure on education ranked as low as 82 among 116 countries for which data were available. As Dreze and Sen point out, "from 1968 onward, successive versions of National Policy on Education have 'resolved' to raise this proportion to six percent, but this target has not been approached to this date."[31] For

---

29. Historical and up-to-date data on many aspects of India's economic development are available on the Internet from the website of the Ministry of Finance of the Government of India: http://www.nic.in/finmin/

30. Pravin Visaria, "Structure of the Indian Workforce, 1961–1994." *The Indian Journal of Labour Economics,* vol. 39, no. 4, December 1996, pp. 725–740.

31. Jean Dreze and Amartya Sen, *India: Economic Development and Social Opportunity* (Delhi: Oxford University Press, 1995).

more details see the United Nations Development Program's Human Development Report.[32]

What Went Wrong?

As we have seen, the objective of India's development strategy until 1991 had been to establish a socialistic pattern of society through economic growth with self-reliance, social justice, and alleviation of poverty. The institutional framework of a mixed economy was used in which both public and private sectors coexisted and the NPC set targets for sectoral development and various social welfare programs. The desired sectoral allocations were to be realized through industrial licensing and by using permits to restrict imports. For some time, self-reliance was equated with import substitution, and whenever a product was domestically available, imports were generally not permitted. To further self-reliance, a particular technology could be imported only once, followed by assimilation of the imported technology. Thus, the drive toward self-reliance was shaped more by a reduction in imports rather than by any drop in the domestic cost of production.

This is, admittedly, a very broadbrush picture of India's development strategy until 1991. It led to a number of problems, which had been recognized by some and are now obvious to many with 20/20 hindsight. Heavy industries required large sums of investment with high capital-to-output ratios, long gestation lags, and large imports of capital goods. Inadequate infrastructure, lack of experience, and the necessity of learning by doing further stretched the period of gestation. Costs increased and cascaded into all industries using these inputs. To protect the high-cost domestic industry against foreign imports, trade was restricted and protection through high tariffs and quotas was provided. To stimulate investment in spite of the high costs of domestically produced capital goods, capital was subsidized and factor prices got distorted, resulting in the choice of more capital-intensive techniques than would have been appropriate given the factor endowments of the country. Even if such a strategy were properly implemented, a capital-intensive slow-growth economy was bound to result. Given the tremendous scope such an economy provided for rent-seeking activities to industrialists, traders, bureaucrats, and politicians, it was much

---

32. United Nations Development Programme, *Human Development Report: 1994* (New York: Oxford University Press, 1994).

more profitable to seek these rents rather than to increase the efficiency of domestic production or improve the functioning of the domestic economy. The domestic industry, which was already protected from foreign competition through import restrictions against any domestically available product and from domestic competition through industrial licensing, thus had no incentive to be efficient.

The slow growth of the economy (3.6 percent on the average over 1950–80) and employment did not help much in reducing poverty, as the population kept growing at a rate exceeding 2.2 percent. Why didn't employment increase faster? For that we need to look at some aspects of industrial and labor policy.

Employment

Employment in the organized sector, for which data are available, is a good indicator of employment level. Unemployment numbers, particularly rural ones, are somewhat difficult to interpret. According to Dev, "In the absence of unemployment insurance, very few people in rural areas can afford to remain idle over a long period, and most of them would accept any available work."[33] The problem of employment in India is one of low productivity employment.

Employment in the organized public sector grew at annual rates of 4.3 percent, 3.7 percent, and 2.1 percent over the 1960s, 1970s, and 1980s, respectively, whereas in the organized private sector the corresponding growth rates were 2.9 percent, 0.9 percent, and 0.4 percent. After the reforms of 1991, the growth rate of employment in the organized private sector improved, and over the period 1991–95 it was 1.2 percent. Because of the de-emphasis on the public sector, employment there grew only at 0.5 percent over 1991–95.

It is ironic that employment did not grow more rapidly. The plans had always had employment targets, which were mostly not realized. Considerable emphasis was laid on small-scale industries for which products and activities were reserved. Unfortunately, small-scale industries were not any more employment-intensive or less capital-intensive than large-scale industries. Moreover, the sum total of the various policies of the government discouraged employment creation. Employ-

---

33. S. Mahendra Dev, "Growth, Employment, Poverty and Human Development: An Evaluation of Change in India Since Independence with Emphasis on Rural Areas," *Review of Development and Change,* vol. 2, no. 2, July–December 1997.

ment thus was driven not by any employment-promoting policies but mainly by growth, and growth was low.

Industrial Policy

India's growth rate in the organized sector may be compared with the growth of manufacturing employment in some other countries. In Indonesia, this grew at 6.0 percent per year in 1977–85, in Malaysia at 10 percent per year in 1971–81, in the Philippines at 9.3 percent per year in 1972–85, in Thailand at 7.7 percent per year in 1972–80, and in Korea at 13.4 percent per year in 1971–78.

The slow growth of manufacturing employment in India can be attributed, as argued above, to the broad development strategy that India pursued, which promoted a more capital-intensive development. By the end of the 1980s, one-third of the industrial sectors could be classified as highly protected and half of the sectors as low-protected. The highly protected industries showed a capital-to-labor ratio that was five times higher than that for the low-protected industries. The low-protected industries employed 78 percent of the total workers engaged while using only 43 percent of the total fixed capital; the highly protected industries, with 53 percent of the fixed capital, engaged only 19 percent of the labor. The output of some of the highly protected industries may not be easily tradable. However, if only 50 percent of the capital from highly protected industries were to use the same capital-to-labor ratio as the low-protected industries, industrial employment would have been 40 percent higher. This indicates the cost of the development strategy in terms of lost employment.

But why did employment growth slow down over the years? In 1989, the World Bank claimed that there was a significant trade-off between the real cost of labor and employment.[34] This explained how employment growth in the organized sector employment slowed down due to the negative effect of increases in the real cost of labor, which could not be adequately offset by the positive impact of faster growth in added manufacturing value.

The real cost of organized labor had been far above the cost of unorganized labor. Labor laws to protect employment make it extremely difficult to retrench any worker. Even economically nonviable

---

34. World Bank, *India: Poverty, Employment and Social Services,* A World Bank Country Study (Washington, DC: The World Bank, 1989).

units are not permitted to close down. In fact, such units are often taken over by the government. Along with job security, a number of other benefits are provided to workers, including one month's pay as an annual bonus, which is considered as deferred pay and is not linked to productivity or even to profitability of the enterprise.

As a consequence, entrepreneurs had incentives to restrict regular employment. One could have expected that recourse would be taken to subcontracting and ancillarization. The observations that unemployment had gone down in terms of person-days but had increased in terms of usual status are consistent with such an explanation. Thus, in some sense, in spite of government policy some benefits of growth were considered as additional person-days of employment. This can be expected to have a positive impact on poverty reduction as the economy accelerates.

The Public Sector

The public sector has played a dominant role in India, and its impact on the economy, and consequently on poverty, cannot be neglected.

Roughly 50 percent of capital formation in the Indian economy since 1965–66 has been in the public sector. At the height of its dominance in 1991 it had reached the "commanding heights" in the sense that more than 70 percent of the employment in the organized sector was in the public sector, and it generated around 55 percent of the value added activity in the organized sector. Unfortunately, the public sector has failed miserably in generating surpluses, and its gross savings have never exceeded 40 percent of the investment in the public sector over 1950–95. Thus, instead of accelerating investment as it was supposed to do, the emphasis on public sector has drawn substantially from private savings. The profitability of the public sector has been abysmal. All commercial public sector enterprises together showed an after-tax net profit of less than 5 percent on their sales over 1960–90. Given the generally high capital-to-output ratio of these enterprises, this indicates a very poor return on investment.

One objective that the public sector has at least partly fulfilled is that of being a "model employer": this is true from the viewpoint of those employed but not from the viewpoint of economic efficiency. The public sector has become a high-wage island in the economy. Even in 1995 public sector employees accounted for only about 7 percent of the labor force but received almost 40 percent of the wages and salaries in the entire economy. In 1994–95 the per capita emoluments of public sector employees were more than Rs.84,000. This was twice the average income of a family of five. While consumer prices increased by 6.3 times over 1971–72, the emoluments of a public sector employee increased by 13.3 times.[35] The situation must have become even more skewed after the revision in government pay scales in 1997. The dismal performance of the public sector has had serious consequences for the poor as it has significantly lowered the growth rate of the economy and has pushed wages higher in the organized sector as a whole. As already pointed out, this has led to the choice of relatively more capital-intensive techniques and further constrained the growth of employment.

In addition, the location of public sector enterprises to promote regionally balanced industrialization has not been very successful. Politically determined locations involve some economic costs. While these may be considered acceptable from the viewpoint of regional equity, the location of large public sector enterprises does not seem to have stimulated development of other industries in the area. Thus, Bihar remains industrially underdeveloped in spite of having many public sector heavy industry units and in spite of its large mineral resource base. Perhaps a labor force spoiled by public sector indulgence does not attract entrepreneurs.

India could have continued to muddle through this way for several more years. Fortunately, however, a macroeconomic crisis built up rapidly in early 1991, and India had to act.

The Crisis of 1991 and the Reforms

Background and Objectives

When the new government took over in June 1995, India was in the midst of a serious balance-of-payments crisis. The origin of the crisis and the reform measures undertaken have been dealt with in great detail in earlier *India Briefing* volumes by Khatkhate,[36] Dehejia,[37] and

---

35. Ministry of Finance, Government of India, *Economic Survey 1996–97* (New Delhi: Government of India, 1997).

36. Deena Khatkate, "India on an Economic Reform Trajectory," in *India Briefing: 1992,* eds. Leonard A. Gordon and Philip Oldenburg (New York: The Asia Society and Boulder, CO: Westview Press, 1992).

37. Jay Dehejia, "Economic Reforms: Birth of an Asian Tiger," in *India Briefing: 1993,* ed. Philip Oldenburg (New York: The Asia Society and Boulder, CO: Westview Press, 1993).

Desai.[38] I therefore deal with it only briefly. In early 1991 the country did not have enough foreign exchange to import the bare essentials and to meet its repayment obligations. Reserves had fallen to about $1 billion, adequate to meet the cost of just two weeks of imports. The inflation rate was running at 13 percent per year for the consumer price index. The mounting budgetary deficit was threatening to push the country into an inflationary spiral. The confidence of the international financial community in India's ability to meet its obligations was shaky.

These problems required immediate action. The need for economic reforms had never been so pressing or so urgent. This was also an opportunity to change course, to get India out of the slow-growth track and put it on the fast track.

The economy was trapped in a plethora of controls, procedures, permits, and bureaucratic restrictions. Worse, such a maze had been created that the net effects of these policies were not at all obvious. While the nominal tariffs remained extremely high, averaging 117 percent in 1989–90, a World Bank study, in a review of sixteen subsectors, found that effective protection rates ranged from –16 percent to 162 percent. In another study, a detailed review of 60 projects showed that half the firms studied received negative protection. It was thus not a case of the right hand not knowing what the left hand was doing but rather a case of the right hand not knowing what the right hand was doing!

By now, a number of economists argued that efficient utilization of resources was even more important than the Indian planners' preoccupation with optimal allocation of resources. For example, during the discussion on the Fifth Five-Year Plan in the early 1970s, debates were held on whether the target for steel capacity should be 17 million tons or 17.5 million tons. Even while this was being discussed, the annual output was 8 million tons, with an installed capacity of some 13 million tons. Clearly, the target was quite irrelevant, and any gain from making the target precise was more than offset by the waste caused by the improper utilization of created capacity. In 1970, Bhagwati and Desai argued that Indian planning was inadequate and that "you cannot have growth first and efficiency next."[39] By 1990 a much wider con-

---

38. Meghnad Desai, "Economic Reform: Stalled by Politics?" in *India Briefing: Staying the Course*, ed. Philip Oldenburg (New York: The Asia Society, and Armonk, NY: M.E. Sharpe, 1995)

39. Jagdish Bhagwati and Padma Desai, *India: Planning for Industrialization* (Delhi: Oxford University Press, 1970).

sensus had emerged on the evils of the permit-quota raj. Bhagwati described the interest groups spawned by the regime of controls as an iron triangle consisting of businessmen who enjoyed squatters' rights and benefited from protection, bureaucrats who wielded enormous power to confer rents, and politicians who became "addicted to the use of licensing to generate illegal funds for election and then for themselves."[40] I.G. Patel had suggested that "a bonfire of industrial licensing was in order;"[41] and Parikh had also urged liberalization and outward orientation.[42]

Since the initiation of major economic reforms in June 1991 by the government of Mr. Narasimha Rao through the finance minister, Dr. Manmohan Singh, and the commerce minister, Mr. P. Chidambaram, the Indian economy has undergone a remarkable transition. The objective of the reforms was to make the Indian economy grow quickly. Rapid growth was considered essential as a method of dealing with poverty. This rapid growth was to be achieved through more efficient resource use for which competition, both domestic and global, was considered essential.

For three years, the reforms continued in a blitzkrieg, but in the last two years of Narasimha Rao's government they somehow lost momentum and were reduced to a trickle. The coalition United Front government sought to revitalize the process of reforms but was stalled by the political instability of a minority coalition government dependent on support by the Congress Party. The new Bharatiya Janata Party (BJP) government has promised to continue the reforms but with its own twist of *swadeshi*.

The Specific Measures

To appreciate what has been accomplished, the various reform measures undertaken are briefly described below.

On the industrial front the government removed licensing requirements for all but eight mostly environmentally sensitive industries.

---

40. Jagdish Bhagwati, *India's Economy: The Shackled Giant* (Oxford: Clarendon Press, 1993).

41. I.G. Patel, "On Taking India into the Twenty-First Century (New Economic Policy in India)," 15th Kingsley Martin Memorial Lecture, *Modern Asian Studies,* vol. 21, no. 2, 1986.

42. Kirit S. Parikh, "Eighth Plan and Beyond: Strategies and Tactics," Discussion Paper DP-89–013 (Bombay: Indira Gandhi Institute of Development Research, March 1989); and "An Outward Oriented Strategy: Even More Relevant Now," Discussion Paper DP-91–050 (Bombay: Indira Gandhi Institute of Development Research, March 1991).

Industries were free to decide what to produce, how much to produce, with what technology to produce, and where to produce. All these decisions had earlier been controlled. The restrictions on large houses were removed. The list of industries reserved for the public sector was reduced from seventeen to six. In addition, private sector participation was allowed even in industries on the reserved list. Technology imports were made much freer. The ceiling on royalties that a firm could pay was greatly relaxed. These reforms deregulated industries and introduced domestic competition, and they generated tremendous excitement among Indian industrialists, who welcomed them.

To liberalize trade the Indian rupee was devalued by 35 percent; tariffs were significantly reduced; and imports, except of consumer goods, were freed in the sense that no import permit was required, although, of course, customs duty still had to be paid. Subsequently, the rupee was made convertible on current account. Tariff reduction and devaluation has continued. The maximum duty was lowered to 150 percent in July 1991, 110 percent in February 1992, 85 percent in February 1993, 65 percent in 1994, and 50 percent in 1995. Duties on capital goods have been reduced to between 25 and 35 percent and have gone even lower for export schemes. The import-weighted average tariff rate has been brought down from 87 percent in 1990–91 to 27 percent in 1995–96. Imports of gold and silver were liberalized, which has reduced incentives for smuggling. These measures of trade liberalization have boosted exports, improved the quality of products, and increased competition from foreign goods. This has also put some pressure on Indian industries to become more competitive.

In recognition of the role that foreign investment can play in accelerating economic growth by bringing in new technology, rules governing foreign investment were greatly relaxed. Foreign investment up to 51 percent was permitted in thirty-four primary industries, and even 100 percent was permitted in certain infrastructure sectors such as power. Indian companies were permitted to commercially borrow funds abroad and to sell equity abroad. Foreign investment in Indian equity was permitted and even encouraged by tax concessions.

These reforms have led to a substantial inflow of foreign funds. In reality, foreign direct investment, however, is obstructed, as the various procedural and bureaucratic clearances required still have not been streamlined. For example, in 1991, the government opened up the power sector to private-plant operators. By 1993, some 240 Memorandums of Understanding were signed by private parties willing to set up plants and by the various state electricity boards. However, by December 1997 only three of these had been cleared.

Fiscal reforms to reduce the fiscal deficit were critical for price stabilization. This required both increasing government revenues and cutting expenditures. At the same time, there was a need to reform taxes to reduce, if not eliminate, various distortions and disincentives that the old tax structure entailed. Among the tax reforms, the following important measures have been taken: Tariff rates (customs duties on imports) have been lowered, and differences in tariff across commodities have been substantially reduced. When duty rates vary across commodities, the effective protection provided across commodities may be surprisingly different. Thus, it is conceivable that a product nominally protected may turn out to be unprotected if the import duties on the inputs needed to produce it are high. These reforms, however, lower government revenue from customs duties. Excise duties that are imposed on domestic producers have also been rationalized, and only a few rates are imposed now. Many economists argue that a value-added tax (VAT) should replace such excise duties. A VAT is more difficult to evade and is more efficient as it does not cascade over the various stages of production. Some progress has also been made in enlarging the coverage of the modified VAT scheme. Income tax rates were dramatically lower in the budget presented in February 1997. The maximum tax rate on personal income is now a modest 30 percent. This may be compared with the maximum marginal tax rate of over 90 percent that India had during the 1960s. Of course, hardly anyone paid such a rate. In fact, lowering the tax rate has increased collection. In spite of these reductions, tax revenues have gone up because of better compliance and the higher growth rate of the economy.

Nonetheless, reducing government expenditures is very critical in attaining a fiscal balance. Here the progress has been minuscule. In the early years after the reforms, the government was able to restrict the increase in spending by practices such as not filling job vacancies. This, however, is likely to be neutralized by the very generous wage revisions for government employees agreed to by the government in September 1997. Subsidies are a major element of government expenditures. Many of these subsidies no longer serve the economic or social purpose for which they were introduced. In fact, many cause distortions that lead to inefficiencies. Although they were initiated in the name of the poor, only a small fraction (less than 20 percent) of these subsidies reach the poor. Yet the not-so-poor who benefit from them constitute a powerful political force. Thus, subsidies for food, fertilizer, power, petroleum products, urban transport, higher education, and health care continue to increase.

Another major item of expenditure is support for loss-incurring public sector enterprises. Many people suggest that the government ought to close them down or sell them to private parties, but very little progress has been made. Instead, the government has sold to private investors part of the equity of some of its profitable enterprises. Moreover, the revenues from these sales have been used to meet current expenditures rather than to retire government debt or increase investment in health and education.

As discussed, public sector units (PSUs) earn a very low return on investment. Many observers believe that the poor performance of PSUs has been largely due to political and bureaucratic interference in management. Public sector unit managers do not have the needed freedom and autonomy to allow the PSUs to perform as surplus-generating enterprises. While the government has talked a lot about various reforms, not much has been done so far. Only as recently as September 1997 were steps initiated to provide some autonomy to selected PSUs. How well this will translate into real freedom has yet to be seen.

A steady stream of measures have been taken to make the financial sector healthy, competitive, and transparent. To restore the health of the nationalized banks, internationally accepted prudential norms have been introduced. These require that the risk-weighted portfolio of loans given out by a bank maintain a reasonable relationship to the bank's assets. Interest rates have largely been freed and are now market determined. Firms have been freed to price their capital offerings. Such pricing was earlier controlled. Stock markets have been made transparent through electronic open-order-book trading and the establishment of a regulatory body, the Securities and Exchange Board of India. These reforms seem revolutionary compared with India's earlier policies.

The Impact of Reforms

The unleashing of private initiative from the stifling constraints of the permit-quota raj through deregulation and liberalization led to a remarkable transformation of the Indian economy over a short period of five years. Foreign exchange reserves exceeded $20 billion by March 1995, equivalent to seven months of imports. They have remained at a comfortable level and reached $24 billion by February 1998. Exports grew at approximately 20 percent a year in U.S. dollar terms from 1993–94 to 1995–96, and they reached a level of $34 billion by 1997–98. The trade-to-GDP ratio increased from 16 percent in 1990–91 to 24 percent by 1995–96. Current-account deficits, for example, have fallen from –3.2 percent of GDP in 1990–91 to –1.7 percent in 1995–96. The country's external debt indicators have also shown a marked improvement, with the external debt-service ratio declining from 35.3 percent in 1990–91 to approximately 26 percent in 1995–96. The economy has shown growth in excess of 6 percent for four years in a row, from 1992–93 to 1996–97, averaging 6.6 percent. Prior to the reforms, growth rates above 6 percent were typically due to recovery from poor growth in the preceding year. The year 1989–90 was the only exception to this regularity. A standard method of measuring efficiency is through what is known as incremental capital output ratio (ICOR), which indicates the additional capital (investment) required to produce one unit of additional output. Conclusive data is not yet available, but available evidence suggests a fall in ICOR in recent years compared with the prereform period. Each of these accomplishments was unprecedented in India's economic history.

The public buffer stock of food grain was 25 million tonnes in July 1996, and inflation has been brought down to around 5 percent in 1997–98. Perhaps the most remarkable transformation has been in perceptions. In early 1996, a 7 percent growth rate per year seemed a reasonable target to everyone, including the thirteen-party coalition government of Mr. Deve Gowda.

Even Left-leaning economists' criticism of liberalization opposes not the reforms but only the mechanistic pursuit of some instruments. Thus for example, Bhaduri and Nayyar[43] question the Washington consensus for its emphasis on fiscal deficit and argue that public deficit does not necessarily lead to inflation, that good public expenditure is required for development, and that what is required is not a reduction in public expenditure but only a restructuring and reorientation of it. This

---

43. Amit Bhaduri and Deepak Nayyar, *The Intelligent Person's Guide to Liberalization* (New Delhi: Penguin Books, 1996).

is a position that many liberalizing economists might agree with. This consensus is an important achievement of reform.

Reforms in a Time of Political Uncertainty

By the end of 1996, the optimism of March 1996 was overcast by apprehension. In the first six months of 1996–97, industrial growth had slowed to 8 percent as compared with 12.5 percent in 1995–96, and export growth had dropped to around 10 percent. Real interest rates were very high and credit was difficult to obtain, even though banks were flush with funds as the Reserve Bank of India had injected considerable liquidity into the system, both by injecting money and by permitting banks to give out a larger part of their funds as loans. Infrastructure bottlenecks, shortage of power, congested roads, delays at ports, and expensive telecommunications were and still are widespread. The stock market, which reflects interest rates and expectations about future growth in dividends, had fared badly: the level of the NSE-50 (Nifty) had dropped from a peak of 1,385 in September 1994 to 909 in December 1995 to around 890 in December 1996. The Bombay Stock Exchange (BSE) Sensex had dropped from around 4,000 in December 1995 to 3,100 in December 1996.

The picture seemed to change dramatically with Chidambaram's budget in February 1997. The budget drastically cut tax rates and introduced a number of reforms to stimulate economic growth. A mood of optimism swept over the economy. There was talk of an 8 percent growth rate. The stock market zoomed. On April 25, 1997, in spite of the political events of the first half of April, the BSE Sensex reached 3,825, and Nifty reached 1,069.

The political events that initiated the withdrawal of the Congress Party support from the United Front government; the fall of Deve Gowda's government; the installation of the new government headed by Gujral and its subsequent fall; and the new general elections led to a near paralysis of economic policy and reforms. The BJP-led coalition government has now taken over. The possibility of continuing the process of economic reforms in India's uncertain politics has become questionable.

Foreign investors are often troubled by the uncertainty of India's democratic politics. At every election, they fear reversals of policy. The Indian press contributes to these fears as it finds it profitable to do so. "After Nehru, who?" and "After Indira, who?" have helped sell many news copies, but this uncertainty is exaggerated. For fifty years, Indian democracy has made many peaceful transitions to new governments, but there has always been a certain consistency in the economic policies.

The differences between the policies of different political parties have been minor. The most radical step concerned the policy of reservations by V.P. Singh's government, and there too, the policy was, in principle, accepted by the earlier Congress government. Except for the reforms of 1991, which were acclaimed by most of the political parties, dramatic reversals of economic policy have not taken place.

Another feature of India's democracy must be noted: after each election, one feels that the voters of India seemed to have voted wisely in response to a shared sense of national priorities. In many elections, India has had national waves. Although the peasants in the Punjab, Gujarat, Andhra Pradesh, and Orissa do not talk to each other, they vote with similar concerns and swing the vote in similar ways; therein lies the secret of India's political stability.

Despite this, one has to admit that the decision-making process in India is long and frustrating, and keeps getting longer. Deregulation has eliminated many bureaucratic steps in the decision-making process but still too many are left. The bureaucracy and the politicians who have lost opportunities for dispensing favors naturally cling to the remaining requirements. India has some way to go in streamlining the bureaucracy.

Fortunately, the people of India have become aware of, and now demand, transparency. They have also begun to use public interest litigation to question bureaucratic decisions. While this is a good sign and should lead to transparency, the length of time India's courts spend on proceedings delays matters. The solution to the delays is not to ban public litigation but to make the judicial process speedier.

Even if one agrees that Indian democracy is following a stable course on the whole and is moving toward greater transparency, one may be concerned about the damage political compulsions can do even in the short regime of a coalition government that might accept far-reaching populist but economically damaging decisions. Another concern is that a multiparty government may find it difficult to accept significant decisions that do not have wide support. By the same token, it would be difficult to reverse reforms, as now it is "reversal" that would be the radical step. It would be equally difficult to initiate further radical reforms; only a gradualist movement is possible.

In short, a drastic reduction in subsidies is unlikely. One can, however, hope that the counterproductive nature of many of these subsidies for the very people for whom they are intended would be understood by the various political parties, and one can further hope that a consensus for reforms will emerge.

The Tasks Ahead

The Unfinished Reforms

When one looks back at the goal of a fast-growing globalized Indian economy with which the reforms were initiated in 1991, it is clear that much remains to be done. Some of the most important reforms are genuine reforms of the public sector so that businesses can operate with true commercial autonomy as profit-making enterprises. Reform of labor laws is also important: at present, an organized industry cannot fire a worker without the permission of the state government—permission that is almost never given. This discourages firms from expanding employment and encourages them to invest in labor-saving technology. Judicial reforms to speed up justice are extremely critical. Today, anyone with resources can escape punishment for years, and civil disputes can sometimes take decades to settle. Without judicial reforms, the economic costs of delays caused by the public scrutiny that is increasingly necessary in today's complex world become very large. When justice is swift, challenges from all affected parties can be accommodated.

While reforms of the public sector and labor laws pose difficult political problems and may not be carried out by a coalition government, legal reforms do not pose such problems. Unfortunately, the importance of legal reforms is not fully appreciated by many politicians in India. Therefore, one may not expect much action in the near future on these needed reforms. However, there are critical sectors in which the problems are important to politicians and are pressing enough that action will soon be needed. These include the issues of poverty, energy, power, and environment.

This situation raises a number of questions: Is it likely that a significant dent in poverty can be made soon? What can India do to meet its energy and power needs? What is the role of the private sector in energy? How can India deal with pressing environmental issues, which can no longer be neglected? These are the questions addressed below:

Poverty and Public Policy: A Mixed Record

Poverty has persisted, despite the rhetoric. Even after fifty years of tackling poverty, more than 200 million of India's population remain poor by any measure. Reforms required the dismantling of a policy regime that had often been justified as being in the name of the poor. The reform process also involved significant changes in the relative prices of various goods and the relative profitability of different sectors. This was bound to have an impact on poverty. It is natural to ask what the reforms have done to the level and depth of poverty in the country.

While there are many alternative ways of measuring poverty and while there are also nonincome dimensions to poverty, we employ the commonly used measure of the proportion of the population below a defined poverty line. Even in this head-count ratio, as it is called, there are differences among researchers as to how the poverty line should be adjusted to account for changes in inflation and relative prices over different periods and across different states. An advantage of using the head-count ratio is that estimates for these adjustments are for the most part widely known. The poverty line was defined at 1960–61 prices to be Rs.20 per person per month for urban areas and Rs.15 for rural areas, enough to provide 2,250 calories in urban and 2,400 calories in rural areas per day.

What has been the impact of reforms on poverty? Rural poverty increased significantly in the first two and a half years of the reforms beginning in July 1991. Rural poverty, at 39.7 percent, was higher by two percentage points in 1993–94 compared with 1990–91 (before the reforms). Urban poverty increased in 1992 and 1993 before declining significantly in 1993–94 by four percentage points to 30.9 percent. These differences are within the statistical error limits and the expected range of fluctuations due to rainfall.

The wholesale price index and consumer price index for agricultural workers showed increases in 1991–92. Higher agricultural prices provide higher incomes to farmers who have a marketable surplus. But, by and large, the poor are net purchasers of food, and they suffer when food prices increase. In addition, the poor are hurt because agricultural wages adjust to agricultural prices with a time lag. Thus, the increase in rural poverty was higher than that in urban poverty in the first few years of reforms.

Another reason for the increase in rural poverty could be the increase in the issue price of food grain through the Public Distribution System (PDS) and the consequent narrowing of the price difference between the open-market and PDS-issued prices, particularly since January 1993.

The decline in urban poverty in 1993–94, compared with the previous two years, could be due to lower inflation, relaxation of fiscal compression, significant increase in expenditure on employment programs, and better food management. The severity of both urban and rural poverty declined as measured by the Foster, Green and Thorbecke (FGT) index. Thus, changes in poverty were more likely to be due to agricultural performance and management of the food economy, including food prices and stabilization measures, rather than due to structural adjustment. However, in the first few years of planning it was difficult to distinguish between some of the stabilization measures and structural-adjustment-related reforms.

Other measures of poverty include real wages, unemployment, and subjective feelings of hunger. All these measures showed an optimistic trend. In 1983, the proportion of rural households that claimed they had two meals per day was 81 percent. In 1991, this percentage was 88 percent. By the end of 1993, this proportion had risen to 93 percent. Per capita availability of food grain has been rising since 1993. Real wages also have improved. It is difficult to say whether reforms have adversely affected health and education in the 1990s, although one can give broad indications based on public expenditure in these areas. Many studies have shown that social sector expenditure declined considerably during the first few years of the reforms, and this could have adversely affected human development indicators. In any case, India's performance in human development is very poor. Out of 174 countries, India stands 135 on the human development index scale. Moreover, there are great regional disparities within India.

What are the most cost-effective antipoverty measures? Whether poverty has increased or decreased, there are still many poor people, and there is a broad consensus that India needs to take antipoverty measures. Since the needed expenditure is large, these measures should be cost-effective.

The government has a variety of antipoverty programs. The PDS is often considered the most important among these. Many empirical studies based on the 1986–87 National Sample Survey data on PDS purchases have shown that the poor did not benefit much from the PDS. Parikh says, "the cost effectiveness of reaching the poorest 20 percent of households through PDS cereals is small."[44] The problems with PDS are leakages, inefficiencies of the Food Corporation of India (FCI) in storage and distribution, and a narrowing of the differences between PDS prices and open-market prices.

Many attempts have been made to restructure the PDS. One launched by the prime minister in 1992 was the revamped PDS (RPDS), under which the old system was extended to the 2,446 Employment Assurance Scheme (EAS) blocks. An evaluation of the RPDS by the Programme Evaluation Organization of the Planning Commission has identified several shortcomings, including bogus cards, inadequate storage, and targeting failure.

In 1996, the United Front government promised in their Common Minimum Programme that, through the PDS, the poor would get ten kilograms of food grain per family at half the issue price. Accordingly, they announced that food-grain allocation to states would be based on their poverty ratios according to Expert Group (Lakdawala Committee Report) estimates. The distribution was to be done by the states themselves, who were to identify the poor.

The main problem is the difficulty of identifying the poor. Regional targeting may redistribute the grain in favor of the poor in "backward areas," but the poor in relatively rich areas may be adversely affected. Based on Dreze and Srinivasan,[45] I estimate that regional targeting increases the amount of grain reaching the poor from 25 percent to only 30 percent.

There seem to be two solutions available for restructuring the PDS. The first is to use wage-employment programs, because these lead to self-targeting. Examples are the Employment Guarantee Scheme (EGS) of Maharashtra, the Jawahar Rojgar Yojana, and the EAS. The second solution consists of giving the *panchayats* the responsibility of identifying the poor and managing the PDS.

The EGS has been found to be the most cost-effective of the wage-

---

44. Jyoti K. Parikh, Reddy B. Sudhakar, and Rangan Banerjee, *Planning for Demand Side Management in the Electricity Sector* (New Delhi: Tata McGraw-Hill Publishing Company, 1994).

45. Jean Dreze and P.V. Srinivasan, "Poverty in India: Regional Estimates 1987–88," Discussion Paper DP-96–120 (Bombay: Indira Gandhi Institute of Development Research, 1996).

employment programs, as a much higher fraction of the money spent reaches the poor. The EGS has also been shown to have reduced the depth of poverty, or how far below the poverty line are the poor. It cannot be expected to eliminate poverty because the wages are low; even if one were to work for 300 days on EGS, one would still be below the poverty line. But it is important to keep in mind that when one poor person earns income from the EGS, another job, which often pays even less than the EGS, is open. Thus, even though the net gain to the EGS worker might be small, another poor person can replace him or her in the alternative job, and the gain to the poor as a whole from the EGS remains large.

Energy and Power

The energy sector claims the largest allocation in India's plans and is the biggest item of imports such as oil and petroleum. Its performance and the macroeconomic development of the nation are, thus, highly interdependent.

There are endemic power shortages, and the Indian power sector has not been able to match the growing need for more generating capacity. Over the next five years, depending on the growth rate of the economy, India needs to add another 35,000 to 50,000 mega-watts (MW) of capacity, even though it added no more than 20,000 MW over 1991–97 whereas the target was to add 38,000 MW. The root of this inability to expand capacity lies in the financial sickness of the State Electricity Boards (SEBs). Almost all of them sustain losses and some are even unable to pay for the coal or power they purchase. This is because the SEBs have often implemented the social-subsidy policies of state governments, leading to inefficient patterns of energy consumption and even to nonrecovery of their own costs. Also, there is a great deal of theft of power from the distribution networks, which is classified in the official statistics as transmission and distribution (T&D) losses.

If the SEBs were financially sound, they could have invested in capacity creation, and private power producers would not have re-quired counterguarantees by the central government. These coun-terguarantees provide that if the SEBs do not pay their bills, the central government will. Naturally, the central government is reluctant to pro-vide such guarantees. As already mentioned, this has restricted the growth of private power. The loss due to subsidies to agricultural consumers alone runs to Rs.7,000 crore per year. If the SEBs had that much more money, they could leverage it in the financial markets and set up an additional 7,000 MW every year. Thus, apart from the current losses they represent, the subsidies have serious repercussions for the SEBs' ability to meet future demands.

In order to fill the gap between the demand for and the supply of power, the government has decided to encourage private investment in power generation. However, the entry of the private sector raises a new set of issues concerning the price of power, guaranteed availability, choice of least-cost projects, and so on. The government in India has little knowledge about or experience with these issues. Until December 1997, there was no clearly defined framework to evaluate bids for power projects so that power would be available at least cost. The need to quickly develop transparent and competitive procedures for this is obvious.

The importance of taking action is seen clearly in the government's experience with private power. Within a couple of years of opening the sector, some 240 Memorandums of Understanding (MOUs) were signed to produce private power by 1993. Yet, nearly four years later, only one small plant is functional, one is under construction, and a third has finally been cleared. Some observers believe that even in the face of such dismal evidence, it is possible to have competitive bidding and obtain fair deals through the MOU route by doing the proper homework on both the practical and legal aspects of competitive bidding and benchmarking.

In the long run, institutional reform of the SEBs is inescapable. These reforms should aim at strengthening the SEBs through financial and managerial autonomy and by enhancing competition. However, there are also short-term measures that can help solve the problem of shortage through systems improvement (supply-side management) and demand reduction (demand-side management).

Integrated grid operation and proper management could reduce system costs, improve system utilization, and meet a larger demand. Research at the Indira Gandhi Institute of Development Research has shown that, with integration of the western and southern grids, 5 percent more demand could be met without any additional investment.[46]

---

46. Jyoti K. Parikh and S.G. Deshmukh, "Policy Alternatives for Western and Southern Power Systems in India," *Utilities Policy*, vol. 2, no. 3, July 1992.

India's regional grids are at present operated not as a truly integrated system but merely as a set of interconnected state networks that only occasionally exchange electricity. India needs to overcome transmission bottlenecks, formulate commercial agreements between the SEBs, and ensure grid discipline to avoid frequency mismatches. Also, measures to improve power-station efficiency could mean substantial savings in terms of both energy and costs. It is estimated that a potential savings of 2 percent could be obtained at some thermal power stations by reducing the plant's own consumption of electricity.

Demand-side management (DSM) options induce consumers to use energy more effectively. This can reduce both the economic and the environmental costs associated with power-plant construction and operation. The basic insight behind DSM is that each watt of power that is not required due to reduced demand, in turn, reduces the T&D losses and thus is worth more than one watt of generation. To estimate the scope of savings through a specific energy-efficient option, options need to be identified that are economically attractive to everyone, including the consumer, the SEBs, and society as a whole. If only such options are used, Parikh, et al.,[47] estimate that in the industrial sector alone, a saving of 15,000 MW is possible over the next twenty years at less than half the cost of creating new capacity and with a much smaller gestation period. For DSM programs to be successful, customer awareness is crucial. The government, the SEBs, and the energy service companies all have to play appropriate roles to promote DSM.

The Environment

Environmental issues have become serious in many parts of the country and can no longer be neglected. Environmental problems are affected by the level of economic development, the availability of natural resources, and the lifestyle of the population. Poverty presents special environmental problems for a heavily populated country with limited resources such as India. India cannot afford to continue ignoring environmental issues, as doing so may be costly to society; some problems may reach the point of total disaster, claiming a heavy toll of lives, productivity, and quality of life in general. The growing activism in

---

47. Jyoti K. Parikh, Reddy B. Sudhakar, and Rangan Banerjee, *Planning for Demand Side Management in the Electricity Sector* (New Delhi: Tata McGraw-Hill Publishing Company, 1994).

recent years of voluntary agencies, the explosion of public-interest litigation, and the active interest shown by the courts to redress the situation all reflect the demand for better implementation of existing laws as well as new regulations in response to the worsening environmental situation.

India's most pressing environmental issues are air and water pollution, disposal of solid waste, deforestation, land degradation, and loss of biodiversity.

Air Pollution

Urban air quality has deteriorated in all Indian cities. In particular, air pollution in metropolitan cities has reached intolerable levels due to a combination of vehicular and industrial emissions. Vehicular pollution is related to the failure of public transport to cope with the transportation needs of the population, to the poor pollution standards of vehicles currently sold in India, and to the extremely poor emission standards of older vehicles on the roads.

Even the rural population is not free from the ill effects of air pollution. The rural population uses a substantial quantity of noncommercial fuels, such as crop residues, animal dung, and wood. Air pollutants from these biofuels are released inside or near homes at mealtimes everyday. The amount of health damage per unit of emission for pollution released indoors can be more than a thousand times greater than that from a smokestack outside a town.

Air pollution can cause respiratory illness, damage to materials, and loss of visibility. The main health hazards include respiratory infections, chronic lung disease and lung cancer, and adverse pregnancy outcomes such as low birth weight and stillbirth for women exposed during pregnancy.

Emissions from vehicles that use leaded fuel account for about 95 percent of airborne lead pollution, causing substantial damage to health and property. The number of motor vehicles in India has increased almost thirty-two-fold over the last three decades. The concentration of pollution is particularly high on highways, at road signals, and at traffic junctions. The level of suspended particulate matter, which causes respiratory diseases, exceeds the safe level many times over. Exposure to lead from the leaded fuel that is still prevalent in India is associated with reduced intelligence among growing children.

To reduce air pollution, it is essential to introduce rapid mass transit systems in urban areas, to improve the fuel efficiency and emission-control standards of vehicles, and to reduce transport needs through better urban design coupled with improved means of telecommunication.

Water Pollution and Poor Sanitation

Pollution of water is another growing problem. The discharge of untreated sewage and industrial effluents to bodies of water including, in some cases, groundwater, has made much of India's water unfit for drinking and most rivers unfit for bathing. Water pollution not only aggravates the health of the poor who cannot afford to take defensive measures, it affects both the rich and the poor in less direct ways: fruit and vegetables are grown with untreated water, and fish from affected bodies of water are diseased. As much as 28 percent of the urban population does not have piped water supply. The situation in rural areas is worse as almost all surface-water sources are contaminated and unfit for consumption by either humans or animals.

Due to inadequate sewage-disposal facilities in almost all Indian cities and towns, refuse invariably gets mixed with open-water resources, leading to waterborne diseases. Rivers are highly contaminated for many kilometers downstream from each major city in India. Some of the health problems commonly caused by contaminated water are diarrhea, trachoma, intestinal worms, and hepatitis. Malaria, filariasis, and even epidemics such as cholera can easily spread. Eighty percent of the children in Indian villages suffer from parasitic helminthic diseases caused by the mixing of human waste into open water sources. Recent World Bank and World Health Organization data show that about 21 percent of all communicable diseases in India (11.5 percent of all diseases) are waterborne.

The sanitation problems of large metropolitan cities have grown tremendously in the last forty to forty-five years. There has been an increase of 36 percent in the urban population in one decade without a corresponding increase in investment to augment or improve water supply and sanitation systems. As of today, only 64 percent of the people in urban areas have sewage facilities. Poor sanitation generates health hazards through several routes. These include direct exposure to feces near homes, contaminated drinking water, ingestion of fish from polluted water, and ingestion of produce that has been irrigated with wastewater.

Solid Waste

Based on an average figure of 0.5 kilograms per capita per day of refuse generation, the quantity generated in a large city with a population of one million exceeds 500 tonnes a day. Clearly, systematic efforts are needed for effective disposal of waste.

With increased incomes and the resulting changes in consumption patterns, the composition of waste is changing from biodegradable organic material to plastic and other synthetic materials, which take much longer to decompose. When not collected and disposed of efficiently and effectively, these solid wastes attract rodents and flies, which then spread disease. While refuse can be utilized, after sorting, to generate energy and other useful resources through composting, vermicomposting, and anaerobic digestion, the burning of wastes, which may contain plastics, causes air pollution.

India's air and water have become polluted despite environmental legislation and appropriate emission and effluent standards. The problem is that the central and the state pollution-control boards are not able to enforce these laws. Some observers suggest that India should consider more cost-effective economic instruments to deal with industrial pollution and should develop them quickly, as they are needed with great urgency. Such instruments could control pollution with minimal economic cost, for example, through collecting taxes. Another major alternative is to use emission quotas that are traded on financial markets.

Forest Cover

Deterioration of village commons, deforestation, and soil degradation are other major environmental problems that affect a large part of the population directly.

India has 18 percent of the world's population and 15 percent of the world's livestock, but it has only 2 percent of its geographical area, 1 percent of its forested area, and 0.5 percent of pastureland area. Per capita availability of forest in India is 0.08 of a hectare, which is approximately one-tenth of the world average of 0.8 of a hectare.

India has a forested area of 64 megahectares, which constitutes only 19.5 percent of its total land area compared with the target of 33 percent set in the National Forest Policy Resolution of 1988. Large areas of these forests are highly degraded. Actually, the closed forest that has a forest-cover density of 40 percent or more is only approximately 11 percent of the country's total land area. The average annual production of wood per hectare is 0.7 of a cubic meter as compared with the world average of 2.1 cubic meters, and the total estimated annual increment of growing stock was only 1.24 percent in 1987. It has been estimated that about 157 million tonnes of firewood are required for fuel each year by the rural population, whereas the recorded production is only 58 million tonnes. The rest of the demand is met by illegal lopping, cutting, and encroachment of the forest. While the poor looking for firewood and fodder do cause some deforestation, the main cause of deforestation is commercial, and often illegal, logging to meet industrial demand.

The pressure on existing forests is quite high in India at present, with its high population density and very low per capita forested area. A wide range of flora and fauna are fast disappearing as their natural habitats are destroyed. This further impoverishes the remaining Indian forests. Although there is now an upward trend in the land area and quality of forest, many observers believe that there is a need for massive reforestation programs, greater control over clearing and grazing, and provision of cheap fuel through alternative technologies such as solar power and biogas plants. Some also suggest that more kerosene be made available to save the forests from denudation.

Soil Degradation

Of the total land area of approximately 330 million hectares, some 64 million hectares are forested. In the remaining area, which includes mountains, deserts, and cities, the estimate of the amount of land that is degraded varies, with some estimates as high as 130 million hectares. Unfortunately, since "degraded" is not defined, one estimate is as good as another. It is nonetheless clear that substantial degradation of soil does take place, and it incurs a cost. It has been reported that the loss of a one-millimeter layer of soil from a cultivated area could mean the loss of ten kilograms of nitrogen and two kilograms of phosphorus.

The main cause of degradation is the use of common property resources (CPR) by villagers for purposes such as grazing of livestock and cutting of trees in excess of its regenerative capacity. Since CPR belong to everyone, individuals feel that if they do not use it, someone else will. The regeneration of wasteland, particularly of CPR, has been shown to be feasible and economical. The main elements of such regeneration schemes are a just and well-defined scheme of sharing the costs and benefits from the regeneration of the land and the availability of finance.

Biodiversity

India has a rich heritage of species and genetic strains of flora and fauna. Overall, 8 percent of the world's species are found in India. It is estimated that India is tenth among the plant-rich countries, eleventh in terms of the number of endemic species of higher vertebrates, and sixth in the world among the centers of diversity. Out of twelve biodiversity hot spots in the world, India has two: one in the Northeast and the other in the Western Ghats.

But as the forests become bare, many of the flora and fauna have become extinct or are on the verge of extinction. These species and varieties provide a challenge and a resource to geneticists, animal behaviorists, botanists, zoologists, economists, and many others who have much to learn about and from them. About 1,143 types of animals comprising 71 species of mammals, 88 species of birds, and 5 species of reptiles are now rare and endangered. Many plant species, for which forests are the sustaining source, are also disappearing rapidly. In order to preserve them, special bioreserves should be created and maintained. In the preservation of biodiversity, large contiguous sanctuaries are far more useful than isolated pockets formed by small sanctuaries. It is also easier to focus preservation efforts on a few highly prominent sanctuaries instead of dealing with numerous, partly degraded reserves.

It is important to recognize that the pressure of population growth is a transient phenomenon, whereas reduction in biodiversity is a permanent and irreversible loss. Rapid economic growth can create many nonagricultural jobs and can eventually relieve the population pressure from rural land. However, there is no way to recover lost biodiversity. Thus, even for the sake of the environment, India needs strong and rapid economic growth.

The Next Fifty Years

The next fifty years will surely belong to India. There is much to accomplish and a great deal of possibilities exist. What India needs is a guiding ambition; without one, India will not achieve its full potential. Let me outline what India is able to achieve.

It is possible for India to have a per capita income of $30,000 by the year 2047. If the Indian economy does as well as some of the world's fast-growing economies have done, it could be even higher. Over 1950–73 Japan grew at 9.1 percent, and over 1950–90 Taiwan grew at 8.6 percent. Over 1960–90 South Korea grew at 8.3 percent, and China had growth of 8.3 percent over 1980–93. For India to grow at 8.5 percent over the next two decades and at 7.5 percent thereafter is certainly not impossible. This would bring its per capita income from $320 in 1997 for 970 million people to about $10,000 for 1.4 billion people in 2047. But history has shown that when a country grows rapidly, its currency appreciates. This has happened in Germany, Japan, Taiwan, and Singapore. Today, the purchasing-power parity between India and the United States is 4.0. What this means is that while the exchange rate is Rs.38 to the dollar, Rs.38 can purchase goods and services in India that would cost $4 to purchase in the United States. As a country develops and becomes rich, its purchasing-power parity with the United States tends to move toward 1.0. The Indian rupee, which today is Rs.38 to the dollar, would then have an exchange rate of less than Rs.10 to the dollar. Thus, $10,000 would become $38,000. I suggest a goal of $30,000, just to be cautious.

Of course, the realization of this goal is contingent on curtailing population growth. If India's leadership makes family-planning knowledge and tools available to women so that population growth is at the desired level; conducts a campaign of female literacy to attain near 100 percent adult literacy within three years; makes primary and middle-school education compulsory; and sees that every child goes to school, India should be able to restrict its population to 1.4 billion by 2047, as assumed above.

Doing so would require India to double its expenditure on primary and middle-school education, or to spend roughly Rs.30,000 crore more per year. If appropriate prices were charged on all the economic services provided by the government, India would have ample resources. But, of course, money alone cannot deliver education. What is needed is to transfer control and funds for operating rural schools to the *panchayats*. Villagers should be informed about the performance of their neighbors in order to generate pressure on the *panchayats* and ensure that they perform.

India needs a bold vision, ambition, and self confidence. With these, it can reach the goal of $30,000 per capita by 2047.

India's antipoverty programs should be restructured. While India spends a great deal of money on antipoverty measures, most of them do not effectively reach the poor. If all the resources spent on the various measures were directed to more effective measures, such as employment guarantee schemes, India could help the poor better without using additional resources. Furthermore, rapid growth would provide additional resources for such measures. Best of all, with an educated population and a growth rate exceeding 8 percent, poverty would be nearly eliminated in ten years. India should begin the next 50 years with measures to accelerate growth and, above all, with a campaign for compulsory elementary education.

Will India attain this? As a congenital optimist, I believe it will.

Society

D.L. Sheth

The caste system is invariably seen not only as the enduring system of traditional social stratification in India but also as something that has been unaffected by change over time at its core. This chapter will assess the nature of the changes that have occurred in modern times, especially after independence, and will show that they have contributed to the growth of a new type of system of social stratification.

The theoretical perspective that has long dominated the analysis of social change in India has emphasized certain structural and cultural continuities that Indian society has experienced in the course of modernization. The changes that have occurred in the caste system are usually seen in terms of functional adjustments the system has made for its own survival and maintenance. The ideological and structural changes brought about in Indian society through the processes of industrialization, urbanization, and political democracy are seen as representing elements exogenous to the self-perpetuating system of castes, which selectively incorporates and recasts these elements in its own image. Changes in the caste system are thus analyzed in terms of its adaptation to changes in its environment. In this process, the system may "find new fields of activity" or assume new functions, but it does these only in order to retain its basic structure and ideological (religious) core. In effect, caste continues to be regarded as a system of social stratification governed by the ritual status hierarchy, one in which the religiously sanctioned ideas of purity and pollution serve as its ultimate validation.

In the first section of this paper I critically examine this perspective, with a view to showing how its continued predominance in the field of sociology has prevented recognition of certain (nonritual) aspects of caste, and more important, has prevented the awareness of changes that have directly undermined ritual hierarchy as a principle of social stratification. The second part of the paper provides an overview of changes that occurred in the caste system during colonial rule and then goes on to show how fifty years of the constitutionally created nation-state of India and political democracy have introduced profound and far-reaching changes that are qualitatively different from those of the colonial period in their principles of organization and forms of consciousness in the Indian society. In the third section, I show how these changes were embodied by the institutions of competitive representational politics, which in turn gave rise to new categories of stratification in Indian society. The last section describes, by way of conclusion, some salient features of the newly emergent stratification system in India.

Perspectives

The entire stratification system of Indian society has been equated by many Western scholars with the caste system and has been characterized as the only extremely rigid and closed system of status hierarchy that has survived for so long in the history of any complex society. The system of *varnas* (the four ranked broad categories of caste that appear in the Hindu religious texts) and *jatis* ("castes" proper, that is, the numerous hereditary occupational and endogamous local groups) has been analyzed as being produced and reproduced continually by the perennial religious culture and ideology of Hinduism. This view continued to be elaborated in comparative sociology even in the recent postindependence years, which have actually witnessed profound and far-reaching changes in India's social structure.[1] It conceived caste as not so much a dimension of social stratification as a building block of the stratification system itself—a unit that could be ranked on a purity-pollution scale in a particular local hierarchy. At the macro level, the caste system has been conceived as a vertical hierarchy of statuses created and sanctioned by the religious culture that produced not only the *varna-jati* system, but also a metasystem of classification peculiar to India. This metasystem classifies everything, every conceivable object, human or nonhuman, in the social, physical, and even spiritual world, in terms of its being pure or impure, noble or base. Accord-

---

1. See Louis Dumont, *Homo Hierarchicus: The Caste System and Its Implications,* (Chicago: Chicago University Press, 1970) and Murray Milner Jr., *Status and Sacredness: A General Theory of Status Relations and an Analysis of Indian Culture* (New York: Oxford University Press, 1994); see also F.G. Bailey "Closed Social Stratification in India," *European Journal of Sociology,* Vol. 4, no. 1 (1963), pp. 107–24.

ingly, in the social world, the hierarchy of statuses is seen in terms of the purity or impurity inherent in each caste and in any occupation attached to it.[2]

In this perspective on social stratification, elements of power—intellectual, political, and economic—are thought to be subsumed by the ritual hierarchy as a whole, which endows power to particular statuses in terms of certain specific, but inalienable and inexpansible, resources. These resources are supposed to be used by the ritual social groups (castes) vis-à-vis one another within the limits set by the system. In this view, a particular type and a fixed quantum of power inhere in a status within the hierarchy. However, that power cannot be converted into any other form of power that may legitimately belong to other statuses in the hierarchy, nor can it be transferred to or appropriated by the other statuses. Put simply, in the ritual hierarchy of castes the power attached to a status is a nonconvertible currency. It thus prevents the play of power—economic or political—from disturbing the stability of the hierarchical relationship of statuses. For example, a *brahmin* is placed at the top of the hierarchy, but he cannot legitimately use his high status for exercising political power (that is assigned to a *kshatriya* status) or economic power (inhering in the *vaishya* status) in society. It is a *brahmin*'s status in the hierarchy that legitimizes his priestly and intellectual power and not the other way round. Similarly, a learned *shudra* may command respect but cannot exercise priestly and intellectual power as a *brahmin* can, and a *brahmin* does not lose his high status just because he is poor or lacks political power. Since status, or rather its ritual purity, is the source and sanction of power in the system, it is conceptualized not in terms of the power of a group but as a status resource, or a particular set of entitlements, privileges, and obligations endowed to each status group in the hierarchy.[3]

Of course, in reality, this has not prevented social groups from

---

2. In this view of caste, status is an ideologically derived notion, i.e., from the caste system's overall ideology of purity and impurity; its empirical manifestations may vary in time and space, but the validation of status lies in the idea of purity and pollution, which is supposed to be a perennial idea pervading the whole of Indian society. Consequently, the ideological view of caste makes an absolute distinction between status and power and conceives status as a location on the purity-impurity scale, which remains by and large insulated from the changing distribution of power in society. Thus, the caste system remains *by definition* a closed and unchanging status system. See Dumont, pp. 65–91.

3. For the concept of "status resource" and how that resource is inalienable and inexpansible in the caste system, see Milner, pp. 18–28. Milner conceives status as a

creating and using different forms of power for social mobility and, in the process, changing the arrangement of strata in society. But since such power remains ideologically unlegitimated by the ritual status hierarchy, it is treated as extraneous to the caste system of social stratification. The consequences of the use of such power by social groups for mobility are thus not seen as indicative of any structural changes in the stratification system itself but rather as anomalous phenomena occurring at the periphery of the system. The result is a view of caste as constituting a stratification system peculiar to India, a system continuously produced by a uniquely Indian (South Asian) mentality of *Homo hierarchicus* as opposed to one of *Homo aequalis*.[4]

Such ideally typified status hierarchy of castes (ritual status groups) provided Western scholars of India a much-needed construct from another complex society with which they could contrast and understand better, even celebrate, their own society as one based on the "progressive" principle of equality as opposed to the traditional and static principle of ascriptive hierarchy. Moreover, this is an Orientalist construct that depends almost exclusively on one set of brahminic texts, the *dharmashastras*.[5] These texts indeed espouse the principle of ritual hierarchy, which prescribes statuses within the overall ideological context of the four *varnas* and assigns functions and powers to each on the

---

particular form of power. In that sense, he does not make an absolute distinction between status and power, as Dumont does. Instead, he views status as incorporating a specific kind of power. Nevertheless, Milner, like Dumont, finds in the caste system an ideal-type manifestation of a closed status system, never produced by any other human culture, in which power is codified and organized by the principle of ritual hierarchy and remains subsumed in the status as a resource, such that power cannot significantly affect the relationship of statuses sanctified by the hierarchy.

4. The view of total binary opposition between the Indian status system of caste and the Western stratification system of class held by Dumont is, however, not shared by some Western comparative sociologists. They often see the difference in relative rather than absolute terms. For example, Milner sees the source of insularity of the ritual status system of caste not in the Hindu ideology of purity and impurity but in the Indian culture as a whole that embeds the caste system: "It is useful to conceptualize India as a culture that, *relatively speaking*, has been singularly able to insulate status power from the effect of other forms of power . . . it gives rise to a society in which status not based on other (non religious) forms of power is exceptionally important; hence it provides a unique site for testing general theory of status groups and status relationships." Milner, pp. 53–54.

5. See Amar Farooqui, "Some Comments on Louis Dumont and the Orientalist Understanding of Caste," *Trends in Social Science Research*, Vol. 3, no. 3 (December 1996), pp. 50–62.

principle of purity and pollution. In their theorization of the caste system, the comparative sociologists thus largely depended on the literature created and the practices devised by the creators and standard-setters of the system, the *brahmins*. They usually ignored the counterideological literature and movements created by the *shramanic* traditions of the Buddhists and the Jains and by several *tantric* and *bhakti* sects, which gave a different account of the caste system and had, in effect, produced significant changes in it even in the precolonial past. It is true that the comparative sociologists, while primarily depending on scriptural sources, did not ignore, and could not have ignored, the ethnographic data that were accessible to them. In fact, they used them quite profitably, insofar as these data fitted their theoretical perspective. But when the findings of ethnographic studies did not quite fit the theory's hierarchical frame, the complexities were often explained away as representing so many "exceptions" highlighting, rather than undermining, the general rule of ritual status hierarchy. The sociologists' concern with identifying dominant tendencies of the system as a whole often ended up privileging the brahminic categories of thought and practice in describing the system and discounting those of the lower strata, even if the latter were often articulated more persistently and widely in actual reality.

The point here is not to deny the fact that the Indian stratification system has traditionally been a status system of a particular type, with distinctive cultural features. It is rather to emphasize that just as the role of status and other "nonclass" elements (such as gender and ethnicity) is routinely ignored by comparative sociologists in their account of the functioning of Western stratification systems, the relative but persistent autonomy of the nonstatus power elements, which has all along been undermining and reshuffling ritual hierarchies, has not been adequately considered in their theorization of the caste system. For example, an excessive concern with hierarchy made them see castes only in terms of strata of a hierarchy, and the self-consciousness of castes almost exclusively in terms of their belonging to higher or lower strata.

The reality that castes were substantive communities of people and not just the strata of a system, that they were separate communities, each with its own legend of origin, its self-identity, and often its own rules of internal governance, and that each caste had its own way of relating to other castes, often flouting the prescribed rules of hierarchical obligations, was of little interest to the comparative theorists.[6] The reality that castes, even as they were vertically differentiated in the ritual dimension, interacted with one another horizontally and often negotiated their status claims vis-à-vis each other in a horizontal non-ritual space was largely ignored. For example, the theoretical significance of certain phenomena remained by and large underexplored. This includes the formation of "caste-clusters" among castes occupying different locations in the ritual hierarchy. It also includes the practice of hypergamy, by which a ritually low-status caste or a segment of such a caste could claim higher ritual status in relation to other castes of similar status in the hierarchy by forging marital relations with a high-status caste.

The historical memories of castes *qua* communities, their pride and prejudices vis-à-vis one another through which some among them have nursed a deep social hurt for centuries as well as an ambition for political and economic power, rarely entered the sociologists' accounts of intercaste relations. In fact, several communities occupying disadvantageous structural locations at the bottom of the hierarchy had launched religious and other movements to bring about their upward social mobility, and quite a few of them had succeeded in achieving higher status or some kind of social autonomy from the brahminic ritual hierarchy.

It is, for example, surprising that little attention has been paid to the role of religious sects—such as the Swami Narayan movement in Gujarat, the Narayan Guru movement in Kerala, the Arya Samaj movement in the Punjab and Haryana, the Lingayat movement in Karnataka, and the Vaishnavite movements in Orissa and Bengal—in effecting upward mobility for several lower castes and thus changing the structure of local hierarchies in various regions. Instead, such movements have been viewed by the theorists as illustrating nuances in

---

6. G.S. Ghurye, the founding father of sociology in India, was the first to draw attention to the community aspect of caste. But he did not see it as representing a counter principle to hierarchy. Instead, the nationalist in him disapproved of it as "caste patriotism" that undermined the process of national integration in India. See G.S. Ghurye, *Caste and Race in India* (Bombay: Popular Prakashan, 1969), p. 300. Ghurye, however, did not shut his eyes, as did many of his successors, to institutional changes brought about by castes, especially the lower castes, by separating and organizing themselves into intercaste associations for the purpose of seeking collective social and economic upliftment, which the ritual hierarchy in a village ordinarily did not encourage. Ghurye notes, somewhat ruefully, "Conflicts of claims and oppositions have thus replaced the old harmony of demand and acceptance" (p. 301).

the operation of the invariant structural principle of ritual status hierarchy. On the whole, what the theorists of caste have given us is a reductionist principle of social stratification in India in which every aspect of relationship among actors in the system is seen and explained as a function of a fixed hierarchy of ritual statuses. What is not explainable in these terms simply does not exist at least in any material way. In the process of formulating this principle, the brahminic view of castes not only formed the theoretical framework for understanding the caste system but also became a basic referent for interpreting every aspect of Indian society and culture.

A dominant strand in Indian social anthropology, despite its devotion to ethnoempiricism, often derived its interpretative frame from the comparative theory based on structuralism.[7] It rejected the scripturally derived view of the caste system and, instead, provided thick empirical accounts of the structure and function of caste at the village level. These studies keenly observed and carefully recorded variations in status ranking of the occupationally similar castes across local hierarchies. More important, they pointed to situations of competition and conflict among castes occupying vertically different locations within the ritual hierarchy. But in their theorization of changes in the caste system, they still saw continued primacy of the scripturally sanctioned principle of ritual hierarchy in the determination of statuses in the stratification system.

A phenomenal increase after independence in the incidence and spread of competition and conflict among castes, which in fact severely disrupted the traditional system of social and ritual interdependence among them, was seen in these studies as the system's response to the new functional requirements posed by the politics of representative democracy and the policies of the homogenizing nation-state. The phenomena of separation and division among castes and the forging of new social and political unities among them were seen as adjustments the castes made by stretching themselves horizontally into wider territorial spaces, but the system as a whole was seen as retaining its overall vertical structure of ritual hierarchy. For example, it was not enough for a lower caste or a segment of it endeavoring for upward social mobility to acquire economic and political power, it was also

7. For an elaboration of this point, see D.L. Sheth, "Future of Caste in India: A Dialogue," *Contributions to Indian Sociology*, Vol. 25, no. 2 (1991), pp. 331–341.

necessary for it to validate its claim to a higher status by attaining ritual purity (e.g., through sanskritization). But since the scriptures did not permit change in the ritually prescribed status of a caste, a sanskritized caste could acquire only a new cultural image for itself, not a higher location in the hierarchical structure. At best, a lower caste that acquired new economic and political power was recognized by the social anthropologists as a dominant and powerful group in the local hierarchy but not as one that could register a higher status. In a strange way, the scriptural principle and the theoretical principle of hierarchy (elaborated in some social anthropological studies) converged: both viewed caste as an insulated system of statuses that remained structurally unaffected by changes in the arrangement of power in society. In effect, the postindependence changes in the caste system were viewed as suggestive of adaptations and adjustments by virtue of which the system had not only survived but had even strengthened itself in modern times.[8] In actuality, however, these changes had penetrated so deeply into the system that they had greatly weakened its principle of hierarchy and in some contexts had rendered it inoperative.[9]

Such a view of caste persisted because, in their theorization, the social anthropologists failed to take into account what was happening to castes in urban areas, which constituted much more than just another context in which to observe castes. After decolonization, the industrial system of production and distribution of goods had penetrated further in urban than in rural areas. It radically altered the old preindustrial urban organization of division of labor that was by and large patterned on caste-based occupations. Put simply, the industrialization of old urban centers and the growth of new urban-industrial towns had significantly changed the nature of urban social organization and consciousness, making it difficult for the ritual hierarchy of caste to sustain itself. In cities, castes functioned more as separate collectivities providing a degree of cultural identity, even sociopolitical solidarity, to its members, but they did not constitute a system of urban social stratification. With the growth of a national economy and market, made pos-

---

8. See M.N. Srinivas, *Caste in Modern India and Other Essays* (New Delhi: Asia Publishing House, 1962), pp. 15–41.

9. For an empirically grounded argument showing how castes are breaking away from the ritual hierarchical system and are interacting in horizontal social spaces and forming themselves into new social strata, see I.P. Desai, "A Critique of Division and Hierarchy," in A.M. Shah and I.P. Desai, *Division and Hierarchy: An Overview of Caste in Gujarat* (Delhi: Hindustan Publishing Corporation, 1988), pp. 40–91.

sible by, among other things, the state's policy of economic planning, changes had occurred in the country's production and distribution system. These changes had begun to ramify into the rural areas. In brief, if postindependence studies of castes had been carried out in urban settings, they would have yielded "process-concepts," which would have enabled social anthropologists to observe the impact of urbanization and industrialization on rural social organization, particularly the structural changes that were already occurring in the rural caste system with the change in the village system of food production.[10]

In any event, a large part of the theorization regarding the caste system in India for decades after independence remained theoretically rooted either in Western Orientalism or in the brahminic ideology of social stratification.[11] In either case, the empirical reference for the study of caste was derived from the supposedly static agrarian context. The predominance of these perspectives has given us a lopsided view not only of the traditional caste system but also, and more important, of the changes that occurred in the system during the colonial and postcolonial periods. As we shall see below, the changes that occurred during the colonial period were qualitatively different from those that occurred in the precolonial past. They produced sharp, structural discontinuities in the caste system, which it found difficult to cope with. These changes penetrated deeply into the traditional stratification system after India's decolonization, leading to a new type of stratification arrangement.

Changes

Significant changes took place in the caste system during the colonial period, when the interrelated forces of industrialization, urbanization, and secularization began to make their impact felt on Indian society.

---

10. This point is effectively argued by I.P. Desai. In his view, not studying caste in urban areas prevented Indian sociologists from evolving the "new conceptual frame-work and analytical apparatus" required to grasp the nature and significance of changes that were occurring in the caste system as a whole with the spread of industrialization and urbanization. See Desai, pp. 47–48.

11. Ironically, this theoretical mode acquired greater respectability in the scholarly world in the 1950s and 1960s, soon after India's decolonization, than it had during the colonial period. Commenting on this paradox, I.P. Desai observes, "In my view we failed to emphasize the community aspect of caste, not merely because our model of caste was that of traditional *rural* India but also because of the nature of development of sociological thought in India. After 1951 the influence of Euro-American thought was more direct and dominating than before 1951" (emphasis added). See Desai, pp. 45–46.

The policies of the colonial rulers, aimed primarily at delegitimizing the power of the then-dominant social elite and creating support for their own rule, gave a peculiar twist to these forces, producing some specific but far-reaching changes in India's stratification system.[12]

The most important among these changes was the formation of a new, translocal identity among the lower castes collectively, as a people oppressed by the traditional system of hierarchy. The discourse of rights, until then quite alien to the concepts governing ritual hierarchy, made its first appearance in the context of the caste system. New ideological categories such as "equality before law" and "social justice" began to challenge the idea of ritual purity and impurity. The established categories of ritual hierarchy according to which the traditional stratification system endowed entitlements and disprivileges to various castes began to be confronted with new sociopolitical categories such as "depressed" and "oppressed" classes.[13]

Second, the colonial state, by using the traditional status categories for classifying the population in its censuses, acquired an agency, even a legitimate authority, to arbitrate and fix the status claims made or contested by various castes regarding their locations in the traditional ritual hierarchy. For some lower castes of the *shudra* category, it even opened up "official" avenues to lay claims for a status higher than the one assigned to them in the brahminically ordained hierarchy. Many such castes of *shudras* claimed and often succeeded in registering a status equivalent to that of the *kshatriyas* or the *vaishyas*. For example, in the 1920s, many cultivator castes of Orissa traditionally designated as *shudras* succeeded in being officially, and eventually socially, recognized as belonging to the higher statuses of the Khandayats and the Karnas, equivalent to those of the *kshatriyas* or *vaishyas*, respectively.

---

12. For a detailed discussion of changes in caste under British rule in India and the impact that colonial policies had on the caste system, see G.S. Ghurye, "Caste During the British Rule," in his *Caste and Race in India*, pp. 270–305; see also Marc Galanter "Reform, Mobility, and Politics Under British Rule," in Ghurye's *Competing Equalities: Law and Backward Classes in India* (Delhi: Oxford University Press, 1984), pp. 18–40.

13. Collective self-awareness among the lower castes of a people, oppressed socially and economically by the ritually high-ranking castes, developed and found organizational articulation through their participation in anti-*brahmin* movements that grew in the early decades of this century. See Gail Omvedt, *Cultural Revolt in a Colonial Society: The Non-Brahman Movements in Western India—1873 to 1930* (Bombay: Scientific Socialist Education Trust, 1976); see also Eugene F. Irshick, *Politics and Social Conflict in South India: The Non-Brahman Movements and Tamil Separatism 1916–1929* (Berkeley: University of California Press, 1969).

This is evident from the notes made by the settlement officer for Orissa in his 1922–23 report: "Many families were found to have improved their caste designation since last settlement, or attempted to do so at this settlement. In this way many families designated as Jana [literally, ordinary people] at last settlement sought to be recorded as Rays or Mahapatras ... and Khandyats wished to become Mahalayaks or Karnas, Bariks or Lonkas to become Patnaiks and Chasas [cultivators] to become Khandait [Kshatriya] ... The Census Figures tell the same tale. For instance in Cuttack district there has been an abnormal increase of Khandaits between 1921–31 and decrease of Chasas." The officer also notes that some such claims "were given effect in the records."[14] Further, the enumeration and classification of castes and their ethnographic descriptions compiled by the colonial state highlighted how the ritual hierarchy afforded social and economic advantages to some castes but had relegated others to a state of socioeconomic deprivation and imposed on them degrading and often stigmatized identities. This new awareness led to demands by many such castes for special recognition by the state, not only for an official change of their stigmatized names and upgrading of their statuses but also for receiving educational and occupational benefits. Demands were also made by some of them for political representation; they argued that they belonged to the "depressed classes" or "minorities," categories that the regime had already recognized for such purpose.[15]

Third, by playing the dual role of a super *brahmin* who officially located and relocated disputed statuses of castes in the traditional hierarchy through periodic census classifications and of a just and modern ruler who wished to recognize rights and aspirations of his weak and poor subjects, albeit as social collectivities, the colonial state sought to secure the colonial political economy from the incursions of emerging nationalist politics. This, among other factors, induced people to organize and represent their interests in politics in terms of wider, horizontal caste identities and to participate in the economy on the terms and through mechanisms set by the colonial regime. But all this made it difficult for castes as they entered the new arena of politics—of seeking official recognition and popular representation—to accept simultaneously the functions assigned to their statuses in the ritual hierarchy.

---

14. Final Report on the Revision Settlement of Orissa: 1922–1923, p. 8.

15. For an elaboration of this point, see D.L. Sheth, "Politics of Recognition and Representation," *Book Review*, Vol. 19, no. 11 (November 1995), pp. 34–35.

This resulted in making the hierarchical order increasingly subject to horizontal political competition and conflict among castes, and in the process, the horizontally expanded caste became a recognized and legitimate category for political representation and for administering the social and welfare policies of the state. The principle of ritual hierarchy began to lose its ideological legitimacy.

Fourth, as it became increasingly necessary for them to negotiate their newly defined interests with the state, several castes occupying different locations across local hierarchies but sharing economic (occupational) interests and traditional disprivileges began to organize themselves into regional- and national-level associations and federations in order to project a larger social identity and greater numerical strength.[16]

Fifth, movements of the lower castes for upward social mobility, which were ubiquitous in the history of the caste system, now acquired a qualitatively new dimension as they began to attack the very ideological foundations of the ritual hierarchy, not in terms internal to the system (as had been largely the case with the Buddhist and *Bhakti* movements) but in the modern ideological terms of justice and equality.

Such changes have not only intensified during the fifty years since decolonization, but with India's establishment of a liberal democratic state and institutions of competitive, representational democracy, they have also acquired still newer dimensions and a sharper transformative edge, producing some fundamental structural and systemic changes in the traditional stratification system.[17] The hierarchically ordered strata of castes increasingly function as horizontal groups, competing and

---

16. Galanter sees this development during colonial rule as having brought about some fundamental changes in the caste system: "Caste organization brought with it two important and related changes in the nature of castes. The salient groups grew in size from endogamous *jatis* into region-wise alliances. Concomitantly, the traditional patterns of organization and leadership in the village setting were displaced by voluntary associations with officials whose delimited authority derived from elections." Galanter, p. 23.

17. For a recent argument articulating a contrary position emphasizing that the caste system has, even in the face of such changes, maintained systemic continuity, see A.M. Shah, "A Response to the Critique on Division and Hierarchy," in A.M. Shah and I.P. Desai, pp. 92–133. Shah sees horizontal divisions as intrinsic to the caste system itself, representing another principle of caste organization that has always operated in juxtaposition with hierarchy. The horizontal divisions in caste, in his view, are thus produced and reproduced as part of the continuous process within the system, a kind of change that the system undergoes for its own survival and maintenance. However, for his interlocutor in the debate, I.P. Desai, the horizontal divisions existed prior to caste and were integrated by the caste system through its principle of ritual hierarchy. The divisional aspect of caste that lay dormant for centuries has, in his view, become so pronounced with modernization that

cooperating with one another for the new economic and political power released in society through the process of modernization of the economy and democratization of the political institutions.

Alongside this horizontalization of the organizational structure, the consciousness of caste has also been changing, with members of different castes identified in terms of a community as opposed to hierarchical terms. Caste consciousness is now also articulated as the political consciousness of groups staking claims to power and to new places in the changed opportunity structure. It is a different kind of collective consciousness from that of belonging to a "high" or "low" ritual status group. The rise of such "communalized" caste consciousness has led to the disruption of hierarchical relations and to an increase in competition and conflict among castes. Far from strengthening the caste system, the emergent competitive character of caste consciousness has contributed to its systemic disintegration.

The disintegrating traditional status system is now thickly overlaid by the new power system created, on the one hand, by elections, political parties, and above all by social policies—such as affirmative action—of the state, and on the other hand, by changes in the occupational structure of society that have not only created vast numbers of nontraditional, caste-free occupations but have also given rise to new types of social relations even among the groups following traditional occupations.

The nexus between hereditary ritual status and occupation, which constituted one of the caste system's defining features, is progressively breaking down. It has become unnecessary to justify the occupation one follows in terms of its correlation with the ritual purity or impurity of one's inherited status. The traditional, ritualistic idea of cleanliness or otherwise of the occupation one follows has become unimportant if the work brings a good income to the individual. A *brahmin* dealing in leather or an ex-untouchable dealing in diamonds is no longer looked upon as engaging in shockingly deviant behavior. That the former happens more frequently than the latter has only to do with the resources at an individual's command and not with observance of the

---

castes are now breaking away from the ritual hierarchy and interacting in horizontal social and political spaces. In this sense, for Desai, horizontal divisions represent a new principle for the emerging stratification system that has undermined the caste principle of ritual hierarchy. See I.P. Desai, "A Critique of Division and Hierarchy," in A.M. Shah and I.P. Desai, pp. 40–49.

ritual prohibitions attached to the statuses involved. In any event, the cleanliness or otherwise of an occupation is increasingly seen in a physical or biological sense rather than in ritual or moral terms.[18]

Significant internal differentiations have taken place within every caste. Traditionally, an individual caste, whether located on the upper or lower rungs of the hierarchy, functioned internally as a truly egalitarian community, both in terms of the rights and obligations of members vis-à-vis each other and in terms of lifestyle, such as food eaten, clothes worn, and houses they lived in. Differences in wealth and status (of clans) that existed among households within the same caste were expressed on such occasions as weddings and funerals but rarely in power terms in relation to other members of the caste. Today, not only have households within a single caste been greatly differentiated in terms of their occupations, educational and income levels, and lifestyles, but these differences have led them to align with different socioeconomic networks and groupings in the society—categories that cannot be identified in terms of the caste system.

The caste rules of commensality have become inoperative outside one's household. Even within the household, observance of such rules has become quite relaxed. In "caste dinners," for example, friends and well-wishers of the host belonging to ritually lower as well as higher strata than that of the host are invited and are seated, fed, and served together with the members of the caste hosting the dinner. The caste *panchayats,* where they exist, show increasingly less concern to invoke any sanctions in such situations.

Castes that occupied a similar ritual status in the traditional hierarchy but were divided among themselves into subcastes and sub-subcastes by rules of endogamy are now reaching out increasingly into larger endogamous circles; in some cases, their boundaries coterminate with those of the *varna* to which they supposedly belong. More important, intercaste marriages across different ritual strata, often even crossing the self-acknowledged *varna* boundaries, are no longer very uncommon.

A larger sociocultural category, such as that of the *bhadralok* in Bengal, has emerged in many regions of India. It is variously identified

---

18. For an illuminating discussion on the changed relationship between ritual status and occupation and its implications for the emergence of a new type of stratification system in India, see I.P. Desai, "Should 'Caste' Be the Basis for Recognizing Backwardness?" *Economic and Political Weekly,* Vol. 19, no. 28 (July 1984), pp. 1106–16.

as "upper-caste" or *savarnas*. This category comprises the *dwija* (twice-born) castes as well as the upwardly mobile dominant castes of the erstwhile *shudras*. In this category of (upper) castes, marriage alliances are frequently made by matching education, wealth, profession, and social power of brides and grooms and/or their parents, ignoring traditional differences in ritual status among them. Significantly, such intercaste marriages among the *savarnas* that cross the commonly acknowledged *varna* boundaries are often arranged by the parents or approved by them when arranged by the prospective spouses on their own. The only "traditional" consideration that enters into such cases is the vegetarian-meat-eating divide, which is also becoming somewhat fuzzy. Although statistically the incidence of such intercaste and inter-*varna* marriages is not yet significant, the trend they represent is. A more important point is that when such marriages take place, they attract little if any censure within their respective castes other than perhaps some raising of eyebrows. In fact, the mechanisms through which castes used to exercise such censorial authority have either disappeared or have become defunct.

The ideology and organization of the traditional caste system have thus been deeply eroded. Its description as a system of status hierarchy has lost its meaning.[19] As may be expected, such erosion has taken place to a much greater extent and degree in urban areas and at the macrosystem level of social stratification. But the local hierarchies of castes in the rural areas are also being progressively subjected to this process.[20] In the villages, too, traditional social relationships are being redefined in economic terms. This is largely because in the last three

---

19. Of late, such recognition of systemic changes in caste is reflected in the mainstream sociological writings. For example, M.N. Srinivas, in one of his latest works, characterizes the changes that have occurred in the caste system in modern times as systemic in nature: "As long as the mode of production at the village was caste-based, denunciation of inequality from saints and reformers, or from those professing other faiths proved ineffective. It was only when, along with ideological attacks on caste, education and employment were made accessible to all, and urbanization and industrialization spread that systemic changes occurred in caste." See *Caste: Its Twentieth Century Avatar*, ed. M.N. Srinivas (New Delhi: Viking, Penguin India, 1996), p. xiv.

20. For an overview of the comprehensive, systemic changes that have occurred in local hierarchies of castes in rural areas, see G.K. Karanth, "Caste in Contemporary Rural India," in *Caste: Its Twentieth Century Avatar*, ed. M.N. Srinivas, pp. 87–109. Karanth, in his concluding remarks to the essay, observes, "In the first place, it may not be appropriate any more to refer to caste in rural India as a 'system.' Castes exists as individual groups, but no longer integrated into a system, with the dovetailing of their interests" (p. 106).

decades, particularly since the "Green Revolution" and with the increasing role of the state and other outside agencies in the food production and distribution system in rural areas, the social organization of the village has substantively changed. While it once was a socioreligious system, the Indian village is increasingly becoming a primarily economic organization. The priestly, trading, and service castes, or the social groups not directly related to agricultural operations, are leaving the villages or serving them, if and when their services are still required, from nearby towns. The members of such castes who do continue to live in the villages have largely removed themselves from the "village system" of economic and social interdependence of castes. They increasingly function in the emergent national-market-related rural economy or in the government and public sectors of employment.

In this process, many a caste has structurally severed itself from the system of ritual obligations and rights that once governed its economic and social existence and gave it an identity in terms of its status in the ritual hierarchy. Intercaste relations in the village today operate in a more simplified form, as exemplified by the relationship between castes of landholders and those of landless labor. The relationship between these groups is often articulated in terms of the political consciousness of two groups of castes representing different economic interests.

The socioreligious content of economic relationships in the village has thus largely disappeared; they have become more contractual and almost entirely based upon monetary considerations. The traditional *jajmani* relationships, which regulated economic transactions between castes in socioritual terms, have been replaced by the relationships of employer and employee, of capital and wage labor. When the traditional social and religious aspects of economic relationships, such as traditional obligations of one status group to another, are insisted upon by any caste, it often leads to intercaste conflicts and violence in the villages. In brief, the pattern of social relations sustained by the internal system of food production of a village and by conformity of status groups to their religiously assigned roles in the system and to norms defining those roles has virtually disintegrated.

In sum, while castes survive as microcommunities based on kinship sentiments and relationships, they no longer relate to each other as units of a ritual hierarchy. The caste system, long conceived as a ritual status system, has imploded. Having failed to cope with the changes that have occurred in society at large, particularly since India's decolonization, the caste system is unable to maintain, on the basis of its own principle of ritual hierarchy, vertical linkages of interdependence and cooperation among its constituent units. Nor can it enforce its own rules governing the obligations and privileges of castes vis-à-vis each other. In the few specific contexts where ritual relationships between castes still survive, they have acquired contractual, often conflictual, forms that negate the system's hierarchical aspect. Ritual roles, for example, those of priests and barbers that members of some castes still perform, have been reduced to the roles of functionaries called upon to do a job for payment on specific occasions, such as weddings and deaths. Performance of such functions by a few members of a caste, however, cannot be used for fixing the status of that caste in the changed stratification system. Such roles, it seems, now survive outside the stratification system as a part of Hindu religious practices. Phenomenal changes, however, have occurred in Hinduism itself, such that intercaste relations can no longer be viewed as constitutive of religious practice. The growth in popularity of new sects and even of new deities and shrines, the growing importance of gurus and godmen, and the new practice of public celebration of Hindu religious festivals on a much wider social and geographical scale involving the participation of members of a number of castes across ritual hierarchy and regions have all shored up popular-cultural and political aspects of Hinduism. These have considerably weakened the traditional ritual and social organizational aspects of Hinduism. In this process, intercaste relations have lost not only systemic context but also religious reference. Castes now negotiate their status claims in the newly emergent stratification system.

The simultaneous processes of the detachment of castes from ritual hierarchy and the growth, albeit in varying degrees, of economic, social, and cultural differentiations within each caste have resulted in castes entering into various new, larger sociopolitical formations that have emerged in India's changing stratification system. As we shall see in the next section, each such formation grew from the process of politicization of castes and has acquired a new form of collective consciousness, a consciousness different from that of a ritual-status group. Yet the new consciousness is not that of a class as in a polarized class structure; it is, rather, based on a perception of common political interest and modern status aspirations on the part of members of these new formations. The unitary consciousness of individual castes has become diffused into an expanded consciousness of belonging to a larger sociopolitical formation that cannot be described as a "caste" or a "class."

The Politicization of Castes

For some two decades after independence, the political discourse on caste was dominated by radical-left parties and liberal-modernist intellectuals who saw, rather simplistically, changes in the caste system as suggestive of its transformation into a system of polarized economic classes. The discourse remained bogged down in the dichotomous debate on caste-versus-class politics. "Class politics," or the strategy of mobilizing popular and electoral support for political issues and candidates along class lines, was seen as the only rational, scientific way of representing the forces of social change and modernization in democratic politics. "Caste politics," on the other hand, was seen as harking back to the "atavistic" institution of the caste system, which, it was believed, was rapidly losing its basis in the structure of material interests in society; it survived largely at the level of habit and sentiments. The proponents of this view ignored the fact that, while caste had lost its significance as a ritual-status group, it survived as a community that sought alliances with similar communities with whom it shared political interests and consciousness. Hence, parties of the Left, both Communist and Socialist, by and large sought to articulate political issues and devise strategies of mobilizing electoral support in terms of the economic interests that in their view divided the social classes in India.[21] As it turned out, although these parties could credibly claim to represent the poorer strata and even occupied some significant political spaces in opposition to the Congress Party at the time of independence,

---

21. The writings and politics of Ram Manohar Lohia, a renowned socialist leader, however, constituted an exception to this approach of the Left to political mobilization. In Lohia's view, horizontal mobilization of the lower castes on issues of social justice and ritual discrimination had greater political potential for organizing the poor and deprived populations of India than the ideology of class polarization, which, in his view, lacked an empirical, social basis for mobilizational politics. See Ram Manohar Lohia, *The Caste System* (Hyderabad: Ram Manohar Lohia Samata Vidyalaya Nyas, 1964); see also D.L. Sheth, "Ram Manohar Lohia on Caste in Indian Politics," *Lokayan Bulletin*, Vol. 12, no. 4 (January–February 1996), pp. 31–40; also D.L. Sheth, "Ram Manohar Lohia on Caste, Class and Gender in Indian Politics," *Lokayan Bulletin*, Vol. 13, no. 2 (September–October 1996), pp. 1–15.

they failed to expand their electoral support in any significant measure for decades after independence.[22] The binary opposition of caste and class continued to get more acute in ideological debates, but the actual politics of elections and parties had already begun to adapt to the changed reality of the deritualized caste scene.

Put simply, competitive politics required that a political party seeking a wider electoral base must view castes as a pure category of neither "interest" nor "identity." The involvement of caste in politics fused "interest" and "identity" in such a manner that a number of castes could share their interests and identity in the form of larger sociopolitical conglomerates. The process was one of politicization of castes through which the elements of both hierarchy and separation among castes were reorganized and recast in larger social collectivities.[23] These new collectivities did not resemble the *varna* categories or anything like a politically polarized class structure. The emergence of these sociopolitical entities in Indian politics defied the conventional categories of political analysis, namely, class analysis versus caste analysis. The singular impact of competitive democratic politics on the caste system was thus that it delegitimized the old hierarchical relations among castes, facilitating new, horizontal power relations among them.

The process of politicization of castes acquired a great deal of sophistication in the politics of the Congress Party, which scrupulously avoided taking any theoretical-ideological position on the issue of caste versus class. The Congress Party, which was politically aware of the change in the agrarian context, saw castes as socioeconomic entities seeking new identities through politics in the place of the old identities derived from their traditional status in the ritual hierarchy. Thus, by relying on the caste calculus for its electoral politics and, at the same time, articulating political issues in terms of economic devel-

---

22. See D.L. Sheth, ed., "Social Bases of Party Support," in *Citizens and Parties: Aspects of Competitive Politics in India* (New Delhi: Allied Publishers, 1975), pp. 135–64.

23. Rajni Kothari, in his pioneering work on the Congress Party, saw the aspect of Congress politics that involved expanding its social base through management of caste-based political factions regionally and seeking consensus on issues of development and modernization nationally as crucial to the Congress Party's prolonged political and electoral dominance. See Rajni Kothari, "The 'Congress System' in India," *Asian Survey*, Vol. 4, no. 12 (December 1964), pp. 1161–73; see also "The Congress System Revisited," in his *Politics and People: In Search of Humane India*, Vol. 1 (Delhi: Ajanta Publishers, 1989), pp. 36–58.

opment and national integration, the Congress was able to evolve durable electoral bases across castes and to maintain its image as the only truly national party. This winning combination of caste politics and nationalist ideology secured for the Congress Party a dominant position in Indian politics for nearly three decades after independence.[24] The Congress Party rarely used such dichotomies as upper caste versus lower caste or capitalist versus working class in its political discourse. Its politics was largely addressed to linking vertically the rule of the newly emergent upper caste, English-speaking "national elite" to lower-caste support. The ideology used for legitimation of this vertical social linkage in politics was neither class ideology nor caste ideology; the key concept was "nation building."

The Congress Party projected its politics and programs at the national level as representing the national aspirations of the Indian people. At the regional level, the party consolidated its social base by endorsing the power of the numerically strong and upwardly mobile but traditionally lower-status dominant castes of land-owning peasants, such as the Marathas in Maharashtra, the Reddys in Andhra Pradesh, the Patidars in Gujarat, and the Jats in Uttar Pradesh. In the process, the party created patron-client-type relationships in electoral politics, relationships of unequal but reliable exchanges between political patrons—the upper and dominant lower (intermediate) castes—and the numerous "client" castes at the bottom of the pile, popularly known as the Congress's "vote-banks." Thus, in the initial two decades after independence, hierarchical caste relations were processed politically through elections. This ensured for the Congress a political consensus across castes, despite the fact that it was presided over by the hegemony of a small upper-caste, English-educated elite in collaboration with the regional social elite belonging, by and large, to the upwardly mobile castes of landed peasants. The latter, however, were often viewed by the former (the national elite, with their self-image as modernizers) as parochial traditionalists. Still the alliance held.

This collaboration between the two types of elite created a new structure of representational power in society around which grew a small middle class. This class consisted of the upper-caste national elite living in urban areas and the rural social elite belonging to the

---

24. For detailed empirical studies of the interaction between caste and politics, see Rajni Kothari, ed., *Caste in Indian Politics* (New Delhi: Orient Longman, 1970).

dominant peasant castes as well as members of the upper castes living in rural areas. The ruling national elite, although belonging to upper castes, had become detached from their traditional ritual status and functions. They had acquired new interests in the changed (planned) economy and new lifestyles that came with modern education, nontraditional occupations, and the degree of Westernization that accompanied this process. The dominant-caste regional elite still depended more on sanskritization than on Westernization in their pursuit of upward social mobility. But they encouraged their new generations to take up modern English-language education and to enter new professions. In the process, thanks to their acquisition of new power in the changed rural economy and in politics, several peasant communities succeeded in claiming social status equivalent to the *dwija* castes despite their *shudra* origins. Consequently, such communities as the Patidars, Marathas, Reddys, Kammas, and their analogues in different regions were identified with the upper castes, rather than the backward castes. The acquisition of modern education and interests in the new, planned economy enabled them, like the *dwija* upper castes, to claim for themselves a new social status and identity of belonging to the middle class. At the same time, the caste identities of both these sections of the middle class were far from dissolved. They could comfortably own both upper-caste status and middle-class identity, as the two categories had become concomitant with each other. While the alliance between the upper-caste national elite and the dominant-caste regional elite remained tenuous in politics, together they continued to function as a new power group in society at large. In the formation and functioning of this middle class as a power group of elite, caste had indeed fused with class, and status dimension had acquired a pronounced power dimension. But insofar as this process of converting traditional status into new power was restricted to the upper rungs of the ritual hierarchy, they sought to use that power in establishing their own castelike hegemony over the rest of society. It is this nexus between traditional upper status and new power that inhibited the transformative potential of both modernization and democracy in India.

This conflation of the traditional status system with the new power system, however, worked quite differently for the numerous non-*dwija* lower castes. In negotiating their way into the new power system, their traditional low status, contrary to what the statuses of the upper and the intermediate castes did for them, worked as a liability. The functions attached to their very low traditional status had lost relevance or were devalued in the modern occupational system. Moreover, since formal education was not mandated for them in the traditional status system, they were slow to take to modern education when compared with the upper castes. Nor did they have the advantage of inherited wealth, as their traditional status had tied them to the subsistence livelihood patterns of the *jajmani* system.

In brief, for the lower castes of peasants, artisans, ex-untouchables, and the numerous tribal communities, their low statuses in the traditional hierarchy worked against their entry into the modern sector. Whatever social capital and economic security they had had in the traditional status system was wiped out through the modernization process; they no longer enjoyed the protection that they had had in the traditional status system against the arbitrary use of hierarchical power by the upper castes. On top of that, they had no means or resources to enter the modern sector in any significant way other than by becoming its underclass. They remained at the bottom rung of both the hierarchies, the sacred and the secular, caste and class.

This, objectively, did create a political division between the elite and the "masses," but it still did not produce any societal awareness of socioeconomic polarization. In any event, it did not create any space for class-based politics. In fact, all attempts of the parties of the Left at political mobilization of the numerous lower castes as a class of proletarians or as a "working class" did not achieve any significant results, either in electoral or revolutionary politics. Neither did their politics, focused as it was on class ideology, make much of a dent in Congress-dominated politics, for the Congress Party had established the political hegemony of the upper-caste-oriented middle class with the electoral consent of the lower castes. A very peculiar caste-class linkage was forged in which the upper castes functioned in politics with the self-identity of a class (ruling or "middle") and the lower castes, despite their classlike political aspirations, with the consciousness of their separate caste identities. The latter were linked to the former in a vertical system of political exchange through the Congress Party, rather than horizontally with one another.

It took some three decades after independence for the lower castes of peasants, artisans, ex-untouchables, and members of tribal communities to express their resentment about the patron-client relationship that had politically bound them to the Congress Party. With a growing awareness of their numerical strength and the role it could play in achieving their share of political power, their resentment took the form of political action. An awareness among the lower castes about using political means for upward social mobility and for staking claims as larger social collectivities for a share of political power had arisen during the colonial period, but it was subdued after independence (for almost three decades) by the upper-caste, English-educated national elite, who dominated the political discourse. During this period, the rural elite belonging to the upwardly mobile intermediate castes made a place for themselves in the middle class. But members of the other lower castes remained outside its pale. It was around the mid-1970s that the social composition of the old middle class, consisting by and large of the upper and intermediate castes, began to change. This was largely due to the social policies of the state, of which the policy of reservations (affirmative action) was most important. Despite its tardy implementation, after about three decades of independence the impact of reservations policy became visible. It gave rise to a small but significant section in each of the lower-caste groups that acquired modern education and entered the bureaucracy and other nontraditional occupations. In effect, by the end of the 1970s, several members of the lower castes had entered the middle class. This not only enlarged the middle class but made it socially diversified as well.

This process came to a head at the beginning of the 1980s when the Second Commission for Backward Classes, the Mandal Commission, made its recommendations for extending reservations in jobs and educational seats to the Other Backward Classes (over and above those available to the Scheduled Castes and Scheduled Tribes) in all states and at the central level. This, however, became a highly contentious issue in Indian politics. The Mandal Commission proposal was stoutly opposed by sections of the old middle class. They saw the Mandal proposal as an illegitimate means made available by the vote-hungry politicians for the lower castes to force their way into the middle class (particularly into white-collar jobs). But this opposition of the old middle class to the Mandal Report led to a resurgence of activity by the lower castes in national politics. This resurgent politics, guided by lower-caste aspirations to enter the middle class, was pejoratively derided as the "Mandalization of politics" by the English-educated elite. The so-called Mandalized politics, however, resulted in radical alterations of the social bases of politics in India.

In the first significant change, the Congress Party–dominated politics of social consensus presided over by the hegemony of an upper-caste, English-educated elite came to an end. The Congress organization could no longer function as a system of vertical management of regional-caste factions. The elite at the top could not accommodate the ever-increasing claims and pressures from below, by different sections of the lower castes, for their share of power. From the mid-1970s through the 1980s, large sections of the lower strata of social groups abandoned the Congress and constituted themselves into shifting alliances of their own separate political parties. The vertical arrangement of the regional-caste factions that the Congress had perfected just collapsed. The national parties—the Congress, the Bharatiya Janata Party (BJP), and the Communist parties alike—now had to negotiate for political support directly with the sociopolitical collectivities of the Other Backward Castes (OBCs), the Scheduled Castes (SCs), and the Scheduled Tribes (STs), or with the regional-caste parties constituted by them.

Second, the categories of the OBCs, SCs, and STs, expressly devised for the administrative purpose of implementing the reservations policy, perhaps as an unintended consequence acquired a strong social and political content and surfaced as new social formations in the macrostratification system. They now operated in politics with the self-consciousness of socioeconomic groups. Not content with proxy representations by the upper-caste, middle-class elite, they wanted political power for themselves. Politics now became a contest for representation among horizontal power groups representing social collectivities as identified by the policy of reservations. These groups began to bargain with different existing parties or formed their own new parties. Whatever survived of the hierarchical dimension of the traditional stratification system in politics was thus effectively horizontalized.[25]

Third, the horizontalization of castes in the political arena foreclosed the BJP's option to reproduce a Congresslike social hierarchy in politics and thus to fill the political void created by the collapse of the Congress. The BJP's campaigns of political mobilization of all Hindus (the upper castes, OBCs, SCs, and STs) by using the slogan of cultural

---

25. The concept of "politicization of castes," was first used by Rajni Kothari in the 1970s to describe changes that had occurred in the caste system with its involvement in democratic politics. See "Chapter 1: Introduction" in his *Caste in Indian Politics*, pp. 3–25.

nationalism, or *hindutva*, also remained effectively confined to its support base largely among the upper and intermediate castes. Even emotive issues such as that of the Babri mosque and Ram temple raised by the BJP failed to quell the lower castes' fear that the BJP was using these means to reproduce a Congresslike caste-class hierarchy in politics. The outcome is that the BJP is confronting a social-structural barrier to further expansion of its electoral base, which it cannot hope to cross in the foreseeable future and still emerge as a single-majority party at the national level. To large sections of the lower castes, the BJP campaign of *hindutva* appears to be the ploy of an upper-caste, upper-class minority to project itself as a political majority by claiming to represent all Hindus. Consequently, like any other party today, the BJP has to negotiate with the lower-caste Hindu groups separately as horizontal power groups rather than as constituents integral to the political movement of Hindu solidarity. Unlike the Congress of the past, it is forced to work out coalitional arrangements of power sharing with several lower-caste-oriented regional parties. Put differently, the politics of horizontal caste coalitions, an outgrowth of the "Mandalized politics" of the 1980s, has rerooted national politics in the regions and has greatly diminished the pan-Indian character of the national parties. The claims of national representation by any of these parties have become unsustainable.

Fourth, the "Mandalization" of politics by the generation of aspirations among the lower castes to attain middle-class status and lifestyles prevented the process of class polarization. This politics created new compulsions in the social arena. The old middle class, dominated by the upper and intermediate castes, is now compelled to admit expansion beyond itself and make space, if grudgingly, for different sections of the lower castes. At the same time, lower castes, while forming coalitions in politics, compete among themselves intensely at the social level for entry into the growing middle class.

In sum, the "Mandalization" of politics has prevented political organization of the lower castes into one single class of oppressed proletarians and has generated an aspiration among many of their members to enter the middle class. The possibility of realizing this aspiration has been opened up, among other things, by the policy of reservations.[26]

---

26. See D.L. Sheth, "Reservations Policy Revisited," *Economic and Political Weekly* (November 14, 1987), pp. 1957–87.

Reservations have provided special occupational and educational opportunities to members of the numerous lower castes and thereby converted their traditional disability of low ritual status into an asset for acquiring new means for upward social mobility. What politicization of castes, along with the spread of urbanization and industrialization, has thus done is contribute to the emergence of a new type of stratification system in which the old middle class has not only expanded in numbers but has also begun to acquire new social and political characteristics.

Conclusion: The Emergent Stratification System/Rise of a "New Middle Class"

The macrostratification system of traditional Indian society, which did not have a centralized polity, functioned superstructurally as an ideology of *varna* hierarchy. Lacking structural substance, it served as a "common social language" and supplied normative categories of legitimation of status to various substantive local hierarchies of *jatis*.[27] But after India became a pan-Indian political entity governed by a liberal democratic state, new social formations, each comprising a number of *jatis*—often across the ritual hierarchy and religious communities— have emerged at the regional and all-India levels, and these formations have given a structural substantiality to the macrostratification system that it did not have in the past. The nomenclature that has stuck to these formations is the one that was devised by the state in the course of implementing its social and cultural policies, especially that of reservations. As such, in the macrosystem of social stratification, the new formations are identified as the "forward" or "upper castes," the "backward" castes, the *dalits* or SCs, and the tribals or STs. Over the years, the unitary and hierarchical consciousness of each caste has become diffused; it has expanded to embrace these larger sociopolitical categories, providing a collective self-identification to its members.

Unlike the closed status groups of the caste system, the new social formations function as relatively loose and open-ended entities that compete with each other for political power and for control over economic and cultural resources. In this competition for power and status in the macrostratification system, members of the upper-caste forma-

---

27. See M.N. Srinivas, "Varna and Caste," in *Caste in Modern India and Other Essays*, pp. 63–69; see also Andre Betelle, "Varna and Jati," *Sociological Bulletin*, Vol. 45, no. 1 (March 1996), pp. 15–27.

tion have available to them the resources of their erstwhile traditional higher status, and those of lower-caste formations have the advantages accruing to them from the state's policy of affirmative action as well as from their large numbers, both of which they use politically as well as collectively for upward social mobility. Thus, the new emergent stratification system represents a kind of fusion between the old status system and the new power system. Put differently, the ritual hierarchy of closed status groups has transformed into a relatively more open and fluid hierarchy among the new social groups.

This systemic transformation of the traditional stratification system, particularly the increasing loss of its religious reference and legitimation, is often simplistically perceived as the change from a caste society to a class society. India is far from moving in the direction of a polarized class society; instead, a kind of mass society seems to be in the making in which a vast social space has become available to castes detached from the ritual hierarchy for forming themselves into a new macrostratification category that I call the "new middle class."

In this process, the advantages secured collectively by castes in the political arena are used by members of each formation, as they compete intensely among themselves and with those of the other formations for entry into the new generic social category of the "middle class." Its membership is associated with new lifestyles (modern consumption patterns), ownership of certain economic assets, and the self-consciousness of belonging to the middle class. The ritual purity or impurity of the statuses held by its members in the traditional status system has, for the most part, ceased to be a criterion for their recognition or otherwise as members of the middle class. As such, it is open to members of different castes—which have acquired modern education, have taken to nontraditional occupations, or command higher incomes and greater political power—to enter the middle class.

And yet, the Indian middle class cannot be seen as constituting a pure class category—a construct that, in fact, is a theoretical fiction. It is important to recognize that the Indian middle class carries within it some elements of the antecedent status hierarchy as well as the ethnic and gender divisions that exist in society at large. Further, for the most part, entry to this "class" is dependent on the traditional status resources at one's disposal (as in the case of upper-caste members) or on such modern legal provisions as affirmative action (as in the case of the lower castes). So, it seems the Indian middle class will continue to have a caste element to the extent that modern status aspirations are pursued, and the possibility of their realization is seen, by individuals in terms of the castes to which they belong. But crucial to the formation of the middle class in India is not just that members of lower castes are entering it in increasing numbers but that the nature of their pursuit for upward mobility has radically changed. Their quest is for acquiring modern education, white-collar jobs, wealth, political power, and other such means of modern status, and not for registering higher ritual status.

The process of middle-class formation in India is empirically illustrated by the findings of a recent all-India sample survey. The survey, based on a stratified random sample (probability proportionate to size) of 9,614 Indian citizens drawn from all the Indian states except the state of Jammu and Kashmir, was conducted by the Centre for the Study of Developing Societies, Delhi, in June–July 1996. In concluding this chapter, I present below some *preliminary* findings of the survey.

1. As we saw earlier, the middle class, which was almost exclusively constituted at the time of independence by English-educated members of the upper castes, expanded to include the upwardly mobile dominant castes of rich farmers during the initial three decades after independence. In other words, this period saw the emergence of a small rural-based middle class.

2. The survey reveals that even today, the upper and the rich-farmer castes together dominate the Indian middle class. While members of the two upper categories, the *dwija* upper castes and the non-*dwija* dominant castes, account for about one-quarter of the sample population, they constitute nearly half of the new middle class. But this also means that the representation of upper castes has decreased in today's middle class, for the old middle class was almost entirely constituted by them.

3. The survey conceived the middle class in terms of subjective variables (respondent's self-identification) and objective variables (high level of education, white-collar occupations, ownership of assets such as land, motor vehicles, televisions, water-pumping machines, and houses). Accordingly, 20 percent of the population was identified as belonging to this middle class. About half of this middle-class population came from different lower-caste social formations, namely, the *dalits*, the tribals, the backward communities of peasants and artisans,

and the religious minorities. Considering that members of these social formations constituted 75 percent of the sample population, their 50 percent representation in the middle class is proportionately much lower than that of the upper and intermediate castes. But seen in the context of their inherited lower ritual status in the traditional hierarchy, their 50 percent representation is a significant development. Even more significant is the fact that when members of the lower castes acquire modern means of social mobility, such as education, wealth, and political power, their low ritual status does not stand in the way of their entering the middle class and, more important, acquiring the consciousness of being members of the middle class.

4. Analysis of the survey data also revealed statistically highly significant differences in political attitudes and preferences between the members of the middle class and the rest of the population. More important, on certain crucial political and cultural variables such as support for a political party and belief in the *Karma* theory, respectively, the difference between the lower-caste and upper-caste members of the middle class was found to be much less than that between members of the middle-class and others who do not have either the self-image or an actual position in the middle class. Put simply, lower-caste members of the middle class tend to exhibit social and political attitudes more in common with other (upper-caste) members of the middle class than with their caste compatriots.

5. The Indian middle class today has a fairly large rural component, thanks to its inclusion first of the rural-based dominant castes and now of the members of the lower castes participating in the modern economy and in administration. In brief, the middle class in India today is not a simple demographic category comprising sections of different castes and communities. It is a sociocultural formation in which the caste identities of its members survive, but their ritual hierarchical statuses have lost relevance. Individuals from different castes and communities, as they enter this middle class, acquire not only common economic and political interests and modern lifestyles but also a new self-image and social identity as members of a middle class.

To conclude, the nexus of caste and ritual status has broken down. The erosion of the ritual status hierarchy, however, does not mean that castes qua communities have disappeared or will disappear in the foreseeable future. They continue to exist, but as sociocultural entities detached from the traditional hierarchy of ritual statuses. By forming themselves into larger horizontal, as opposed to vertically hierarchical, social groups, their members now increasingly compete for entry into the middle class. The result is that members of the lower castes have entered the middle class in sizeable numbers. This has changed the character and composition of the old preindependence middle class, which was constituted almost entirely by a small English-educated, upper-caste elite. The new and vastly enlarged middle class is becoming, if slowly, politically and culturally more unified and socially more diversified.

Foreign Relations

Howard B. Schaffer

The decision in May 1997 of the newly elected Bharatiya Janata Party (BJP)-dominated coalition government headed by Prime Minister Atal Behari Vajpayee to carry out nuclear tests and to declare India a nuclear weapons state signaled a new, highly nationalist assertiveness in the way the country views itself and its place in the world in this golden jubilee year of its independence. In abandoning the carefully ambiguous stance on nuclear weapons taken for many years by its predecessors in power, and choosing instead to "bring the bomb out of the basement," the Vajpayee government indicated that it intends to pursue foreign and security policies that reflect the BJP's long-held perception of India's status as a great nation and civilization. This view had been spelled out by the BJP and its coalition partners in their National Agenda for Governance that was issued as they took office in March: "We will strive to secure for India a place, role and position in the global arena, consistent with our size and capability. . . ." The agenda also stated that "to ensure the security, territorial integrity and unity of India we will take all necessary steps and exercise all available options. Towards that end we will re-evaluate the nuclear policy and exercise the option to induct nuclear weapons."

India's decision has been widely condemned by the world community as a violation of international norms that severely damaged the longstanding global nuclear nonproliferation regime. New Delhi's action, and the arguments used to justify it, worsened Indian relations with the countries most important to its security and well-being. The Clinton administration, whose dismay was heightened by its sense that India had deliberately deceived the United States about their nuclear intentions, immediately imposed congressionally mandated sanctions. Chinese leaders reacted angrily to India's claims that security concerns about the nuclear-armed People's Republic had significantly contributed to their decision. The Japanese government suspended further loans and grants.

Pakistan's concerns over the implications of its unfriendly neighbor's nuclear ambitions were heightened soon after the tests by saber-rattling statements from senior Indian government figures about the India-Pakistan dispute over Kashmir. It came as no surprise when, despite a major effort by President Clinton and other world leaders to persuade them not to do so, Pakistan followed India's lead with tests of their own seventeen days after the first Indian detonations. In India itself, the near-universal euphoria with which the blasts were welcomed was gradually replaced by skepticism and even condemnation on the part of some opposition politicians, leading newspapers, and political commentators. Both at home and abroad, critics argued that contrary to the Vajpayee government's claims, India's journey down the nuclear weapons path had neither improved its security nor enhanced its standing in the world.

The BJP leaders who dominate the coalition government's foreign and security policy process will no doubt continue to be imbued by the nationalist fervor that led them to declare India a nuclear weapons state. Meanwhile, the international community is still scrambling for ways to limit the impact New Delhi's decision will have on the spread and potential use of nuclear weapons in the subcontinent and elsewhere. Stung by the adverse world reaction, which was probably more severe than it had anticipated, the Vajpayee government is examining its options with regard to both the further development of its now-demonstrated nuclear weapons potential and its broader foreign and security policies. At the time of this writing, only a month after the tests, it is not possible to forecast with any precision how these countervailing forces will interact.

As New Delhi considers further steps, it will have to decide to what extent it intends to continue to give priority to the quest for international recognition and prestige and for regional predominance, as reflected in the nuclear tests, over other longstanding objectives such as economic development, Third World leadership, economic autonomy, and global disarmament. To assess its strategic environment in the wake of the tests and the international reaction afterward, India will need to calculate how all these objectives relate to its most fundamental requirement—to maintain the country's integrity and defense. It must also judge how best to interpret and carry out these security needs in a world made more dangerous by its nuclear decisions.

Although circumstances have dramatically changed, and the Vajpayee government differs in ideology and core constituency from its predecessors, its efforts to develop fresh policy lines are, in an important sense, a continuation of the search for new directions in foreign policy that has gone on in New Delhi for the past decade. The changes that transformed international affairs after the end of the Cold War called into question or made irrelevant some of the most fundamental and longstanding features of India's approach to the world. These included "ideological" elements, such as nonalignment with the Western and Soviet-led blocs, as well as more explicit policies and practices, such as New Delhi's priorities in dealing with the Middle East. At the same time, major policy developments on the home front, especially the replacement of a government-controlled, inward-looking economy by a more free-market-based economic system that encourages trade and foreign private investment, significantly changed India's foreign policy needs.

The required reexamination and reworking of India's foreign policies in the 1990s would have been a daunting task under any circumstances. But it was complicated by developments that significantly changed the domestic political environment in which foreign policy decisions are made. The end, at least for the time being, of the dominance of a single, powerful "umbrella" party; the advent of often shaky, short-lived coalition governments; the spread of regional and single-state parties led by politicians of narrow, parochial backgrounds; and the appeal of strident Hindu communalism as a political platform distracted India's leaders from foreign policy and distorted their customary ways of dealing with it.

Against this unpromising background, the three Indian governments that held power early in the 1990s—the Congress Party regime led by Prime Minister Narasimha Rao (1991–96) and the United Front administrations headed by H.D. Deve Gowda (1996–97) and I.K. Gujral (1997–98)—were able to make some important adjustments in foreign policy. These included fresh approaches in India's relations with some of the major powers and regional blocs, most notably the United States and the Association of Southeast Asian Nations (ASEAN), as well as unprecedented changes in the substance and style of New Delhi's dealings with its South Asian neighbors.

The coalition government's Agenda for Governance and its subsequent policy decisions make clear that it is determined to change some of these new approaches. Other initiatives undertaken earlier in the decade by the Congress and the United Front regimes have already been significantly undercut by foreign reaction to what the coalition regime has done. But despite this, and for all the winds of change that have blown across India and the rest of the world in the 1990s, the Vajpayee government will inevitably be influenced by the ways in which its predecessors have defined and pursued India's foreign policy objectives since the country won independence in 1947. Like them, it will work from India's peculiar circumstances as a country that is huge, ethnically and culturally diverse, and poor, yet in many respects technologically advanced—a subcontinent-sized state that looms over its neighbors in South Asia but whose history has taught it to be wary of the challenges posed by nations outside the region. The excitement over the nuclear tests should not obscure the fact that these earlier governments, too, were guided by the concept of India as a great nation whose size, population, resources, and status as a major world civilization entitle it, or even oblige it, to play an influential role on the global stage.

This concept reaches back to the era when Jawaharlal Nehru dominated India's foreign (and domestic) policy stage as prime minister, minister of external affairs, and leader of the nationally dominant Congress Party. The seventeen years between independence and Nehru's death in 1964 marked the high point thus far of India's role on the world scene. They saw the development of many of the principles and practices that were to distinguish Indian foreign policy for years afterward. Although some policies underwent important changes in the course of Nehru's long innings—or, as in the case of friendship with the People's Republic of China, were scrapped altogether—a consistent core remained that was inherited by his successors.

Nonalignment with a pro-Soviet tilt, opposition to colonialism and racism, a stress on world peace and disarmament, and Indian ambitions to play a leadership role on the international stage to promote these causes trace back to these early years. So does the top priority independent India has always given to the safeguarding of its territorial integrity and national security, a goal that was underscored by the country's recent experience as a victim of imperialism. India's desire to become the security arbiter for the South Asian region, which some analysts argue inevitably derives from its geography and historical experience, also dates to that period, as does the longstanding antagonism toward

Pakistan that has been such a highly visible, distracting, and ultimately sterile feature of New Delhi's approach to the region and the world.

Nehru's foreign policies were strongly influenced by what he was trying to do at home to promote national unity and to foster economic development through semisocialist, autarkic programs that gave priority to the buildup of heavy industry and largely isolated India from the global economy. Most of his preferences and goals were shared by his successors, although sometimes in forms that were significantly altered from the Nehruvian originals. His daughter Indira Gandhi (prime minister 1966–77 and 1980–84) and grandson Rajiv Gandhi (prime minister 1984–89) put greater stress than he had on the development and use of military force as a foreign policy weapon, and it was during Mrs. Gandhi's first government that India conducted in 1974 its initial nuclear test. But this significant militarization of India's policy, which included the projection of power into three neighboring countries, can also be said to have had its origin in Nehru's time. The expansion of India's military might following its defeat in the China-India 1962 border war and the conviction, heightened by the unsympathetic reaction of other nonaligned countries to that Indian debacle, that battlefield victory is more persuasive than moral argumentation in international forums date back to the final years of Nehru's government. And even earlier, Nehru had made possible his daughter's decision—and ultimately Vajpayee's as well—to conduct nuclear explosions by initiating and giving high priority to India's atomic power programs.

Under Nehru and his successors, India won outstanding foreign policy successes and suffered serious setbacks. These will be discussed in greater detail later in this chapter, but some of the high points are worth mentioning here.

A noteworthy achievement was India's ability to play a major role on the international stage that for years went well beyond what its military and economic strength warranted. Although New Delhi's pretensions to world moral leadership during the Nehru years were frequently scoffed at, especially in the United States, India's persistent promotion of nonalignment as an appropriate and legitimate foreign policy approach encouraged many other Third World countries to adopt the concept. This advocacy was eventually instrumental in making it acceptable to the contending power blocs as well. India's nonaligned status made it possible for the country to garner sizeable financial support for its economic development programs from both these blocs. Yet despite that achievement, India made only limited progress in raising the living standards of its impoverished masses and, internationally, it failed to become a model for economic development that other Third World countries would seek to emulate.

India's efforts to ward off any significant external political influence or military presence in South Asia except on its own terms did not achieve lasting success until the end of the Cold War sharply eroded the security interests that powerful outsiders had in the region. India's stunning defeat of Pakistan in 1971 in the third—and, so far, last—of the India-Pakistan wars and the resulting breakup of its longtime antagonist were monumental achievements of Indian arms and diplomacy. But they did not lead to Pakistan's permanent acquiescence in India's regional predominance or resolve their bitter, long-running dispute over the status of Kashmir. In the long run, India's victory has only heightened the fears and suspicions of India's smaller neighbors of what these countries consider New Delhi's quest for hegemony in South Asia. They tend to regard India as a regional bully. Their relations with New Delhi have been embittered by the presence within India of ethnic and religious groups with ties to their countries who have sought to influence Indian policies in ways the smaller countries resent. Neither these South Asian nations nor India itself have displayed any serious interest in creating a regional bloc in international forums that would have the advantages, among others, of helping New Delhi achieve its ambition to play a more influential role on the world stage.

During much of the period, India's relations with the United States followed a course that some observers likened to a roller coaster. Washington's decision to develop and maintain with varying degrees of intensity a security relationship with Pakistan was a major setback for India and seriously damaged bilateral ties. Along with other Cold War–related issues on which Washington and New Delhi differed sharply, the U.S.-Pakistan link helped limit to brief periods the beneficial impact of such positive factors as sizeable U.S. economic assistance, the valuable support the United States quickly provided India in its 1962 border war with China, and the democratic values the two countries share. Until recently, efforts to improve relations were also hobbled by the negative stereotypes supposedly well-informed people in India and the United States had of the other country, and by the lack of serious substance in bilateral ties, notably in the economic area. This thinness in the relationship encouraged successive U.S. administrations to give little attention to the impact on the U.S.-India connection of the global agendas they pursued, not least those policies that brought Washington into conflict with New Delhi's positions on nuclear proliferation issues.

In the 1990s, at the end of the Cold War, the development of more substantial ties, especially in trade and investment following the Rao government's decision to adopt more market-oriented economic policies, and the increasing prominence in U.S. public life of a sizeable Indian immigrant community opened the way to a steadier and stronger relationship. The Indian nuclear tests were a severe setback to the substantial progress already made—the roller coaster moved downward again, at a fast clip. How lasting and far-reaching the damage will prove to be is likely to depend primarily on New Delhi's future behavior in the nonproliferation sphere and on its relations with its neighbors.

Nehru's greatest foreign affairs setback was the failure of his policy of friendship with the People's Republic of China, which he had cherished as a key element in his vision of a new Asia that could change the world for the better. India's defeat in the China-India border war led to a lengthy, hostile freeze in relations. It was not until the past ten years that a series of visits and agreements finally brought about a thaw. The agreements fell well short of a settlement of the territorial dispute that had sparked the war. The two governments had apparently consented to let that sleeping dog lie. They were moving gradually toward an easier relationship, if not a close one, when New Delhi detonated its nuclear tests and justified them in part by citing security concerns about China. Beijing's incensed reaction has prompted fears that the two countries may be heading toward another prolonged period of strained bilateral relations.

Elsewhere in the East, Indian foreign policy has given importance to Southeast Asia, a region adjacent to its own with which it has historical and cultural ties and hopes for important economic ones. In Nehru's day, New Delhi tried with some success to play a role in arranging and administering the settlements that followed French withdrawal from Indochina, and Indira Gandhi's government later became outspoken in opposing U.S. intervention in the area. Indian policies in Southeast Asia were long driven by concepts that were key to New Delhi's approach to many other parts of the Third World: anticolonialism, usually defined as opposition to the assertion of Western, specifically U.S., influence; a preference for radical, anti-Western regimes such as the Democratic Republic of Vietnam; and, especially after the end of the Vietnam War, a hostility to the spread of Chinese power in the region. More recently, economic objectives—trade and investment—have come to dominate India's Southeast Asia policy, as they have its policies in many other parts of the world. New Delhi has sought to develop closer ties with ASEAN with these goals in mind, and these goals have also become the main element in its relations with the countries of the European Union. Similar economic concerns have long been the principal basis for India's relations with Japan as well. The two countries have never been politically close despite their common allegiance to democracy, in important measure because of New Delhi's disdain for Tokyo's security alignment with Washington.

From the mid-1950s, India looked to the Soviet Union for effective diplomatic support, advanced weaponry, economic assistance, special trade arrangements, and nuclear power facilities. The collapse of the Soviet Union in 1991 was a grave blow to India and had immediate, far-reaching repercussions that New Delhi had to scramble to contain. Its efforts to deal with these have included the development of a new, if less significant, relationship with post-Soviet Russia. India has quite sensibly recognized that although Russia is no longer a superpower with whom it shares a broad range of major interests, or even a near neighbor, it can be useful to India in a variety of fields. New Delhi seems wisely determined to develop strong and constructive ties, although these will obviously never match the pre-1991 relationship that had been such a key element of Indian foreign policy.

Among the interests the two countries share is a concern about the former Soviet republics of Central Asia. There, as in neighboring Afghanistan, India seeks to forestall the spread of Islamic political fundamentalism and Pakistani influence (seen by New Delhi as closely linked) and to develop economic opportunities. Indian policies toward Iran have also been driven by anti-Pakistan designs and economic interests. These economic objectives, not least India's interest in securing its oil supply and fostering the welfare of Indian migrant workers, have also become dominant in New Delhi's approach to the Middle East. They have largely replaced the political interests, highlighted by favor for radical, secular Arab regimes and ostracism of Israel, that India had long pursued in the region.

The Nehruvian Legacy

Nehru had been interested in foreign policy long before India won its freedom from the British. His travels had made him familiar with the European scene, and his attendance as a rising star in the Indian National Congress at the Brussels Congress of Oppressed Nationalities in 1927 brought him into contact with other aspiring Asian nationalist leaders. In the two decades leading to independence, he developed firm views on what free India's role in the world should be. His party colleagues deferred to him and accepted the foreign policy resolutions he drafted at Congress Party sessions. Like many of their contemporary political heirs, they had other priorities.

Nehru looked to a resurgent Asia as a transforming agent in the postcolonial world politics in which India would play a leading role.[1] He was a dedicated foe of the colonialism and racism that India had experienced under the British and believed that a free India could help eradicate them elsewhere in Asia and Africa. As a socialist and anti-imperialist, he was suspicious of the capitalist countries. His attitude toward the Soviet Union, which he had visited in 1927, was ambivalent. Although he was repelled by Soviet methods, he was impressed by the regime's performance in developing the economy and by what he took to be its generous ethnic policy in establishing separate republics for its non-Russian nationalities. He was more concerned by the evils and dangers of fascism than of communism.

Implicit in Nehru's approach was a determination to have free India pursue an independent foreign policy. He made this more explicit as freedom neared. As leader of the interim government in 1946, he pledged that, as far as possible, India would "keep away from the power politics of groups, aligned against one another."[2] He saw this nonaligned policy as a major part of the effort to preserve Indian independence, to which he gave top priority once freedom had been won. A strong advocate of the amicable resolution of disputes, he

---

1. For a particularly perceptive study of Nehru's view of Asia, see Thomas P. Thornton's chapter, "Unclear Focus: Five Decades of Indian Policy in Asia," in *India: Fifty Years of Democracy and Development,* ed. Yogendra K. Malik and Ashok Kapur (New Delhi: APH Publishing House, 1998). I am grateful to Professor Thornton and to my wife, Ambassador Teresita C. Schaffer, for going through the draft text of my article and offering me many valuable substantive and stylistic suggestions.

2. Jawaharlal Nehru, *India's Foreign Policy* (Ministry of Information and Broadcasting, Government of India, 1961), "Future Taking Shape," broadcast from New Delhi, September 7, 1946, p. 2.

attached great importance to the maintenance of world peace.

All of this suggested not only that independent India would play an active and purposeful part on the international stage but also, given Nehru's vision of India as a benign and constructive force in the world, that it had an obligation to do so. The extent to which it was subsequently able to carry out this self-appointed mission probably exceeded Nehru's hopes and expectations. His foreign policy activism, which his daughter and grandson continued in differing contexts and different ways when they were in power (with a brief interruption, from the mid-1960s to the late 1980s), encouraged Indian elites to recognize that their country was a serious international player that could legitimately aspire to an even more far-reaching role. Although this public interest has waned since the end of the Nehru-Gandhi dynasty, a high-visibility foreign affairs role will probably continue to pay political dividends for the government of the day, at least if it can be portrayed as successful. Even governments whose priorities lie elsewhere will take this into account.

Nehru made the preindependence ideas he had championed the core of free India's foreign policy when he took the reins of power. The heightening of the East-West confrontation that coincided with Indian independence, and the importance the Nehru government gave to rapid economic development of the impoverished country the British had left, led the new prime minister to put particular stress on the quest for peace—in his view a necessary ingredient for growth.[3] This emphasis on peace further fueled his commitment to nonalignment. He persistently urged it on other newly independent Third World states as a legitimate, appropriate, and beneficial approach for them to adopt in the Cold War world. They could form a "zone of peace" between the contending blocs and thereby reduce the danger of a global conflagration. At the same time, Nehru's overriding concern for India's security and territorial integrity made him prepared to use force when the country's own immediate interests seemed threatened.

To the strands of foreign policy thought dating from the freedom struggle, Nehru added important concepts that stemmed from the precepts and experience that had guided the British rulers of India. The British had taken great care to ensure that their Indian raj would not be

---

3. See Michael Brecher, *Nehru, A Political Biography* (London: Oxford University Press, 1959), p. 566.

successfully challenged by any rival power. They developed a variety of protective relationships with neighboring states and territories with this end in view. The importance to them of the security of India was heightened by its role as the hub of Britain's eastern empire. It was from India that armed forces and diplomatic envoys went forth to project British power and influence to the Far East, the Persian Gulf, and the littoral of the Indian Ocean, which was rightly termed a British lake in those imperial years.

The secession of Pakistan ruled out independent India's inheriting all of the ramparts the British had erected and maintained over the years to protect their subcontinental possessions, famously including those in the northwest designed to ward off a long-feared challenge from Russia. Nor did the Nehru government have the naval and air power that had enabled the British to project their armed forces into nearby areas. It was only in the 1980s, following a sizeable buildup of Indian military capability under Indira and Rajiv, both of whom saw the use of military power as a major foreign policy instrument, that New Delhi launched armed interventions in the Indian Ocean area.

Nonetheless, these imperial legacies became an important influence on Indian foreign and security policy as Nehru developed it. For all his faith in the resurgence of Asia and his fond hope that Indian friendship with China would start a new phase in world affairs, he promptly negotiated security treaties with the strategically placed Himalayan buffer states similar to those they had had with the raj.[4] His attitudes toward the smaller countries of South Asia and India's aspirations to become the security manager for the region and the seas that surround it also reflected to an important measure this British inheritance.

Nehru dominated the Indian scene in a way present and future prime ministers cannot realistically hope to match. Foreign policy was always a special interest for him, and he retained the external affairs portfolio throughout his prime ministership. Until trouble erupted with the People's Republic of China in the Himalayas, his role as architect, manager, and principal spokesman of India's approach to the world went essentially unchallenged either by politicians, civil servants and military officers, or the intellectual community. Foreign-service officers became the prime minister's privileged assistants, developing in

---

4. For Nehru's early attitudes toward China, see S. Gopal, *Jawaharlal Nehru: 1947–1956* (Cambridge, MA: Harvard University Press, 1979), Vol. 2, p. 139.

the process the impressive professional competence that remains their hallmark. Self-confident, talented, and articulate, they were an effective instrument in the pursuit of India's ambitious foreign policy objectives. Although the foreign service is no longer the prized career it once was, its officers will no doubt continue to serve Indian interests well. They will also be a force for activism in New Delhi's conduct of international relations.

Nehru's allegiance to an independent, nonaligned foreign policy stemmed from his strong conviction that India needed to chart its own course, judging each issue on the basis of its ideals and self-interest. "I do not think that anything could be more injurious to us from any point of view—certainly from an idealistic and highly moral point of view, but equally so from the point of view of opportunism and national interest—than for us . . . to try to align ourselves with this power or that and become its camp follower in the hope that some crumbs might fall from their table," he told the Indian Constituent Assembly in 1948.[5]

Nehru practiced his independent foreign policy with a flair and skill that soon made him an internationally renowned figure. Under his leadership, India was able to play a role on the global stage that went well beyond the part its limited economic and military strength warranted. Nehruvian diplomacy became involved in a host of issues, many of them of seemingly limited relevance to immediate Indian interests.

This Indian involvement and the pretensions to moral superiority that often accompanied it raised hackles in the West, notably in Washington, whose diplomatic style was marked by a similar tone. As the Cold War intensified and came to dominate the world's agenda, India was scored for its unwillingness to adopt a firm anti-Communist position despite its democratic form of government. Its interest in a "zone of peace" was seen as a bid by Nehru to organize and head a third force. This the prime minister denied, although in fact Indian diplomats took the lead in mobilizing like-minded Third World countries in international forums. He was a major figure in the decision on the part of the nonaligned countries, by then far more numerous, to establish a formal movement in 1961.

Western, especially U.S., distress about Nehru's foreign policy

---

5. Nehru, *India's Foreign Policy*, "We Lead Ourselves," speech in the Constituent Assembly, March 8, 1948, p. 31.

deepened in the early 1950s when India adopted positions on the Korean War and other major Far Eastern issues that seemed to tilt in the direction of the Soviet Union and the newly established People's Republic of China, which India had promptly recognized. These Indian policies led the Communist powers to reexamine their attitudes toward the Nehru government and set the stage for their accepting India in the post-Stalin era as an important, genuinely independent country worth cultivating.

Nehru's activist, independent foreign policy was popular with the public and benefited him politically. As he recognized, it helped foster independent India's unity during the country's troubled early years by providing Indians with a source of national pride. By adopting nonalignment, India avoided the domestic political discord the country's taking sides in the developing Cold War might have sparked. With the exception of the right-wing Swatantra Party that came to brief prominence in the late 1950s and 1960s, opposition political parties, including the Communists, joined the ruling Indian National Congress in lauding or at least accepting the policy. Often working in conjunction with factions and individual leaders within the Congress, these parties sought not to overturn nonalignment but to move its practice in the directions they favored. Leftist elements that sought closer ties with Moscow were more active than pro-Western forces in such efforts.

While the Soviet Union moved toward acceptance of India's independent line, and soon came to benefit from it, the United States, which in 1954 had forged a security alliance with Pakistan, took more time to change its disdainful view. A breakthrough came at the beginning of 1957, with President Eisenhower unexpectedly leading the way. John Foster Dulles, Eisenhower's powerful secretary of state, who had earlier termed Indian nonalignment immoral, followed reluctantly. India was thereafter criticized not for its nonalignment per se but for not practicing a "genuine" version of it. Washington would over the years find much cause for complaint on that score.

Although neither Washington nor Moscow had any realistic expectation of enlisting New Delhi as an outright ally, both sought to win its favor. India benefited from this competition and extracted substantial economic assistance from both sides. The Soviet Union considered this aid an important weapon in its drive to persuade major Third World countries to support its foreign policy line. The United States, acting initially to counter the Soviet initiative, came to see its large-scale funding as a way to promote a model for economic development in a democratic setting.

Nehru was quite content to receive economic assistance from both East and West provided it came "with no strings attached," or at least none that interfered with his freewheeling policies abroad or his socialist preferences at home. While he mistrusted capitalism and pursued economic policies that discouraged foreign private investment in India, he did not advocate a redress of the economic grievances of India and other Third World countries through a reallocation of global financial resources. This Indian approach changed in the 1970s when Indira Gandhi was prime minister. India then played a prominent role in the ultimately unsuccessful effort Third World countries mounted in international bodies to bring about a "New International Economic Order" and other changes in the global economic system.

It is that latter-day role that some Indians look back to when they advocate a continuation, or resumption, of Indian nonalignment in an age when the end of Cold War blocs seems to offer scant scope for it. For them, nonalignment means Nehruvian-style Third World leadership for post-Nehru economic causes. It is attractive to some leftists and may also have appeal to other Indians who are seeking a *raison d'être* for a revitalized Indian leadership role in world affairs.

The independent, vigorous foreign policy Nehru practiced and bequeathed to his successors gave New Delhi a seat at the international high table (if below the salt) and avoided the association with a single bloc that the prime minister so disdained. But it had important flaws damaging to Indian interests. These included the practice of viewing many foreign policy issues through the prism of New Delhi's global approach, a tendency not uncommon among great powers or ones aspiring to greatness. Its zeal for nonaligned foreign policies and anticolonial causes led India to deride Third World governments that preferred association with the West. Its preference for radical regimes, connected both to these anticolonial prejudices and its socialist leanings, would have a deleterious impact on India's interests in Southeast Asia and in the conservative, oil-rich Arab countries. Most important, as it focused on the world scene and became involved in issues remote from immediate Indian concerns, New Delhi made no serious effort to develop a regional base for its broader aspirations.

Nehru's inflexibility toward Pakistan and the overriding role he and his successors gave to Indian concern over the Kashmir dispute and other aspects of New Delhi's Pakistan policy were also costly in many ways. A similar inflexibility on his part in dealing with the issue of India's disputed borders with China was an important factor in wrecking his policy of friendship with Beijing and bringing on the China-India war, a military and diplomatic disaster for the Indians. Also needlessly complicating Indian interests at many important junctures was New Delhi's often loudly voiced suspicion of U.S. policies and motives. Nehru had struck this attitude soon after independence, and many influential Indians came to believe that Washington was systematically engaged in efforts to undermine India and limit its power and influence. This credo, which suggested a sustained interest in India on the part of U.S. policymakers far greater than was actually the case, became for generations of Indians the politically correct view. Significantly, it also heightened their preference for Soviet positions and made advocacy of policies that Washington favored often politically risky business. This belief continued to influence Indian perceptions of the United States at a time when the two countries were seeking new, more positive directions in their relationship, and it may become more prominent in the political fallout of the Indian nuclear tests.

The Region

In practicing nonalignment and promoting it as the proper course for newly independent Third World nations, it doubtless occurred to Nehru that adoption of the policy by other South Asian countries would assure the natural preeminence that India's size and strength give it in the region. One of India's most basic objectives from Nehru's time to the present has been to emulate the British in staving off any significant outside political influence or military presence elsewhere in South Asia, except on New Delhi's own terms.

In this context, India has aspired to become the security manager for South Asia. It has sought, with varying degrees of intensity and success, to persuade the smaller nations of the region to look to India to provide order and stability and to protect them from outside threats, real or imagined. These smaller neighbors have not welcomed India's role as regional policeman. Pakistan, of course, has forcefully rejected it.

Pakistan's joining the Western alliance system in 1954 was a grave blow to Indian foreign and security policy. By bolstering its military and economic strength and providing it with diplomatic support, the association with the West enabled Pakistan to challenge Indian subcontinental preeminence and, in disputed Kashmir and elsewhere, its territorial integrity. It worsened the already bad bilateral India-Pakistan relationship that had led to one limited war in Kashmir in 1947–48 and set the stage for a major conflict between the two countries in 1965. As Nehru was quick to charge, it introduced the Cold War into the subcontinent. (He promptly substantiated this allegation by reciprocating Moscow's interest in providing India with diplomatic and economic support.) The one clear advantage India gained by Pakistan's membership in the Western alliance system was that Pakistan was barred from participation in the Nonaligned Movement and could not challenge Indian leadership there.

The special relationship between the United States and Pakistan initiated in the mid-1950s also complicated U.S.-India bilateral relations. Even when the special relationship no longer existed, its negative impact continued. Many Indians suspect that Washington may again revive the relationship, even though the Cold War circumstances that prompted it have vanished. They regard any U.S. move to bolster Pakistan's security as a possibly dangerous blow to India in the context of the zero-sum game in which they still assess Washington's ties with Islamabad and New Delhi. Although it was ultimately not accepted by Islamabad, the Clinton administration's recent offer to Pakistan of a package of supportive measures in return for its not following India's nuclear tests with its own probably heightened Indian suspicions.

Perhaps just as important, the rise of Pakistan as a rival to India that Western support made possible has distorted India's approach to foreign policy. It has given the relationship with Pakistan a far more prominent place in Indian foreign policy than it would otherwise enjoy and has distracted policymakers from paying attention to what would probably have been more promising and deserving areas of interest. This remained the case even after India's 1971 victory broke Pakistan in two and confirmed Indian regional preeminence. The enormous Indian expenditure of resources to defeat any Pakistani military challenge, including a nuclear one, has made the distortion even more glaring. New Delhi's antagonistic relationship with Islamabad, the persistence of their noisy, half-century-old dispute over Kashmir, and what outsiders often see as Indian intransigence on the issue have also significantly, and negatively, influenced the way the rest of the world views India, not least with regard to its aspirations to greater international influence.

This enmity between India and Pakistan has also been important in stalling the development of an effective regional grouping in South Asia similar to the political and economic associations that have been established in other parts of the world. The efforts of the Bangladesh government to launch the South Asian Association for Regional Cooperation (SAARC) were long frustrated by Indian concern that such an organization would provide an opportunity for the other countries in the region to gang up on India, no doubt with Pakistan in the lead. Ironically, Pakistan feared that India would use a regional group to develop a bloc under *its* leadership, and was similarly reluctant to move forward.

Once it was finally launched in 1985—long after regional bodies had been set up almost everywhere else—SAARC was handicapped by rules that prevented it from formally considering political issues and bilateral problems. India and Pakistan's indifference to SAARC has further limited its effectiveness. The organization has conducted some useful activities on such matters as narcotics control and antiterrorism programs, but its principal benefit has been to provide a venue where South Asian leaders can thrash out controversial issues on the margins of formal meetings. Recent efforts on the part of India and several other members to use SAARC to promote regional trade and investment have been limited by Pakistan's reluctance to improve economic ties with India until progress has been made toward a resolution of the Kashmir dispute.

Over the years, New Delhi has shown little interest in cultivating the smaller South Asian countries and relieving their fears of their giant neighbor and their sense of vulnerability to Indian military and economic pressures. India's insensitivity in dealing with them may reflect the way some well-placed Indians handle their relations with those of lesser standing and caste. In any event, India is neither liked nor trusted in its immediate neighborhood. Relationships between the smaller countries and New Delhi have been worsened by the presence within India of politically important groups with ethnic and religious ties to neighboring states. They have been able to use their clout with the Indian government to influence its policies toward those countries.

Aside from its 1971 military intervention in East Pakistan, which paved the way for the establishment of an independent Bangladesh, and its move into Goa and other Portuguese Indian territories a decade earlier, India has sent troops to Sri Lanka and to the small Indian

Ocean republic of Maldives. Both these actions, ordered by Prime Minister Rajiv Gandhi in the late 1980s, came at the request of the local governments. Nonetheless, they soon created backlashes in the two island countries that damaged India's standing and interests. The Sri Lankan intervention also caused a backlash in India, especially within the military. Originally dispatched to the island to disarm Tamil separatists (whom India had earlier supported), the sizeable Indian Peace Keeping Force (IPKF) soon found itself fighting them. It suffered heavy casualties in an inconclusive operation some called "India's Vietnam." The intervention ended ignominiously when a newly elected Sri Lankan government publicly demanded the withdrawal of the IPKF.

Other South Asian states have viewed India's military interventions with considerable concern. They do not welcome India playing the role of regional policeman, whether asked for or not. Indian efforts to limit the influence of outside power, such as its insistence on restrictions on Voice of America broadcasts from Sri Lanka, have been similarly resented.

India's approach to its regional neighbors was both highlighted and significantly modified during the brief rule of the two successive United Front governments that ended in March. As foreign minister in the Deve Gowda government and, subsequently, as both prime minister and foreign minister in his own, I.K. Gujral demonstrated an unprecedented willingness to offer other South Asian countries important concessions without demanding reciprocity or more. Gujral's initiatives led to successful negotiations with Bangladesh and Nepal on sensitive economic issues that had long roiled India's relations with both countries. The so-called Gujral Doctrine won considerable praise across the Indian political spectrum and was accepted even by leaders who in the past had opposed such forthcoming approaches either on grounds of Indian national interest or because of their own parochial concerns.

Gujral's initiatives, and the favorable reception they received in India, may have reflected a sense that with the threat of outside interference in the region reduced by the end of the Cold War, New Delhi could afford to adopt more benign policies toward its neighbors that would replace the tough big-brother attitude that had shaped them earlier. The fate of the Indian expeditionary force in Sri Lanka may also have been an influence.

Gujral's approach could have been a reflection, too, of a growing concern on the part of thoughtful Indians (shared by some in neighboring countries) that South Asia was being left out as the world organized itself into regional groupings. From the South Asian perspective, ASEAN is the best example of these political/economic blocs. Indeed, Gujral identified regional integration and globalization as the two main elements in the post–Cold War world. Accommodation to both were leading elements in Indian foreign policy under his direction.

In its National Agenda for Governance, the Vajpayee government pledged to promote peaceful relations with all of India's neighbors on a reciprocal basis. This represents a stepping back from Gujral's more forthcoming position, which some BJP leaders have derided since they came to power. The national agenda also declared that India "will promote and strengthen regional and civilizational grouping on the line of SAARC and ASEAN."

How these generalizations will translate into concrete policies will only become clear once the diverse parties that make up the governing coalition have had some time to work together. The dependence of the Vajpayee government on regional and state parties to maintain its narrow majority in Parliament is likely to influence the way it deals with foreign policy issues more in South Asia than anywhere else. Although the favorable popular reaction to the nuclear tests has strengthened the BJP's position vis-à-vis its coalition partners, it is not at all certain how long the party will be able to maintain this new dominance. In time, parliamentary politics may well revert to the maneuvering and manipulation that marked the coalition's first, pre-test weeks in office, when the BJP leadership was obliged to pay more careful heed to its partners' views.

It is noteworthy in this connection that Vajpayee's coalition includes important political parties based in the states of Tamil Nadu and West Bengal. As other Tamil and Bengali parties have done in the past, they can be expected to claim a role in formulating New Delhi's policies toward Sri Lanka and Bangladesh, where India's Tamils and Bengalis, respectively, have important ethnic ties.

Although New Delhi's relations with Islamabad seem unlikely to improve significantly while the BJP remains in power, it would be wise for the new Indian leadership to give the rest of the South Asian region at least some of the prominence and positive attention Gujral did in his brief time in office. India can gain from the better economic ties that a more cooperative relationship will promote, especially if these were eventually to lead to the creation of a free trade zone in the region, as New Delhi has been urging. Such a relationship could over time reduce the smaller South Asian countries' fear of India, recently rekindled by its nuclear tests. It could also enable their governments and New Delhi to deal more effectively with a host of bilateral problems as well as with the broader regional issues they are all concerned with—the environment, narcotics, terrorism, migration, and water management, to name the more prominent. India's voice in world affairs would have greater resonance if it were regarded as the leader of a friendly regional grouping, rather than as a regional tough at frequent odds with its neighbors.

Pakistan and the Kashmir Issue

For reasons of its own, not least its perilous economic situation, Pakistan joined the other South Asian nations in welcoming the Gujral Doctrine. But as the deadlock in efforts to resume their high-level dialogue soon again demonstrated, improving relations between India and Pakistan is far more difficult than bettering ties between India and the smaller regional countries. Efforts to do so have been affected by the legacy of animosity and distrust that continues to poison attitudes on both sides of the border long after most of those who lived through the horrors of the 1947 partition have died or retired from active political roles.

The dispute over Kashmir remains the principal obstacle to normalization of bilateral ties, if not the development of friendly ones. Both governments continue to hold—at least publicly—to the conflicting positions they adopted in 1947–48 on the future of the Muslim-majority state, officially termed Jammu and Kashmir. The Indians claim that the state is now, and has been since its Hindu maharajah's accession to India in October 1947, an integral part of the Indian Union. For them, the only issue to be discussed with Pakistan about Kashmir's future status pertains to the need for Pakistan to "vacate" those parts of the old princely state that it illegally occupies. India-Pakistan talks on Kashmir should be held within a strictly bilateral framework that conforms with the agreement the governments of prime ministers Indira Gandhi and Zulfikar Ali Bhutto reached at Simla in 1972.

Pakistan, for its part, maintains that Jammu and Kashmir has always been disputed territory. Talks between New Delhi and Islamabad over its future must focus on securing the right of self-determination for the

Kashmiri people through the conduct of a free, fair, and internationally supervised plebiscite in which, as agreed in United Nations resolutions adopted in 1948 and 1949, Kashmiris would choose between India and Pakistan. The international community led by the United States should involve itself in the effort to resolve the problem.

While maintaining these longstanding positions, both New Delhi and Islamabad have indicated that they are prepared to settle for less. India would accept the territorial status quo, converting into an international frontier the present Line of Control that separates the portions of the state each side holds. Pakistan would agree to some form of regional self-determination that would lead to the division of the state on ethnoreligious lines. Under such a settlement, it would expect to acquire the predominantly Muslim Vale of Kashmir and to retain the exclusively Muslim areas in the former princely state's northern and western reaches that it has controlled since 1947. India would keep the largely Hindu (Jammu) and Buddhist (Ladakh) regions. Neither India nor Pakistan countenance the establishment of an independent Kashmir. Many Kashmiris have long favored this "third option." It was forcefully revived by influential dissident groups in 1989, when an insurrection that still continues broke out in the state against Indian rule.

Compromise between these positions is not in the cards, at least not if it entails the two governments signing a formal agreement that finally settles the future of the state. At least since the 1965 war, when Pakistan's effort to force the Indians out of Kashmir by military action failed, Indian political and public opinion has been firm in its insistence that, other than minor modifications that would make the Line of Control more rational on security and economic grounds, those parts of the state India holds must remain within India. While many Indians now recognize that their government has over the years botched its relations with the Kashmiri Muslim majority and thus helped alienate them deeply from India, they continue to subscribe to views widely shared since the Kashmir issue first developed. These range from the conviction that inclusion of a state with a Muslim majority within India serves to confirm the country's secular character while refuting Pakistan's two-nation ideology,[6] to the expressed fear that "another

---

6. Under the leadership of M.A. Jinnah, the Muslim League called for a separate Pakistan on the grounds that Hindus and Muslims were two distinct nations, not, as the Indian National Congress insisted, a single Indian people.

partition" would lead to the slaughter and flight of India's Muslim minority. Pakistanis, displaying similarly inflexible attitudes, claim that until Muslim Kashmir joins Pakistan, their country—established as a homeland for the subcontinent's Muslims—will remain incomplete.

Under these unpromising circumstances, probably the best course the two countries, and the Kashmiris themselves, can follow over the next few years is to set aside the issue of the ultimate status of Kashmir. With international encouragement, they should instead focus on measures that can head off the specter of a fourth India-Pakistan war, this time with possible nuclear dimensions. A cease-fire and thinning out or withdrawal of forces along the tense Line of Control that separates the two armies would help; so would a genuine undertaking by Pakistan to curb movements across the line. Infiltrators armed and trained in Pakistan have not been primarily responsible for the Kashmir uprising—largely a homegrown development fueled by Kashmiri frustration with Indian rule—but they have significantly contributed to it.

These measures could also help restore normal civil life in Indian Kashmir, long disrupted by the insurgency. Other useful steps in such a normalization process include a significant reduction in the presence of Indian armed forces on internal security duty in Kashmir; an improvement in India's unsatisfactory human rights performance there; the initiation by the Indian government of talks with representatives of a broad spectrum of Kashmiri opinion; and a parallel commitment by all of the armed militant and countermilitant Kashmiri groups to give up violent methods and participate constructively in such a dialogue.[7]

Aside from serving as useful confidence-building measures, such steps would relieve the suffering of the Kashmiris themselves and could, over time, diminish the Kashmiris' alienation from India, especially if they were eventually accompanied by adjustments in the state's constitutional position within the Indian Union. A commission set up by the Jammu and Kashmir government has been examining the advantages of greater autonomy for the state, or at least for the Muslim-majority areas, including the pivotal Vale of Kashmir, where dissatisfaction with the Indian connection is strongest. But the advent of a Hindu nationalist-led government makes it highly unlikely that

---

7. These and other recommendations are spelled out in *1947–1997, The Kashmir Dispute at Fifty: Charting Paths to Peace*, a report on the visit of an independent study team to India and Pakistan sponsored by the Kashmir Study Group in 1997.

New Delhi would countenance a looser relationship for Kashmir except in the context of an India-wide devolution of power to the states.

The measures could also, and importantly, set the stage for normalization of other elements in India-Pakistan relations. Pakistan has long maintained that Kashmir is the unresolved "core issue" that stands in the way of normalization of bilateral ties. It has resisted the Indian argument that the two countries should deal first with less knotty matters, then tackle Kashmir in the better atmosphere created by their success in resolving these other problems. Not without reason, Pakistan maintains that, as the status quo power in Kashmir, India will pocket the gains scored in negotiations on such issues as trade and cultural exchange and in the end will hold to its hard-line position on the future of the state. By providing political cover for those in Pakistan who seek better relations with India, Indian concessions on the stationing of troops, human rights, and dialogue with the Kashmiri dissidents could encourage movement by Pakistan on other bilateral differences.

The likelihood of India making these or any other significant concessions to Pakistan on Kashmir or anything else has been reduced by the BJP-led coalition's election victory. Historically, the BJP and its pre-1977 predecessor, the Jana Sangh, have made India-Pakistan relations central to their foreign policy approach and have taken a hard line on them. At the insistence of the BJP's coalition partners, the national agenda that the Vajpayee government adopted omitted the demand made in the party's election manifesto that Kashmir's special status within the Indian Union be abrogated. Also left out of the agenda were domestic policy items in the manifesto that were regarded as anti-Muslim and had produced a negative reaction in Pakistan. Nonetheless, there was considerable apprehension in Pakistan and elsewhere that bilateral relations would deteriorate with a coalition headed by the BJP at the helm despite the brakes the other parties in the government might apply; despite Vajpayee's pledge in his first address to the nation as prime minister to "go the extra mile" to improve ties; and despite his constructive record on India-Pakistan issues as foreign minister in the broad-based Morarji Desai government in the late 1970s. The "good-neighbor" policy India initiated at that time was one of the highlights of its conduct of foreign relations, and it significantly, if briefly, improved India's ties with Pakistan and other South Asian countries.

India's nuclear tests led many Pakistanis to conclude that their worst fears about the hostile character of a BJP government had been confirmed. The heightening of animosity and invective that accompanied the tests, and Pakistan's conduct of reciprocal detonations, make it even more important for the international community to encourage an India-Pakistan dialogue on Kashmir and broader security issues and prevent the danger of strategic miscalculations—both nuclear and conventional—from leading to a new war. Any measures the great powers propose will be difficult to sell, not least those regarding Kashmir. The Indians have long resisted any internationalization of the Kashmir dispute and have insisted that they and the Pakistanis deal with it on a bilateral basis. The Pakistanis, for their part, have objected to measures that do not force the Indians out of Kashmir or respond to the demand for self-determination for the state. But with Kashmir now a potential flash point for a nuclear war, the situation has become too perilous to continue untended.

The United States

Over the past fifty years, U.S.-India relations have experienced a series of substantial ups and downs. Spells of sometimes bitter antagonism over major global, regional, and bilateral issues have alternated with briefer periods in which what Dennis Kux has called the two estranged democracies[8] found reasons to improve their ties. India's regard for the United States has been seriously hurt by U.S. support for Pakistan, and for a long time this limited the beneficial impact of more positive aspects of the relationship.

Ironically, in light of Indian perceptions, no major power has been more concerned about India-Pakistan relations and more interested in seeing them normalized than the United States. India has generally considered Washington's efforts unhelpful or worse. From 1948 on, New Delhi believed that the positions taken by the United States on the Kashmir issue at the United Nations and elsewhere were biased in Pakistan's favor. In 1962, the Indians resented the British and U.S. efforts to get them to negotiate a Kashmir settlement with Pakistan at a time when India was weakened by its defeat in the border war with China. India had been convinced earlier that the U.S.-Pakistan security

---

8. Dennis Kux, *India and the United States: Estranged Democracies* (Washington: National Defense University Press, 1993).

relationship lessened the prospect of a resolution of the Kashmir dispute and other India-Pakistan differences. This was true enough if by a resolution India meant one primarily on its terms.

Since the 1972 Simla Accord, Washington has accepted bilateralism as the best way to resolve the issue. In recent years, it has added that the wishes of the people of Kashmir should be taken into account. But many Indians remain convinced that the United States seeks an opportunity to become involved in resolving the dispute in ways unacceptable to India. This attitude has persisted despite countless reiterations of Washington's longstanding Kashmir policy by U.S. officials, whose statements are carefully scrutinized in India for evidence of such unwelcome purposes. President Bill Clinton's reported assurance to I.K. Gujral in New York in September 1997 that the United States will only be prepared to assist actively in the search for a settlement if both India and Pakistan want it to do so was well received by India, particularly since it came on the heels of a baseless but widely accepted report that the president was planning to organize a tripartite session with Gujral and Pakistan's Prime Minister Nawaz Sharif to deal with India-Pakistan differences. But the renewed expression of U.S. and international concern about Kashmir following the South Asian nuclear tests has revived New Delhi's apprehensions about Washington's intentions.

India's worry over the U.S. role in India-Pakistan relations in general and Kashmir in particular is part of a broader conviction, to which many Indians have subscribed, that Washington has been persistently unsympathetic, even downright hostile, on issues that New Delhi considers important to its interests. These suspicions date back to the earliest years of Indian independence. Nehru resented not only what he considered Washington's pro-Pakistan tilt on Kashmir but also the broader global strategy pursued by the Truman administration. To the prime minister, this strategy went against the foreign policy principles and objectives he most valued—the pursuit of peace and anticolonialism prominent among them. He believed that the U.S. initiative in mobilizing Western Europe into an anti-Communist bloc could lead to a third world war. He was disturbed by evidence of U.S. support for Western colonial rule in Indochina, Portuguese Goa, and elsewhere.

Many who dealt with Nehru in those days were persuaded that he had a dislike for Americans as a people that helped fuel his suspicions about U.S. policies and motives. Some contemporary Nehru watchers attributed his bias to the influence of British socialism, others to the prime minister's upper-class education in Edwardian England. Nehru's prejudices fitted into the unfavorable stereotype many Indians had developed about Americans—crassly materialistic, prone to violence, and prejudiced against the nonwhite races—at a time when contact between the two peoples was far more limited than it later became.

The charge that Washington has been deliberately antagonistic to India's interests has been rightly rejected over the years by U.S. policymakers and knowledgeable observers. As noted, in the mid-1950s this Indian perception of U.S. malevolence was intensified by the U.S.-Pakistan security agreement and by the military hardware, diplomatic backing, and large-scale economic support the United States subsequently provided to Pakistan. This agreement sent bilateral relations between the United States and India to a low point. In the years that followed, India's attitude toward the United States was improved by the more forthcoming approaches of the second Eisenhower administration (1957–61) and by the Kennedy administration (1961–63), and especially by the latter's prompt support for India in its border war with China. Afterward, periods of brief hope and expectation on both sides continued, all too often, to give way to disillusion, exasperation, and, in Washington, indifference. The "mature relationship" that visiting political leaders and foreign policy officials bravely spoke of did not come about. Yet across those often troubled years, U.S. and Indian professional diplomats worked hard and successfully to maintain a dialogue and to head off confrontations when the policies of the two governments on important issues drifted dangerously far apart.

Some of the swings in this roller-coaster relationship were prompted by Cold War events such as the Vietnam War and the Soviet occupation of Afghanistan. Because of New Delhi's tendency to lean toward Moscow on Cold War issues, as a general rule a worsening of the U.S.-Soviet confrontation damaged U.S.-India relations, while an improvement helped better them. To some extent, the 1971 India-Pakistan war, which sent bilateral relations plummeting to an all-time nadir, fitted into this category, at least from the viewpoint of President Richard Nixon and Dr. Henry Kissinger. They saw the conflict in global terms, with Moscow and New Delhi in lockstep. The much publicized Nixon-Kissinger tilt toward Pakistan and the dispatch to the Indian Ocean of a U.S. naval flotilla led by the aircraft carrier USS *Enterprise* are still all too well remembered in India.

These frequent swings have been aggravated by the relative lack of substance to the bilateral relationship. India's economic policies for years discouraged U.S trade and investment, effectively ruling out a meaningful business connection between the two countries. Shared cultural and intellectual ties, a tradition of close political consultations, active political lobbies, and, until recently, a substantial, politically involved Indian ethnic group in the United States have also been largely absent. A substantial drop-off in Washington's political interest in South Asia after 1965 contributed to keeping the overall bilateral relationship skimpy.

This thinness in bilateral relations made India more vulnerable— than were countries with which the United States had more substantial associations—to the implementation of the global agendas of successive U.S. administrations, especially those concerning nuclear nonproliferation, human rights, and intellectual property rights. As one State Department official put it, U.S. policy toward India became a "theme park" for advocates of a host of special issues who believed they could make an impact because the U.S.-India relationship had few staunch or influential defenders.

The end of the Cold War held out the possibility of a major improvement in U.S.-India relations. The "tilt to Moscow" that New Delhi had adopted in return for Soviet diplomatic support and sophisticated military hardware, as well as for broader policy considerations, was suddenly a thing of the past. It could no longer complicate New Delhi's relations with Washington, as it had done with greater or lesser intensity since the mid-1950s.

The disappearance of East-West confrontation also meant that the United States would no longer involve itself in the affairs of South Asia as part of a worldwide endeavor to contain communism. Indeed, in the post–Cold War environment, the United States became less interested in involvement *anywhere* except in areas in which it perceived that important and immediate U.S. interests were clearly at stake. Until the Indian and Pakistani nuclear tests, these areas were usually defined to exclude South Asia. Coupled with the ending in 1990 of further military supply and most forms of economic assistance to Pakistan because of its continuing nuclear program, U.S. loss of political interest in the region (which had revived in the 1980s when the Soviets occupied Afghanistan) meant, in effect, that India had largely achieved its longstanding goals of closing off South Asia to outside "interference" and assuring the "natural" predominance there that its size and strength give it.

In this more promising atmosphere that prevailed in the near decade between the end of the Cold War and the South Asian nuclear tests, New Delhi tried to improve its bilateral ties with Washington. As it had since Nehru's time, it sought U.S. recognition of its importance on the world stage, to be symbolized in the 1990s by India becoming a permanent member of an expanded United Nations Security Council. It also wished to ensure that the United States held fast to its stated policy of avoiding intervention in South Asian political issues, especially the quest for a Kashmir settlement. It looked to the United States for high-technology products and for a degree of security cooperation, an area in which some limited progress had already been made. It wanted to engage in a serious and sustained dialogue with Washington on major global developments. This goal was made even more attractive by the United States' becoming the "sole remaining superpower"—and by the Soviet Union's no longer being around to express concern about U.S.-India exchanges.

To these rather familiar political and security objectives, updated by the end of the Cold War, India added in the 1990s an important array of financial and commercial objectives that called for better ties with the United States. Many of these stemmed from the major reforms in Indian economic policy initiated by the Congress Party government of Prime Minister Narasimha Rao in 1991. The reforms were extended slowly and unevenly by Rao's United Front successors. The Vajpayee government is trying to advance them somewhat further, although with an unhelpful twist designed to safeguard the interests of Indian enterprise.

For all their limitations, the reforms brought India into the global economy and opened unprecedented opportunities for foreign trade and investment. The United States became India's leading trading partner and source of foreign private capital. By 1997, total bilateral trade totaled almost 11 billion dollars—a 111 percent increase over the 1991 figure. During the same period, U.S. direct investment in India increased from negligible levels to over a billion dollars.

The United States warmly welcomed the reforms and the gradual dismantling of India's enterprise-inhibiting regulations. As has so often happened before, U.S. officials tended to be overexuberant about future prospects, at least in the earlier years of Rao's programs. Their exuberance faded as reform initiatives ran into opposition from political leaders both within and outside the government who were concerned about the impact they would have on constituencies important to them. United States diplomats and businesspeople also found that bureaucratic foot-dragging and inertia hamstrung implementation of those reform measures that *were* enacted, notably by delaying approval of foreign investment proposals.

Nonetheless, the changes of the 1990s suggested for the first time that the Indian economy could become one of the major forces in the twenty-first-century world. Whether it will actually do so depends not only on the pace and scope of future reforms but also, of course, on how the reformed economy is managed by governments that may well remain dependent on unsteady coalitions and uncertain mandates.

Not surprisingly, the development of more substantial economic ties brought its own problems. Washington's insistence that India promptly open more sectors of its economy to U.S. exporters and investors and New Delhi's demands for improved access for its manufactured goods to U.S. markets have been two especially vexing issues.

In the longer term, however, these irritating problems are likely to be overshadowed by the major impact that the changed economic equation can have in helping bring about the long elusive strengthening of the U.S.-India relationship. This is already beginning to happen. Influential Americans in business and industry whose attitudes toward India were negative, if they ever thought of it at all, are now paying serious attention. Along with the sizeable population of Americans of recent Indian origin who have begun to play a role in political life in this country, these people and their representatives in Congress have energized a lobby that advocates a more constructive and involved U.S. government approach to India on a variety of issues. Remarkably, it is the first time such a significant lobby has operated since the 1950s and 1960s, when pro-India sentiment in the United States was spearheaded not by conservative businesspeople but by liberal politicians and intellectuals impressed by Nehruvian democracy. The greater substance that enhanced economic ties and other positive post–Cold War developments have brought to the relationship has also encouraged academics and others long concerned with India and U.S.-India relations to weigh in with studies that call attention to the neglect of India among senior U.S. policymakers and recommend new, useful approaches.[9]

Economic issues had, of course, been an important element earlier in U.S.-India ties. In the late 1950s and 1960s, when economic assistance was a major feature in the bilateral relationship, U.S. ambassadors and aid mission directors regularly engaged in far-reaching dialogues with senior Indian officials, urging them to adopt measures that, in the U.S. view, would speed Indian development and promote social equity. But the donor-recipient relationship, however well meaning, is essentially an unhealthy one between unequal partners. This was especially true when it brought together Americans who saw aid as a tool to promote U.S. political objectives and Indians who resented not only those motives but also, in many cases, the avuncular economic advice the Americans offered them. Some observers have even argued that for all its magnitude (in overall dollar terms, although not, compared with aid to many other recipients, on a per capita basis), U.S. economic assistance damaged relations with India more than it benefited them. In the years leading to the imposition of congressionally mandated sanctions triggered by the Indian nuclear tests, the aid that the United States provided New Delhi went almost entirely through international financial organizations such as the World Bank or through nongovernmental organizations. Direct bilateral economic assistance had become only a small fraction of India's capital imports.

This hopeful, post–Cold War near decade of gradual, if sometimes fitful, progress toward more constructive and stable U.S.-India ties was abruptly interrupted when India conducted nuclear explosions and declared itself a nuclear weapons state. Washington's strongly negative response reflected and brought to a new intensity the longstanding policy differences it had with New Delhi over weapons of mass destruction. Their disagreement on the issue had seriously troubled the relationship since 1974, when India's detonation of a nuclear explosive device helped prompt a major worldwide U.S. effort to stem the further development of nuclear weapons. Even earlier, the United States had been concerned by India's refusal to sign the Nuclear Nonprolifer-

9. Recent examples include the Council on Foreign Relations report, *A New U.S. Policy Toward India and Pakistan*, prepared by an independent task force led by Richard N. Haass and Gideon Rose; and a CFR book, Sharin R. Tahir-Kheli, *India, Pakistan, and the United States: Breaking with the Past*.

ation Treaty negotiated in the late 1960s. Despite the urging of the United States and others, New Delhi remained adamantly opposed to the treaty, which, it argued, established unacceptably discriminatory double standards between the five nations that the treaty categorizes as nuclear weapons states and other nations, including India. India similarly resisted other proposals, made by the United States and other countries, designed to prevent it from producing nuclear weapons. More recently, in 1996, India angered the United States and much of the rest of the world by refusing to sign the Comprehensive Test Ban Treaty on nuclear explosions absent an agreed timetable to eliminate all nuclear weapons. Meanwhile, it acquired the technology and the material needed to fashion weapons at short notice. It also developed missile systems capable of delivering such weapons.

The sharp differences that Washington had with New Delhi over nonproliferation seemed at times to overshadow other aspects of U.S. policy toward India. The attention U.S. policymakers gave to the issue and the impact it had on U.S.-India ties were heightened by legislation that the U.S. Congress enacted beginning in 1978. Among other things, this legislation barred the United States from having any relationship with India in the nuclear field as long as the Indians did not permit international inspection of all of their nuclear sites. Implementation of the legislation closed off what had, at one time, seemed a particularly promising area of bilateral cooperation. It sparked angry, lengthy confrontations between Washington and New Delhi when the legislation made it impossible for the United States to fulfill obligations it had undertaken earlier.

As the overall bilateral relationship improved, some U.S. commentators called for the repeal or waiver of such antiproliferation measures. They argued that the best, most realistic course the United States could follow was to accept, tacitly, what India had already done in developing a nuclear weapons capability rather than to persist in unpromising efforts to persuade India to cap, roll back, and ultimately scrap its nuclear programs. They saw this as part of a broader effort to "denuclearize" Washington's India policy, namely, to downgrade nuclear issues from their dominant position in U.S. thinking about India.

The nuclear tests have had just the opposite effect. The almost unprecedented attention to India that they have provoked on the part of senior officials, Congress, and the U.S. public has focused on nuclear proliferation. Moreover, the Clinton administration's post-test handling of other aspects of the relationship has largely been shaped by the nuclear issue. Under the sanctions legislation, the Clinton administration has been obliged to cut off most of the limited bilateral economic assistance that the United States provides India. It has also had to suspend further Overseas Private Investment Corporation guarantees to U.S. investors in India and loans from the Export-Income Bank. More important, it is obliged by the legislation to oppose lending to India by such international financial institutions as the World Bank and the Asian Development Bank. The United States does not have veto power in these institutions, but it has taken the lead in an effort to win the support of other important donors for an open-ended delay in bringing new programs forward. Washington has also ended its limited security relationship with New Delhi. And, fearing that the changed circumstances in the subcontinent following the tests have heightened the dangers of war there, Washington has spoken out more forcefully on India-Pakistan issues, including Kashmir, than it has for many years.

The nuclear issue has also provoked what seems, at least for the time being, to be a serious change in attitude in Washington toward India. In the early part of the Clinton administration's second term, the president and other top members of the government had given India more positive attention than it had enjoyed since Jimmy Carter occupied the White House twenty years earlier. Senior officials, led by Secretary of State Albright, visited New Delhi and received prominent Indian policymakers in Washington. Preparations were well under way for a presidential journey later this year—the first since 1978.

This positive and engaged attitude toward India has given way to negative perceptions. The administration believes that the Vajpayee government misled it about its nuclear intentions. It now seems to view India more as an international troublemaker that must be brought back in line than as an important democratic power with which the United States, in its own interest, should seek a strong and friendly relationship. The Indians, for their part, have been affronted and disappointed by the U.S. reaction to their nuclear tests. They have been angered by the lead Washington has taken in seeking to rally other major powers to impose sanctions and in calling for other tough measures designed to stem further proliferation. Some of their old resentments toward the United States dating from Nehru's time seem to have been reawakened.

At this writing, only a month after the tests, it is not clear how lasting or serious this latest estrangement between the two countries will be. From Washington's viewpoint, much will depend on Indian behavior on nonproliferation issues. Should India agree to sign the Comprehensive Test Ban Treaty; refrain from the weaponization or deployment of nuclear weapons; and take other antiproliferation measures the United States and other major powers have called for, Washington's mood and policies will improve and a presidential visit, now postponed, could be rescheduled. Progress in a resumed dialogue between India and Pakistan on Kashmir and on other bilateral issues will also help.

As they deal with the new situation, the two governments and their publics need to keep in mind that the reasons both countries have for promoting a constructive relationship did not diminish on May 11, 1998. If anything, the events of that day made such a relationship more important for them. Washington's interests were spelled out well in a 1997 study published by the Council on Foreign Relations. It rightly mentioned preventing major war and further nuclear proliferation; expanding economic growth, trade, and investment; promoting robust democratic institutions; and cooperating on issues ranging from enhancing stability across Asia to combating terrorism and drug trafficking.[10] India's far-reaching political, economic, and security interests in better ties with the United States are obvious and even more important.

It will certainly be to the advantage of both countries if they can overcome their present difficulties and antagonisms and resume the progress in the relationship made earlier in the decade. Yet even by the most optimistic assessment, this will not lead to their becoming warm friends, as some have unrealistically hoped. As in the past, their foreign policies will be shaped by differing historical experiences, geographic settings, and perceived political, economic, and security needs. Although they share many interests, they also have important differences. The new nuclear dimension makes it even more important that they give their ties the careful and positive attention that was so often absent in the first fifty years of their changing relationship.

China

The stunning military defeat India suffered at the hands of the People's Liberation Army in 1962 effectively froze China-India relations for a

---

10. The Council on Foreign Relations, *A New U.S. Policy*, p. 1.

quarter century. In the poisoned atmosphere that had so quickly replaced what William Barnds called the spurious friendship of the mid-1950s,[11] the Indians regarded China as an inimical force posing a threat to their interests well beyond the Himalayas. China's assistance to separatist and radical elements in northeastern India, its development of nuclear weapons, and the saber-rattling, if ineffectual, support it gave Pakistan in the 1965 and 1971 India-Pakistan wars reinforced this Indian hostility. The U.S. opening to China heightened New Delhi's concerns by conjuring up the prospect of a "Washington-Beijing-Islamabad axis" targeted at India. Little progress was made toward normalizing China-India relations, and none toward resolving the border dispute that had led to the 1962 war.

The disastrous war had a serious impact on broader Indian policy. The reaction of other African and Asian countries gravely undercut Nehruvian faith in its partners in the Nonaligned Movement. Disregarding Indian charges of Chinese aggression, almost all remained neutral in the conflict and subsequent efforts to resolve it. The lesson for India was that winning on the battlefield pays off. It led the Indians to undertake a major buildup of their armed forces that reached its zenith in the 1980s. The 1962 experience, and the Chinese nuclear blast that followed two years later, no doubt contributed to India's decision to go ahead with its own nuclear explosives program.

India resisted Washington's attempts following the war to draw it into U.S.-sponsored efforts to contain communism in Southeast Asia. Among other reasons, the Indians did not wish to jeopardize their ties with the Soviets, to whom they looked for security against further Chinese attacks. But following the fall of Saigon and the souring of relations between Beijing and Hanoi, India's Southeast Asia policy was significantly influenced by its hostility toward China and a desire to limit Beijing's influence in the region. This manifested itself in the strong support New Delhi gave Hanoi, most visibly in recognizing the government that the Vietnamese installed in Cambodia following their military overthrow of the Khmer Rouge. Its pro-Vietnam policy put India at odds with the noncommunist states of the region, then banding together in ASEAN. This would have unforeseen and unfortunate consequences for India later.

11. William J. Barnds, *India, Pakistan, and the Great Powers* (New York: Praeger Publishers, 1972), chapter 7.

The long hostile freeze, punctuated by occasional flare-ups and maneuvers along the Line of Actual Control that separated India and China's armies, began to thaw with the visit of Rajiv Gandhi to China in 1988. Relations gradually improved from that time until the Indian nuclear tests. The border has been quiet, and prospects for its remaining so have been helped by the signing of a couple of agreements to reduce tensions along the Line of Actual Control. The second of these, reached during President Jiang Zemin's 1996 visit to India, provided for specific limitations on arms, air reconnaissance, and maneuvers in the border areas. China-India trade has expanded, reaching almost $1.6 billion in 1996 (excluding Indian trade with Hong Kong), compared with less than $50 million five years earlier. High-level visits have increased. The Chinese have adopted what they term a flexible attitude toward India's 1974 annexation of the Himalayan principality of Sikkim (which they loudly protested for years) and its control of areas in the eastern Himalayas that Beijing claims. They also profess themselves satisfied with what they consider as India's less provocative attitude in its handling of the Dalai Lama and other Tibetans exiled in India.

Important differences remain, and new ones have been created by the Indian tests. As noted, Beijing was angered by the Indian assertion that the danger to India's security posed by its nuclear-armed northern neighbor helped prompt New Delhi's decision to adopt the nuclear option. In making this charge, the Indians may have talked themselves into believing that Beijing's posture is more hostile than it actually is. Ironically, the charges could prove self-fulfilling and lead the Chinese to revert to a harsher line toward India. Meanwhile, Pakistan's tests have given a new salience to Indian concerns over Beijing's supply of missile and nuclear technology to Islamabad.

The settlement of the border dispute remains as elusive as ever. China's offer to accept the status quo, giving up its claims in the eastern Himalayas in exchange for India's abandoning territory it claims in Ladakh, is presumably still on the table. In its election manifesto, the BJP stated that one of its key foreign policy goals was "to improve relations with China by seeking speedy resolution of the outstanding border problem." Although some observers contended that this statement and the emphasis the coalition government gave to the concept of "Asian solidarity" could foreshadow early progress toward a breakthrough, the post-test atmosphere is hardly conducive to this.

Moreover, the Vajpayee government is likely to be cautious in taking a step that might incur political difficulties by exposing it to charges that the government has alienated India's "sacred soil." In any event, there is no reason that this presently sleeping dog cannot lie while the two countries move toward an easier relationship.

It is certainly to India's advantage to improve relations with China. As Raja Mohan argued before the Indian tests, better ties with China would give India much-needed flexibility in dealing with the major powers with a stake in Asian relations.[12] Better ties could lead to a further erosion of China's support for Pakistan and the smaller countries of South Asia. A border stabilized by confidence-building measures would give India greater flexibility in dealing with perceived security threats from Pakistan and elsewhere. Over time, a more confident relationship with China could also allow India to reduce its defense expenditures.

But even in the best of circumstances—which hardly prevail today—there are likely to be limits to the advance toward better relations from India's viewpoint, and probably from China's as well. A few in India, mostly drawn from the Left, urge a strategic linkup. In their view, the two Asian giants should collaborate in bringing about a "truly just global order." (Russia sometimes figures as a third candidate for leadership of this club of those allegedly excluded from a unipolar, U.S.-dominated world.) Such an alignment is an unrealistic option for an India whose foreign policy is likely to be increasingly influenced by such economic goals as attracting more foreign private investment, winning greater access to Western markets and advanced technology, and persuading the European Union and the United States to accept an opening of India to their products that is more gradual than they want. In that setting, China is more of a rival of India for foreign trade and investment than a potential friend.

This rivalry is nothing new. In the 1950s, India and China were seen to be in competition as role models for Third World economic development. Both floundered badly, and neither India's efforts to bring about economic progress through centralized planning within a democratic framework, nor China's attempts to do so in an authoritarian setting, became a pattern to be emulated. In more recent times, China has clearly bested India on the economic front. The reforms it adopted

---

12. *The Hindu*, December 2, 1996.

in the early 1980s have led to impressive gains. The advances India has achieved following its move toward a market economy a decade later have been substantial, but well below the Chinese mark.

The envy and concern that China's stunning growth have excited in India have been heightened by an awareness of the growing disparity in the two countries' military strength and the greater respect and attention that the rest of the world affords Beijing. This probably influenced the Indian decision to go nuclear, although it was certainly overshadowed by such considerations as the BJP's longtime commitment to nuclear weapons and the Vajpayee government's immediate domestic political concerns. Before the nuclear tests, some maintained that the disparity in power between India and the People's Republic led New Delhi to adopt more cautious positions in dealing with Beijing on such important issues as China's supply of missile technology to Pakistan.

Inevitably, the future of China-India relations will significantly depend on what Beijing does with its enhanced economic and military power and, in the nearer term, how its hostile reaction to the Indian tests plays out. India, for its part, should have little interest in returning to the confrontational mode in which relations were frozen for so long. What would be best from its viewpoint is an early resumption of the unspectacular warming trend of the past decade in the context of a vague and shadowy competition between the two countries. It is unclear at this point whether such a scenario would be acceptable to Beijing or whether it will instead revert to its anti-Indian posture in dealing with South Asia.

Southeast Asia and Japan

Like China, Southeast Asia will remain a high-priority area for Indian foreign policy in the years ahead. An adjacent region with which India has cultural ties reinforced by the presence in Malaysia and Singapore of sizeable Indian ethnic populations, Southeast Asia has come to loom large on India's foreign economic policy map as New Delhi moves toward full participation in the global economy in which the countries of the region now play such an important role.

India had, of course, taken a major interest in Southeast Asia long before its confrontation with China in the Himalayas made thwarting of Beijing's influence there a key element in its policy in the region. India's activist role was shaped by the key pillars of Nehruvian doc-

trine: anticolonialism, nonalignment, a preference for more radical regimes, and a desire for world peace. To these was added, in the 1950s
and 1960s, an interest in playing an important role in the effort to bring
about a settlement of Southeast Asia's colonial and postcolonial conflicts. This objective was exemplified most vividly by the highly visible performance of Nehru's then principal diplomatic operator, the
outspokenly anti-Western V.K. Krishna Menon, at the international
conference convoked in Geneva in 1954 following the collapse of the
French effort to put down the Communist Vietminh insurgency in
North Vietnam. Indian activism was also reflected in its chairmanship
of the tripartite International Control Commissions for the three In-
dochinese states that the conference established.

New Delhi's initial objective in Southeast Asia, as it was elsewhere
on the Asian continent, was to have the region become a Nehruvian
"area of peace," in which regimes followed nonaligned, independent
foreign policies and would be amenable to Indian leadership in an
African-Asian third force outside the two rival world blocs. India
scorned those states that chose to align their foreign and security policies with the West, and India also strongly objected to the establishment in 1954 of the Southeast Asia Treaty Organization (SEATO). It
regarded the U.S.-sponsored body as a device to perpetuate colonial
and neocolonial influence in the region that would only worsen prospects for peace. Its negative attitude was sharpened by Pakistan's
SEATO membership, which gave Pakistan a further claim to Western,
and specifically U.S., support.

As in other parts of the world, India's anticolonial concerns were
targeted at Western influence and presence. New Delhi was not troubled by Moscow's support of leftist regimes and insurgencies in Indochina. Its preference for these groups on ideological grounds
reinforced this bias, as did its own links with the Soviet Union. Problems elsewhere in U.S.-India relations were important in shaping Indian attitudes in the region, especially in heightening its criticism in the
1960s and early 1970s of U.S. military intervention in Vietnam and
elsewhere in Indochina.

The Indians initially viewed ASEAN in much the same negative
way they had viewed SEATO. They also retained, well into the post–
Vietnam War period, the condescending attitude toward most of the
Southeast Asian countries that was the hallmark of their dealings with
the smaller nations of their own region. Excepted, and treated with

careful friendship and admiration, was the triumphant Democratic Republic of Vietnam.

Neither the Indian leaders nor almost anyone else could have foreseen the later emergence of the Southeast Asian nations as economic tigers whose rapid growth—far faster than India's, at least until their recent difficulties—would make them a force to be reckoned with in global markets and potentially valuable trading partners and investment sources for India. Nor did India anticipate ASEAN's becoming an important political and economic bloc that could significantly affect its interests.

New Delhi's decades of disdain for the noncommunist Southeast Asian countries is now a thing of the past that the Indians would prefer to forget. I.K. Gujral made the development of close ties with ASEAN and its member states a major goal in what he called his "Look East" policy. After much lobbying, New Delhi succeeded in 1996 in becoming a full ASEAN dialogue partner. It seeks linkage with the ASEAN free-trade area, and ASEAN support for membership in the forum for Asia Pacific Economic Cooperation. The performance of ASEAN as a successful regional grouping has almost certainly helped prompt India's interest in developing stronger political and economic cooperation in its own region through the vitalization of SAARC and other multilateral and bilateral means.

Thus, India now finds itself playing the part of a suitor for Southeast Asia's favorable economic consideration, a fundamental change from its earlier aspirations to be a major actor in determining the then much-troubled region's political future. Economic matters are likely to continue to be the more significant aspect of the relationship in the future. Despite the financial crisis, the region's long-term economic prospects are bright, and it will continue to be important for India for trade and investment. Except as they relate to economic issues, political matters will probably play second fiddle.

The Southeast Asian response, like the reaction in many other parts of the world to similar Indian interest in more fruitful economic relations, will be significantly influenced by how well India manages its economy, especially the scope and pace of reforms. Meanwhile, New Delhi's efforts to develop closer ties with ASEAN are likely to be complicated by concern over India's size and economic strength. They could also be complicated, unfortunately for the Indians, by recollectioos of India's past performance in the region.

Burma (Myanmar) has been a special concern for New Delhi because of its strategic location close to the restive northeastern region of India and its possible susceptibility to Chinese influence. The inability of the Burmese government to control non-Burman tribal areas along the Indian frontier made possible their use as supply routes and sanctuaries for insurgent groups fighting for independence or greater autonomy within the Indian Union. Although China no longer assists these insurgents, New Delhi remains wary of the possibility of Beijing's acquiring naval facilities on the Burmese Indian Ocean coast. In more recent years, India's problems with Burma have focused on the deplorable human rights record of the Burmese military regime. Indian criticism of the regime on human rights grounds was unusual. Over the years, New Delhi has generally accepted the political systems and practices of other countries, provided these did not include racial discrimination. (India has ordinarily defined this as whites discriminating against people of color.) Lately, New Delhi's sympathy for the Burmese opponents of the regime has waned. The military's evident ability to stay in power despite international and domestic opposition, Burma's acceptance into ASEAN, and the prospect of improved opportunities for Indian business as the regime opens the country to foreign trade and investment may have prompted New Delhi to modify its position.

Disappointing the hopes expressed in the early 1950s by U.S. statesman Chester Bowles and others that, as major countries with a shared allegiance to democracy, India and Japan could become twin pillars for Asian security against communist challenges, New Delhi and Tokyo never developed a close political relationship. Nehru was dismayed by postwar Japan's decision to place itself under the United States' security umbrella rather than to adopt the nonaligned foreign policy he championed. New Delhi pointedly declined to be a party to the treaty Washington had negotiated with Japan to formally end the Pacific War and later signed a separate treaty with the Japanese. The enduring U.S.-Japanese alliance remained an obstacle to better relations until the end of the Cold War. During that long period, neither country seemed to have felt that it was in its interest to make any serious effort to bring about a warming of political ties, and the occasional visits by Indian and Japanese leaders to one another's capitals accomplished little in that direction. Some observers have argued that cultural differences have limited the development of more cooperative attitudes. In any event, the two countries seem to have viewed one another over the years with their own peculiar brands of condescension.

Under these circumstances, the main strands in India-Japan relations have been economic. Japan has been a major contributor to India's economic development programs and in recent years has become its largest bilateral economic donor. More recently, with the advent of India's economic reform, trade and investment have gained new importance in the relationship. Although the end of the Cold War removed an important obstacle to political and security cooperation, economic issues are likely to remain the focus of bilateral ties in the future.

Russia

New Delhi's ties with Moscow in the post–Cold War world are a pale shadow of the robust, supportive relationship that had long been a major pillar of Indian foreign and security policy, but they are still important and are likely to remain so.

As noted, the demise of the Soviet Union was a blow to India. Since 1955, when Khrushchev and Bulganin famously used their tour of the country to dramatize the friendship and support their post-Stalinist regime could give a major Third World nonaligned power, New Delhi has looked to Moscow for diplomatic backing, advanced weaponry, economic assistance, special trade arrangements, and nuclear power facilities.

Unlike the United States, the Soviet Union was prepared to accept Indian predominance in South Asia. Its veto power in the United Nations Security Council prevented the passage of resolutions on the Kashmir issue that New Delhi found objectionable. Soviet backing for India in the Bangladesh crisis, highlighted by the signing of a friendship treaty, assured India that it could safely pursue a forceful policy in its confrontation with Pakistan over the problem. The Soviets were willing to provide, at cut-rate prices and on easy credit terms, sophisticated equipment such as MiG-29 jet aircraft that they ordinarily made available only to their Warsaw Pact partners. Soviet assistance in the development of big Indian public-sector projects was important in making India a major industrial power. The Soviet Union's import on rupee-ruble account—essentially a barter deal—of goods for which India had a limited market elsewhere was matched by its willingness to provide oil, newsprint, and other raw materials that New Delhi would otherwise have had to pay for in scarce hard currency. Its policy on nuclear exports was less restrictive than was Washington's.

The Indians reciprocated such valuable Soviet policies, sometimes at considerable cost to their other relationships. India's willingness to accept with minimal protest the eight-year Soviet occupation of Afghanistan was particularly damaging in setting it apart from the United States, other Western powers, most of the Islamic world, and China. Yet at the same time, New Delhi stopped well short of full acceptance of Soviet positions in Asia and elsewhere. Allegations by American and other critics that it had become a Soviet ally or lackey were highly overstated. When it perceived that its ties with Moscow had become too close, as it did in the late 1950s, the mid-1970s, and the early 1980s, New Delhi took steps to reestablish greater East-West balance in its foreign policy, maintaining a pro-Soviet bias but a less egregious one.

The new Russia cannot, of course, play the same role as did the Soviet Union. But it can still be important and helpful to India. Moscow remains New Delhi's major source of imported military hardware, although it now provides this on less generous terms. Its military supply policies have also been helpful in a negative sense: it has declined to sell weapons to Pakistan and recently prevented Ukraine from doing so. India will want to do what it can to assure that such cooperative attitudes persist. Although trade between the two countries plummeted as Russia opened to Western goods, Moscow can be helpful on the issue of the liquidation of the remaining rupee balances it holds.

Beyond these immediate prospects and problems, there is a more fundamental consideration. Russia remains a major power with far-reaching international concerns. Whatever its present difficulties, it will play an important role on the world stage, not least at the United Nations. As a permanent member of the U.N. Security Council, it will have a major voice in the decision on India's bid for a similar seat should the council expand. It has important interests in parts of Asia of particular concern to India. It can again be useful, if India plays its cards right, should New Delhi face a challenge from Beijing. Although it is no longer a close neighbor of India's, its major role in the once-Soviet states of Central Asia that now separate the two countries can be important to India, which has interests in that area. The two countries share a concern about the progress of militant Islamic fundamentalism there and in neighboring Afghanistan.

During the March 1997 visit to Moscow of Prime Minister Deve Gowda, India and Russia resolved to raise their relationship to a "strategic partnership." This is a much-abused term. But whatever it may mean in this context, it indicates that in the absence of ideological considerations and much of the foreign policy and economic content that gave enormous substance to the Moscow–New Delhi tie in Soviet times, India intends to pay careful attention to the relationship. The positive line that Deve Gowda adopted is likely to continue. It is clearly in India's interest to have a strong and constructive relationship with Russia, although this will obviously be much less far-reaching than the old India-Soviet link. Barring a serious breakdown in Moscow's relations with the West, there is no reason why the two countries cannot achieve and maintain such a relationship.

Europe

In the early years of independence, India's ties with Europe focused on Britain. India continued to look to its recent imperial master for trade and investment, financial links, and cultural associations. It chose to remain within the Commonwealth, a crucial decision that ushered in a new, postcolonial role for the association as a loose, multiracial, worldwide grouping of states. Despite the organization's diminished importance, New Delhi still appears to value its membership in the Commonwealth, where it can put forward its views before a broad international forum and carry on informal diplomacy on the margins of the group's periodic global and regional sessions. At least until the early 1960s, when India developed a defense-supply relationship with the Soviet Union and, briefly, with the United States, the Indian armed forces looked almost exclusively to the British for imported military hardware and technical assistance. Over the years of post-imperial Britain's decline as a significant player on the international stage, India-British ties loosened. The political relationship was hastened on its downward path by Britain's pro-Pakistan position in the 1965 war, and it was eventually superseded on India's U.K. agenda by economic policy matters and issues arising from the presence in the United Kingdom of a sizeable Indian immigrant community. By 1997, Prime Minister Gujral was sneering at Britain as a third-class power.

Although some influential Indians during the Nehru-Gandhi period thought well of the continental Western European countries as nations (like India) with long and rich civilizations and social-welfare, statist, yet democratic approaches sitting uncomfortably between the super-powers, in actual practice New Delhi gave lower priority to its rela-tions with them than it did to its ties with many other parts of the world. In the heyday of bilateral international assistance, India looked to the major continental countries as important sources of aid within the Western consortium of donors led by the World Bank. When Mrs. Gandhi's government became concerned in the 1980s that it was be-coming overdependent on the Soviet Union for advanced military equipment, it turned to France, as well as to England, for sophisticated aircraft. Later in the decade, Rajiv Gandhi strengthened India's mili-tary-supply links with Western Europe by ordering large quantities of artillery from the Swedish Bofors firm. Allegations charging major fraud in the deal played an important part in Gandhi's electoral defeat in 1989. The Indians probably saw these arms purchases, and other positive aspects of their relations with the Western European countries, as ways in which they could make their nonalignment more credible at a time when they were close to Moscow and on poor terms with Washington.

During these Cold War years, New Delhi was careful to maintain good ties with the Eastern European countries as well. Like those on the other side of the Iron Curtain, many of the Warsaw Pact nations provided economic assistance to India, emulating Moscow in targeting much of this to the development of heavy industry. New Delhi long maintained a special relationship with Yugoslavia under Marshal Tito, who uniquely among European leaders played a role in the leadership of the Nonaligned Movement and in that capacity developed warm ties with Nehru.

As it does to countries in many other parts of the world, India now looks to Europe largely in terms of economic benefits. Like the United States, the European Union is seen by India as an important trading partner, a source of investment, and a key negotiator at the World Trade Organization where New Delhi seeks to win favorable interpre-tations of WTO rules.

Other Important Areas

Aside from its relations with the countries of its own immediate re-gion, Southeast Asia, and the major powers, including Japan and the

European Union, India's foreign policy concerns in the coming decades are likely to focus on Central Asia, Afghanistan, the Persian Gulf area, and the Indian Ocean.

Central Asia

India's interests in the former Soviet republics of Central Asia are both political and economic. New Delhi wants to forestall Pakistan's influence in these Muslim countries, which some in Islamabad believe offer the "strategic depth" in Pakistan's confrontation with India that President Zia ul-Haq made part of the Pakistani foreign affairs lexicon in the 1980s. India also seeks to limit the spread of Islamic fundamentalism in the region. It will look for opportunities to expand Indian trade and investment. These opportunities will be more promising if stability is restored to Afghanistan and direct trade becomes feasible. The cooperation of Pakistan will be necessary for such land transit, another reason for New Delhi to seek better ties with Islamabad.

Afghanistan

India's objectives in Afghanistan have always been primarily Kautilyan, to make friends with an enemy's enemy. It has preferred regimes in Kabul that are antagonistic to Pakistan and that distract and weaken the Pakistanis in their face-off against India. To this goal has been added countering the rise of the more militant political forms of Muslim fundamentalism. New Delhi considers these a challenge to communal harmony at home and, especially, a danger in Kashmir, where Kashmiri and foreign Muslim fundamentalists have played an important role in the insurgency against Indian rule. The foreign insurgents include Afghans as well as others who have fought in the Afghan civil wars.

These twin primary objectives, weakening Pakistan and limiting the growth of Islamic fundamentalism as a political platform, are in all probability linked in New Delhi's approach. New Delhi is likely to have concluded that a fundamentalist regime in Kabul will be more favorable to Pakistan than the more secular groups that the Indians have preferred. While a restoration of stability and normal civil life in Afghanistan would have obvious advantages for New Delhi, the Indians would probably prefer continuing division to the establishment of a government exercising authority throughout the country that would lean toward Pakistan.

Iran

Whether Iran is ruled by a shah or by Shia divines, India's policy there, too, has been importantly moved by anti-Pakistan objectives. New Delhi's long-term effort to weaken Pakistan's influence and to limit Tehran's support for Islamabad has achieved some success, notably on the Kashmir issue; Iran no longer backs Pakistan's position in international organizations in any meaningful way.

Aside from this historical anti-Pakistan strand, Indian policy will continue to stress important economic objectives: oil supply, trade, and investment. India's political goals include promoting the regional stability that will serve these economic interests. It may see closer links with Iran as a way of promoting a more moderate approach by Tehran at home and abroad. From India's point of view, such a moderate Iranian line could usefully include reduced promotion of Muslim fundamentalism as a political force in areas with important Shia populations. Shias are not a big group in India, probably no more than 2–3 percent of the total population, but they are significant in some parts of Kashmir.

The Arab World

India's role in the Arab countries of the Persian Gulf and elsewhere in the Middle East was for decades highlighted by its reflexive support of the Arab cause against Israel and by a preference, as in other parts of the Third World, for radical, nationalist, anti-Western secular regimes. India refused to establish normal diplomatic relations with Israel and, shamefully, signed on to the U.N. resolution equating Zionism with racism. Its outspokenly anti-Israel stand traces back to Mahatma Gandhi's opposition to the Zionist effort to found a state based on religion. The antagonistic approach that independent India's governments have long adopted toward the Jewish state stemmed much less from this ideological stand than it did from foreign policy considerations (winning Arab support) and domestic political purposes (catering to the country's sizeable Muslim vote). New Delhi's positions cost it support among Jewish and other Americans. Its ideological preferences in dealing with the Arab world prompted it to favor such men as Egyptian President Gamal Abdel Nasser, who had a strong personal relationship with Nehru, and the Baathist leaders of Iraq and Syria, rather than more conservative, Islamic-oriented Arab leaders. The former were, in any event, more prepared to be forthcoming to India. As elsewhere in the Muslim world, New Delhi's policies were significantly influenced by its interest in reducing support for Pakistan on the Kashmir dispute and other India-Pakistan issues.

Much of this has now changed. India and Israel exchange ambassadors and have developed a robust relationship, reportedly including important cooperation in the intelligence area. New Delhi no longer seeks much of a political role in the region, a far cry from Nehruvian days. Its last effort to do so in a significant way, during the 1990–91 Gulf crisis, was ineffectual and confused. Its focus now is economic: securing its oil supply; looking after the large number of skilled and unskilled Indian guest workers whose remittances are an important source of foreign exchange; and encouraging trade and investment. Its political efforts are designed primarily to promote these important objectives, and its relations with Arab countries of various leanings have become more evenhanded. Its approach is likely to follow a similar pattern in the future.

The Indian Ocean

India's interest in projecting its power into the Indian Ocean, which recalled its British imperial heritage, complicated its relations with some of the other littoral states in the 1980s. In the 1990s, when funds for an expanded blue-ocean fleet were scarce, its Indian Ocean ambitions became more modest. India has recently led the formation of an Indian Ocean Rim Forum, yet another example of its newfound interest in regional bodies. Whether this will amount to very much and what serious purposes, if any, New Delhi sees it accomplishing, are still unclear. In line with India's objectives elsewhere, economic matters will be primary.

Conclusion

Despite the concerns raised by India's nuclear tests, economic considerations are likely to prove the most important element in determining national foreign policies in the next decades. As this study has tried to show, India has already given the achievement of its economic objectives a much higher priority in its approach to the world than it had done earlier. Its interest in doing so has been heightened by its economic reforms, which have given foreign economic policy a new urgency and importance.

Economic considerations will also determine, in a major way, the role India is able to play in the world and the kind of role this will be. The realization of India's longstanding aspirations for great-power status and the respect that accompanies it will depend primarily not on its nuclear arsenal but on how successful it is in managing its economic affairs and promoting the rapid growth that, to its distress, has been a key element in the rise to power and esteem of its Chinese rival. If, as some of its boosters and well-wishers predict, India becomes the world's fourth-largest economy, it will indeed be a force to be reckoned with. If the Indians falter on their economic reforms and enjoy only mediocre gains in their GDP, it will be another story.

What use in its foreign relations would India make of an expanded economy and the political potential that would accompany it? No clear answer can be given. Certainly the record of the past suggests that there will be a strong tendency for it to make its presence felt and again seek a leading role in world politics, as well as on the global economic stage. The political scene at home will, of course, be important. Stable governments undistracted by domestic political crises are more likely to play such expansive roles.

The purposes to which India would put a greater role in the world would be quite different from those that prompted Nehru and his political heirs. India's economic success will have been based on reforms that link it to the world economy. It is unlikely to be attracted to the old shibboleths that inspired Nehruvian foreign policy. Its policies will be much less ideological, and more immediately related to India's interests. Particularly under BJP-led governments, those policies might well include a strong dose of narrow nationalism that other powers are unlikely to welcome.

As they look to the twenty-first century, the United States and other major nations would be well advised to keep these different scenarios in mind as they reexamine their ties with India. The way they deal with India now could influence the choices a stronger India makes in the future.

Culture

Kapila Vatsyayan

Generalization is inappropriate for a country such as India, with its staggering multiplicity of races, languages, religions, levels of society, and artistic forms and styles. Attempts to classify any aspect of Indian culture can only be partial, as categories overlap, forming different configurations. Each section of society, each region, language, and artistic genre, is like a piece in a kaleidoscope: together they form different shapes and patterns, depending on the situation and the moment. And yet there is an unmistakable Indian cultural ethos underlying this plurality. A gigantic, imperceptible net holds the parts and the participants together in a totality that is clearly Indian.

In India, coexistence is the norm rather than the exception. Diverse groups have lived side by side for centuries. This phenomenon, unlike multiculturalism in the United States, is not new. India is home to a vast number of racial types who have inhabited the land for centuries, including the Australoids, Mongols, Dravidians, and many others. India's societal structures range from nomadic herding groups to village communities to urban complexes. The history of each group can be traced to great antiquity.

India's demographic profile can be roughly divided into four parts: tribal, rural, semiurban, and urban. The small, cohesive communities that make up the tribal segment are officially designated as Scheduled Castes and Scheduled Tribes. According to the Census of India of 1991, these diverse groups, which are spread throughout the subcontinent, constitute 16.48 percent and 8.08 percent of the total population of India, respectively. The modes of creative expression of these groups have played a seminal role in effecting changes in the artistic movements of independent India. Many sophisticated forms of individual creativity have drawn inspiration from their vibrant and rich cultures.

According to the same census, 62 percent of India's population is rural. Village society in the rural areas continues for the most part to revolve around agriculture. The semiurban small towns have connections with village societies on the one hand and with metropolises and large town centers on the other. Finally, there is the population that lives in cities and megacities, which is significant although it is small in terms of percentage. The city interacts not only with small towns and villages but also with the world. India's cities, now more than ever, are cauldrons of a plurality of subcultures, with roots ranging from the village to classical India to Europe and the West. A sizeable number of city dwellers are heirs to the twin heritages of Indian tradition and British education. The cultural profile of each of these four groups has undergone far-reaching changes with independence and industrialization.

While there is dynamic interaction among these diverse societal levels within each state, particular sections and societal groups also interact with their cognate levels in other states. Each region of India, in turn, has a distinctive style that is conditioned by its physical landscape and the specificity of its groups. Language and literature, textiles, crafts, architecture, sculpture, music, dance, and theater vary across the states.

States also interact with each other in contiguous and adjoining regions, forming larger cultural clusters that overlap. For example, Assam, Bengal, and Orissa form one cluster, and Orissa, Madhya Pradesh, and Andhra Pradesh form another. Thus two patterns emerge: different societal levels within a state interact, and states interact.

Interaction is undoubtedly conditioned in part by geography and physical proximity, but it is also shaped by tribal groups, languages, and skills and techniques. To give only two examples, the Santhals (in Bihar, Bengal, and Orissa) have been the substratum for many artistic movements, and the Gonds have filled the same role in another region of India. Finally, each state is like a planet in orbit: each rotates on its own axis, but all revolve around the same political and civilizational continuities and changes.

The Indian lifestyle abounds in creative activity in all sorts of daily functions. Music, dance, floor painting, wall painting, written and oral poetry, ballads, and *kathas* (tales) have long been known in all parts of India, from Kashmir to Kanyakumari, from Saurashtra to Orissa. This rich heritage (which reverberates through the annual calendar with the movement of the moon and the sun) had been left comparatively untouched by the political history, but it is slowly being affected by economic and social changes.

In independent India, many national and state tribal research institutes as well as the Anthropological Survey of India have become conscious of the urgent need to preserve, document, and conserve this heritage, and they have launched programs intended to ensure the continuity of these living traditions in the face of rapid developmental changes. The rural development programs have acknowledged the importance of the cultural fabric in their development strategies, but not enough. These programs need to take the fragile ecobalances into account. Conservation of biodiversity and continuation of cultural diversity are closely linked. There is new vigorous movement, both governmental and nongovernmental, to preserve ecocultural zones such as sacred groves and mangroves.

Institutions of the arts—literary, visual, and performing—have arisen in all parts of India. This is a new phenomenon. In preindependence India, training in the arts, particularly the performing arts, consisted of one-to-one transmission from teacher to pupil. This was known as the *guru-sishya parampara*. More recently, there has been a marked trend toward institutionalization. In some cases, the results have been beneficial, but in others they have not. The arts are particularly vulnerable to the demands of rapid urbanization and tourism. By the 1980s it became evident that, unless the local cultural environment were nurtured, many literary modes as well as performing and visual arts would lose their creative vibrancy.

Throughout a long history of wars and invasions, political ups and downs, and making and unmaking of kingdoms and feudal states, the pattern of Indian civilization has been sustained. The creation of poetry, philosophic schools, monuments and sculpture, murals and miniature painting, theater, dance, and music throughout nearly 1,500 years of Indian history has been marked by a dual sense of time. One sense is connected with a perennial worldview, accenting the flow of continuity. The other is situated here and now, where things are subject to change. Thus, in all spheres, but particularly in the arts, the traditional and modern coexist. In fact, the tension between them is not one of opposites; it is instead a symbiotic relationship between the past and the present. Complementarity and coexistence (although not without some conflict) are the norm in India.

It is against the background delineated by these general remarks, that one must view the developments in the broad field of culture in general and the arts and crafts in particular over the last fifty years. Political independence was certainly a moment of great significance and importance; however, it did not bring about a complete break from the spatial dynamics of the regions outlined above or the temporal dynamics of the flow of a civilization with a double lifeline of continuity and change. The transformations that have taken place have sometimes been due to governmental policy and planning and at other times have been unrelated to these. Politics and culture interact, but not necessarily with a cause-and-effect relationship.

The situation in India in the field of culture and the arts a hundred or more years prior to independence must also be viewed in terms of the diverse societal structures and lifestyles of the regions and the powerful articulations by the minority educated empowered elite. Also, it must be remembered that all sections of society in all regions aspired to political freedom and participated actively or indirectly in the struggle for independence. Thus there arose the interesting phenomenon that while a group or a particular section of society retained its local or regional identity, it simultaneously renounced that identity temporarily in the cause of the struggle for political freedom.

At independence, tribal and rural India subscribed to a worldview that considered man and nature to be interrelated. Man was in nature, not against it. Life revolved around flora and fauna according to the agricultural calendar. There was no dissociation of function and art; instead, the artistic act was a daily ritual. While there was trade of artistic products, there was no commodity market for them.

The tribal situation was not analogous to that of the Native Americans. By and large, the British had left the tribal groups alone. There were occasional onslaughts and mass conversions and equally powerful movements of dissent and protest. But despite these, little disruption took place in lifestyle and function. As a result, this group continues to be integral to the vast subcontinental organism.

A striking feature of the postindependence period has been the effort to bring these communities into the democratic process. Each of these communities had its own system of self-governance. Now they have been called upon to follow a uniform pattern of electing leaders. While this major change has brought a sense of participation at a pan-Indian level and an opportunity to assert a distinctive identity politically, it has also caused a disruption in the way of life. Fifty years of developmental efforts have brought literacy, health, and exposure to other parts of India. They have also resulted in the dissociation of arts from function. A deep disjunction is in evidence. While the arts and crafts of the Scheduled Tribes (be they the Nagas of Nagaland, the Garos of Meghalaya, the Marias of Bastar, or the Saoras of Orissa) reach the crafts museums and are displayed in international exhibitions, the makers of these objects are gradually but surely being sucked into the vortex of a semi-industrialized society. The pioneers of the crafts movement in India, who identified this creativity, sought to foster it in its own milieu. But trends in the last three decades have shown that recognition and status have been given to the arts and crafts in terms of their purely commercial value, and not always for their aesthetic and functional worth.

A concurrent movement is the effect of the powerful visual and kinetic language of the tribal and rural arts on the urban-elite painter, textile designer, and dancer. Artists from the cities often turn to tribal sources for inspiration. Innovations in textiles, design, and the handicraft sector rest squarely on inspiration from and even exploitation of the designs, skills, and techniques of the anonymous artists of tribal India. In preindependence India, fragments of this extraordinary creativity were gathered for ethnographic collections in museums of anthropology and natural history; today, tribal creativity permeates the urban-elite levels of Indian society. Not many systematic studies of this phenomenon are available; however, the upward mobility of artistic expression and skills is unmistakable. The pity is that while the products have been given status and recognition, the makers have not.

What is true of the arts and crafts of tribal India is also true of those of rural agricultural India. Life used to revolve around the agricultural cycle despite economic deprivation, famine, and even starvation. The calendar moved around the events of farming (sowing and harvesting) and of human life (birth, marriage, and death). Life was punctuated by a series of fairs and festivals, ritual painting, chants, theatrical spectacles, music, and dance. The specialists (ironsmiths, goldsmiths, masons, stone carvers, weavers, actors, and dancers) were sometimes classes apart but were nevertheless woven into the fabric of caste society.

In preindependence India, atrocities were committed against weavers and some other professionals, as their skills threatened British livelihoods from the machines of Manchester. Some of the village skills diminished, but none vanished. Mahatma Gandhi used the weaver as a symbol of the movement of *swadeshi* (self-rule) and *swaraj* (independence). The making of handspun cloth (*khadi*), both cotton and silk, was a powerful weapon in the struggle for freedom. This movement has continued in postindependence India but with a difference. The *khadi* has become a small-scale industry, and there is an Indian network of Gandhi *ashrams* (hermitages) and *khadigrama udyogas* (*khadi* village industries). Welcome as this is, it is ironic that the *khadi*, once a strategy for socioeconomic and cultural self-reliance and self-sufficiency of the village, has since been dissociated from its relationship with local culture, community, and function. While textiles from around the country have reached international markets, the makers are gradually being attracted to the lifestyle of urban India. They wear polyester at the same time that their rich silk Paithani and Kanjivarama saris are displayed in high-profile textile exhibitions in Indian cities and abroad.

Traditional theater forms have undergone a similar transformation. To begin with, they were an organic part of life. They thrived on village participation and local patronage. Then independent India gave these traditional forms recognition and status and exposed them to national forums. Theater troupes traveled to metropolitan areas and international festivals. They inspired urban directors and actors who felt the need to replenish their creativity. But the actors and directors of the traditional forms of theater have also been affected by the avalanche of mass media. While the reconstructed form with a contemporary sensibility lives, the original authentic lineage is dying, and, in some cases is already dead.

What is evident in the performing arts is also apparent in the visual arts. The most conspicuous case is that of Madhubani paintings by the women of Bihar, which are traditionally created as part of a domestic ritual. The paintings, and even some of the painters, received recognition. The works, formerly largely executed on mud walls, are now painted on paper. They travel to urban centers and decorate the homes of city dwellers. They have influenced the style of modern Indian painters and have been shown abroad. Some individual traditional painters have been honored. However, mass production has begun in the villages, and gender changes are taking place. Once, Madhubani painting was the preserve of women; now many young men in the village have taken to it for a living.

While the artistic product receives recognition, its cultural context is shed or withers away. In the village, mass production begins with the motivation of market returns. As a result, the work of art loses its vibrancy, with some notable exceptions. In short, the dilemma of the contextualized arts surviving in new contexts continues. There are no straight answers in terms of correct choices. This is a common phenomenon, with both positive and negative sides. If the arts remain insular in small environments, they may not grow; if they are uprooted and replanted, they may lose their original essence and spirit.

Institutions

Although political freedom arrived in 1947, numerous fetters of the immediate past persisted, and vast areas of human endeavor remained that did not receive the attention of national or regional governmental policy. One of these areas was culture, understood both in its broadest sense as encompassing all activities of the human being, from the most personal and subjective to large mass congregations in the tribal, rural, and urban milieus, and in the more formal sense of museums, archives, institutions devoted to the fields of archaeology and anthropology, and the literary, visual, and performing arts. At the time India attained political independence, there was a definite estrangement between the institutions of traditional culture—whether supported by the state or fostered by individuals, communities, or the Indian princely states— and the institutions of education.

In the universities, courses were taught on the history and civilization of Europe and of India, but these demonstrated little thought to cultural development. Disciplines such as aesthetics, art history, and the practice of the arts were mostly nonexistent. Except in Shantiniketan, the university founded by Rabindranath Tagore, none of the arts—architecture, sculpture, painting, music and dance, or theater—were part of the formal system of education. Until the 1950s, it would be unheard of to treat these as serious subjects of study.

In 1947, the central government administered and financed a few institutions. Important among these were the Anthropological Survey of India and the all-India network of the Archaeological Survey of India. A few museums existed, principally the Indian Museum in Calcutta, the Madras Museum, and the Prince of Wales Museum in Bombay. There were the National Library and the two great institutions of Oriental learning, the Asiatic Society in Calcutta and the Asiatic Society in Bombay. In addition, the British had established schools of art in Madras, Calcutta, and Bombay. There was a small Department of Education in the government but no Department of Culture existed. Other government institutions included All-India Radio, which was set up primarily for the dissemination of official information but that had begun to patronize the arts, particularly music. No state aid, whether financial or organizational, was available to the crafts. A few significant all-India institutions of culture had been established through pure voluntary effort, some with a cultural goal in view and others with either national, political, or social goal. In this context, the work of the Ramakrishna Mission and Shantiniketan must be recognized. In the main, cultural activity, individual or collective, participative or professional, was the concern of people acting outside of formal institutions.

In 1947, when Jawaharlal Nehru assumed responsibility for the government, there were many problems. Chief among these was the need to shift the emphasis of educational curricula. The government sought to attune educated Indians to their cultural past by bringing culture and science to the educated and enabling them to acquire the intellectual equipment necessary to face the challenge of modern science and technology. Simultaneously, the government sought to bring education, as well as social and economic welfare to the masses. The task was gigantic: at one stroke, it was proposed to provide the capacity to carry the burdens of two civilizations, two dimensions of time and space, and two value systems, which would coexist in harmony and produce an integrated personality at home in two worlds. However laudable the aim, the problems of execution were monumental.

To all this was added the sincere wish and hope that was so symbolically and significantly voiced by Mahatma Gandhi: "I do not want my house to be walled in on all sides and my windows to be stuffed. I want the culture of all lands to be blown about my house as freely as possible. . . . But I refuse to be blown off my feet by any one of them." Such was the inheritance of the great leaders who took the reins of government—leaders rooted in the culture of India, yet always open, like Mahatma Gandhi, to creative winds from other lands. Writers and philosophers in their own right, they were the prime movers in initiating what one might call a cultural policy for India.

They were deeply conscious of the fact that, although the preservation of the monuments and manuscripts of India was fundamental, the cultural programs had to be further strengthened and expanded. They were aware also of the fact that unless bold initiatives were taken to nurture, foster, and promote creative talent in all fields, the continuity of Indian tradition would not be sustained.

In the first eight years of independence, the government launched programs that proved to be of crucial importance for the next five decades. A significant event was the government's initiative to include the creativity of rural and tribal India as part of the annual Republic Day Parade. The consequences were both positive and negative. While it gave a sense of pride to the participants initially, very soon the event became a routine spectacle of little consequence. However, for many urban viewers, it sparked insatiable curiosity about the cultural heritage of tribal and rural India with which they were not acquainted. Some among them traveled to remote corners of India to explore this heritage in greater depth. Others saw this as a veritable storehouse for packaging "exotic India." Similarly, the rural and tribal participants from different states who came to New Delhi experienced inevitable changes and acculturation during their stay. With hindsight, the decision and the consequences did have far-reaching implications.

Equally important were the establishment of the Indian Council for Cultural Relations, the National Museum in New Delhi, and three national academies—Sangeet Natak Akademi (performing arts), Lalit Kala Akademi (visual arts), and Sahitya Akademi (literature). These institutions reflected a concern for creative effort in all aspects of the arts and the desire to cultivate a knowledge of India at the tribal and rural levels. The institutionalization of cultural effort took many shapes and forms. These included the drive to establish Buddhist institutions, institutions of Islamic Studies, Sanskrit Studies, modern Indian, and English and European studies.

Literature and the visual and performing arts were in no small measure stimulated and fostered by the three Akademis and the National School of Drama. The Akademis instituted a system of recognition and awards unknown in preindependence India along with a series of annual meetings, exhibitions, festivals, and plans for financial assistance and support. Over recent years, similar institutions have been established in the states. They foster the regional languages as well as forms of the visual and performing arts. There is active exchange and greater dialogue among regions in the fields of the arts. Translated works have been promoted, and there is a massive program of publishing in nearly twenty-four languages through the Sahitya Akademi and its sister organization, the National Book Trust. Through the enhanced opportunities provided by publication awards, camps, and festivals, there is an active pan-Indian dialogue among painters, theater directors, musicians, and dancers of different regions.

While all this is welcome, one sometimes wonders whether in the feverish anxiety of expositions, exposure, and dissemination there is room for the reflection and silent contemplation so essential for the arts. The festivals of arts organized since the 1980s in different parts of the world—Great Britain, the United States, France, Germany, the Soviet Union, Thailand, and elsewhere—have been great opportunities for presenting Indian arts, although the presentation has been packaged for particular audiences. Perhaps this was to be expected in the absence of any structural link between the education system at both the school (elementary and secondary) and university levels, and cultural activity. As a result, while the education system largely followed earlier patterns that had been instituted by the British, the cultural institutions became the vehicles of preserving, conserving, and disseminating ancient and contemporary creativity without equal insistence on an intensive critical discourse.

It was in response to this hiatus between education and culture that a new institution called the Centre for Cultural Resources and Training was established. It developed a program to train teachers and teacher trainers in imparting knowledge about Indian heritage and arts to secondary schools and colleges. Over the last three decades, it has trained many thousands of teachers and teacher trainers. It has also employed traditional skills such as puppetry and clay modeling to disseminate curricula in other disciplines such as history and mathematics. Through its program of orientation and refresher courses, publications, and audiovisual kits, it has brought about an awareness of the rich plurality of Indian cultural traditions and has succeeded in making students and teachers sensitive to a dimension of Indian life not as yet integrated into the course content and syllabi of the Indian school system. Although thousands have been trained and exposed to the program, this is but a drop in the ocean of India's educational system.

The general mainstream education system has cried out for reforms and transformation since the day of independence. But even prior to that, Mahatma Gandhi's system of basic education was one proposed response solution with minimal results. Several education commissions were set up in independent India in order to free education from the conservative shackles left by Macaulay's vision of educating Indians to be "Indian in blood and colour, but English in taste, in opinions, in morals, and in intellect." There has been some reform but no total transformation. Once again, a voice is being raised to make the content and techniques of education more meaningfully relevant to Indian reality, especially at the rural level. This has been articulated in both governmental and nongovernmental forums. It is also recognized that the emphasis on cerebral skills should be balanced with respect for and development of manual skills. Although change has been slow, it has not been insignificant. In this context, the initiatives taken by organizations such as the Centre for Cultural Resources and Training are commendable. And students have taken it upon themselves to bring the arts in all their variety to schools and universities through organizing an all-India movement. The Society for Promotion of Indian Classical Music Amongst Colleges and Youth (SPICMACAY) represents the young generation's effort to acquaint itself with the creativity of musicians, dancers, theater directors, poets, and painters, all of whom are largely outside the education system. During the last twenty-five years, this movement has spread to all parts of India. Lectures, lecture demonstrations, performances, and exhibitions are organized for small and large groups of students in cities, small towns, and some villages. This has brought about a perceptible change in the attitudes of many young people who would otherwise be confined to the conventional teaching of the sciences and humanities through books.

Archaeology and Anthropology

The Archaeological Survey of India is a large and venerable institution that excavates, protects, and conserves more than 5,000 monuments in India. Established in 1861, it is today a vast network of nearly twenty centers with specialized branches of epigraphy, chemical conservation, and horticulture. It also runs an institute of archaeology. In addition to the central Department of Archaeology, there are state departments of archaeology that look after other monuments and sites of antiquity.

During the last five decades, the Department of Archaeology has

carried out many important excavations that have resulted in a reinterpretation of Indian history. Through these excavations, it is recognized
that the Indus valley and Harappan civilizations did not come to an
abrupt end. The continuation of the Harappan civilization has been
established through recent excavations in Banwali (Haryana) and
Dhola Vira (Gujarat). In addition, many valuable artifacts of the
Kushan period have been brought to light. Water-supply systems and
drainage systems in the complexes of Hampi and Hospet have been
exposed. New excavations have been initiated at Sanchi, in the district
of Raisen in Madhya Pradesh, and elsewhere. Excavations at Aragarh
have revealed new Buddhist sites. Indeed, each decade of archaeological work provides further proof that although much is known about the
material evidence of Indian civilization, at least as much is still embedded in the unexcavated earth of India. Each year, new monuments,
inscriptions, and other artifacts are discovered.

The work of the chemical conservation branch is equally important.
The task of maintaining and conserving thousands of monuments with
regular tourist traffic is not an easy one. In addition to maintaining
sites in India, Indian archaeologists have played a significant role in
the conservation of the monuments of Nubia, Bamiyan, Angkor Wat in
Cambodia, and Borobudur in Indonesia.

In order to be effective, the efforts of the Archaeological Survey of
India have to be matched by an equally strong university system. Alas,
university departments of archaeology are few and far between. The
hiatus between the institutions of education and culture has diminished
but not disappeared. Those concerned with excavating the past and
conserving the heritage that is uncovered are drawn from the university
system, but the active dialogue at the theoretical level is not as vibrant
as it could be. Also, because the disciplines of archaeology, museology, and anthropology emerged in the era of the European Enlightenment and colonial expansion, the theoretical underpinnings born of that
historical situation linger in these disciplines. Although artifacts and
developments are no longer measured against the rise of Greek civilization, there continues to be a marked bias toward establishing linear
chronologies at the expense of recognizing movements of cyclicity,
concurrency, and simultaneity.

The Anthropological Survey of India, which is much younger than
the Archaeological Survey, is also an all-India network and has played
an important role in independent India's attempt to comprehend and

classify its demographic profile. Moving away from the 19th-century definitions and perceptions of anthropology as a discipline for understanding "primitive" peoples, it has studied the physical, biological, cultural, and societal dimensions of all types and levels of the human species in the Indian subcontinent. The result is a vast spectrum of data collection, analysis, research, and interpretation. While some anthropologists continue to adhere to 19th-century notions or are followers of the school of Robert Redfield that classifies India into the great and little traditions, others have taken major strides in evolving new paradigms and theoretical models for the understanding of Indian societies. This community of anthropologists includes a network of those in the university system, tribal institutes, and the Anthropological Survey of India. An active dialogue with vibrant theoretical discourse is taking place with departments of anthropology, religious studies, and sociology in Europe, the United States, Canada, and now Japan. While there is also communication with institutions in Africa, Southeast Asia, and China, it is not as active and dynamic as with the West. How this has affected the quality of research and level of perception is a fascinating and complex field that demands deeper investigation. Nevertheless, here as in other fields, there are concurrent movements of the views of the outsider and the insider, the observer and observed. Mercifully, most have moved away from the attitude of the 1960s that would have referred to "that other exotic and my village informant." There is far greater sensitivity to the indigenous and the authentic, whether seen by the Indian or the foreigner.

Literature, Languages, and Libraries

Village societies in India have traditionally been the repositories of great oral traditions. The oral literatures represent the continuous flow of tradition. When change has occurred, it has been nearly imperceptible, as improvisation and interpretation were part of the very nature of the oral traditions and helped keep them alive. Even when oral works were transcribed, their efficacy lay in their sung, recited, or chanted, rather than their written versions. Every part of India had its special singers, chanters, and narrative tale reciters called *kathavachakas*; some areas continue to have these. While the two great epics the *Ramayana* and the *Mahabharata* were pervasive throughout

India, there were countless local, regional versions. Alongside these were the fables akin to those of Aesop, such as the *Panchatantra*. All these were recited, sung, and dramatically presented. The narrative moved concurrently at many levels—local, regional, historical, mythical, and moral.

In preindependence India, some writers used these epics and fables to arouse national consciousness. Into these stories were woven messages of the struggle for freedom. They were also used for initiating social reforms, and they served as correctives for maintaining social balances. Independent India, especially educated Indians who had been brought up on English or on the written classical literature, gradually became sensitive to the depth and richness of this oral poetry. Many urban writers plunged into the ocean of this oral poetry and its narrative forms and wrote great works of poetry and drama that aroused a sense of national pride. Oral narrative and heroic poetry penetrated into the psyche of the modern writer. This trend continues.

In urban India lived those educated in the schools established by the British and, in some cases, in the remnants of the traditional schools of Sanskrit and Persian, which has been for the most part neglected or actively repressed. There were also temples that fostered the arts, literature, paintings, sculpture, and dance. Alongside these were the princely states that patronized the arts, especially painting, music, and dance. While British rule had depleted village India of its economic resources but not of its language of art, the establishment of the three schools of arts and the modern British system of education deprived urban India of their ability to communicate with their own culture. They were not only decontextualized but were deculturalized.

It was members of this group that had been highly educated through the British system who took a detour journey homeward. Leaders emerged who inspired Indians to know India. Mahatma Gandhi was the greatest of them all, but there were others before and after him, including Gokhale, Ranade, Aurobindo, Rabindranath Tagore, and Vivekananda. Each responded differently to the situation of political and intellectual subjugation and cultural loss.

Equally important was the ferment in the 1930s that involved a host of writers from all parts of India; these writers used diverse languages and European literary forms, but their search was one for national identity. Some used reinterpretation of myth as a means to communicate contemporary concerns, others relied on the historical novel, and still others conveyed their message through short story or drama. Two parallel movements could be discerned in the writings of many of these authors. One was an influence from or dialogue with English and other European literature, including Shakespeare, the Romantics, Ibsen, and the Russian writers Tolstoy, Turgenev, and Gorky. The other was a dialogue with the village, local language, and the archetypal characters of Indian myth.

At independence, the writer was an active participant in the political process. Many writers had been imprisoned and some had been exiled under British colonial rule. Soon after independence, a few among these were elected to the lower and upper houses of the Indian Parliament. The political leaders themselves, including Jawaharlal Nehru and Maulana Azad, were men of letters in their own right; S. Radhakrishnan, the second president of India, was a prominent philosopher. Over the decades, there has been a gradual diminishing of the number of writers who are actively engaged in politics. In addition, few of the politicians of the last decade have been intellectual giants. Thus, there appears to be a widening gap between the intellectual and the political.

The first decades of independence produced a refreshing body of writing in many Indian languages. The paradox of political independence and the trauma of partition were the themes of many distinguished writers from northern India and Bengal. Rural-urban tension and the changing social situation were subjects for others. By the 1960s, fiction reflected the tensions caused by socioeconomic change. The problems of first-generation urbanization and the ills of the *zamindaris* (small feudatory principalities) were often the focus.

In the 1980s and 1990s, the voices of the socially oppressed "backward classes" became louder. The aspirations of the *dalits* (tribal classes) for individual and collective identity are now clearly heard. A feminist literature has concurrently developed. Many age-old myths and archetypal characters from Indian epics are being reinterpreted: Sita is no longer a submissive wife of Rama. She argues, as do Radha, the consort of Krishna, and Draupadi, the wife of the five Pandavas.

In the last few decades, there has been a concern with the inner lonely landscape of the individual, a landscape that has been broken up into a hundred thousand pieces in the vast and complicated milieu of India's megacity culture. This is reflected in the sizeable and significant corpus of creative writing in English that emerged. This poetry and fiction holds its own both in India and internationally. However, there is no danger that it will stifle the literature of the country's many languages. India's vibrant multilingual tradition continues.

Sanskrit is the fountainhead of most Indian languages other than those that belong to the Dravidian, Semitic, and Tibeto-Burman groups. In response to the languishing state of Sanskrit and other classical languages such as Persian and Arabic, the central government has launched many programs intended to strengthen the traditional system of *pathashalas* (recitation schools) and *madrasas* (Arabic and Persian schools). It has established a new Rashtriya Sanskrit Sansthan (National Sanskrit Institution). The Rashtriya Sanskrit Sansthan and the six *vidyapeethas* (schools) impart learning in the diverse traditional disciplines such as *ayurveda* (medicine), *jyotis-shastra* (astronomy and mathematics), *darshanas* (school of philosophy), and *vastu* and *silpashastra* (texts of architecture and sculpture). A program of publications has also been launched that has brought forth a corpus of literature that should be useful for any research student.

Two major programs in the field of Sanskrit that have received support should also be mentioned. The first is the Sanskrit Dictionary, a work based on historical principles. This project, instituted in the Deccan College in Pune, has had a rather long and checkered history. Six volumes have been published, and three others are in press. The project will take another two decades to complete, but once it is completed, the dictionary will have value for another 200 years. The second project, a multivolume encyclopedia on polity-economics and social conduct being given minimal support, is known as Dharamkosa (not to be mistaken for an Encyclopedia of Religion). The editor, the late Lakshman Shastri Joshi, was a doyen of traditional and modern scholarship.

Governmental support has been offered to more than 200 institutions of Sanskrit, Persian, and Arabic studies. The most significant promotion of Sanskrit learning has been through a program that honors Sanskrit, Persian, and Arabic scholars and gives them a lifelong stipend.

The fostering of classical languages and ancient Buddhist studies has not occurred at the cost of modern Indian languages. The necessary attention to ensure a richer vocabulary and a wide range of information in modern disciplines has been given. With a view to giving fresh impetus to modern Indian languages, many national institutions have been established in the last five decades. Foremost among these have been the Central Hindi Directorate, the Commission for Scientific and Technical Terminology, the Central Institute of Indian Languages in Mysore, the Central Institute of English and Foreign Languages in Hyderabad, and the Bureau for the Promotion of Urdu. Each of these institutions has done yeoman service in evolving scientific and technical terminology. A publication program directed toward bilingual and trilingual dictionaries, guides, and readers now exists, not only in the major languages but also in tribal languages. The teaching of English and other foreign languages as second or third languages, and innumerable in-service training programs and correspondence courses have been established. The results of the programs offered through these institutions may not be very evident today, but in times to come, despite the understandable controversy and the criticism, these will have a very important role to play.

Foundations for the growth of languages have been laid. Because of the complexity of the development of languages in a plural society, the situation seems unclear. But there is no doubt that after a period of 200 years of utter neglect of regional Indian languages, a new effort has been made to reestablish these languages of great antiquity. The language program acquires tremendous importance on account of India's linguistic states. Unless bilingualism and trilingualism are fostered and unless each language group is nurtured, supported, and allowed to grow into a full-fledged tree, tension and hostility are bound to arise.

A concerted effort has been made to strengthen India's library system. Besides the National Library in Calcutta, which is one of the most important libraries of Asia, the Central Library in Bombay, the Asiatic Society in Calcutta, and the Central Secretariat Library in New Delhi were strengthened. Alongside these was the institution of the Delhi Public Library, which serves a very useful role for the general public. As support for the massive Adult Education Programme, the Raja Rammohan Roy Library Foundation was later established. It became possible through this foundation to reach district, village, and even block-level libraries. The Library Foundation movement has also made it possible to create a continuing system of dialogue among the libraries of different states. Many programs of assistance and support to voluntary educational organizations and libraries have been launched. Among the most important is a program that provides financial assistance to voluntary organizations for the preservation, cataloging, and publication of unpublished manuscripts.

It is not often realized that there are over 30 million unpublished manuscripts stored in Indian and foreign collections. Although many of these have been cataloged, they await research and publication. A beginning has been made toward this monumental task. The physical preservation of these manuscripts, scattered in thousands of private and public collections, was a first step. Plans were devised to give financial support to private and public institutions to preserve public and private records. Further steps have included the formulation of a National Archival Policy and the establishment of the Indian Historical Commission.

Music and Dance

Music and dance present contrasting scenes. Apart from tribal music and the congregational music of village India, there are distinct but not unrelated highly sophisticated forms of music commonly termed "classical." These fall into two broad schools, Hindustani and Carnatic. The schools are further broken up into a number of family traditions passed down from father to son and from mother to daughter. Traditionally, temples and courts patronized these forms. When, in the 1930s and early 1940s, the resources of these patrons diminished, many court musicians and singers migrated to cities. In the early 20th century, musicians, nationalists, and social reformers such as Vishnu Digamber and Bhatkhanda rehabilitated the court arts in a new middle-class milieu; they took the music out of seclusion and spread it to another sector of society. This is an excellent example of artistic content and artistic process traversing social milieus. As a result, music attained a respectability shorn of its association with a decadent feudal society.

While music gradually found its way into the middle class, the case of dance was slightly different. Temples and courts had fostered distinctive styles of dance. In the south, there were Bharatanatyam and Kathakali, and in the east, Manipuri. In Orissa, there flourished a tradition of women temple dancers called *mahari* and men dancers called *gotipuas*. In the north, there was Kathak. Of the various forms, only Manipuri was part of the mainstream social fabric. The other styles, particularly Bharatanatyam and Kathak, were out of bounds for the respectable middle class.

Then, in the 1930s, Rabindranath Tagore in Bengal, Rukmini Devi in Tamil Nadu, and Vallathol in Kerala began to restore and reconstruct these styles. A neoclassicity emerged. The dynamics of this process were different in each case; however, all represented the reconstruction of fragments of ancient and medieval styles into a new contemporary mode. The classical dances of India today are indeed eclectic efforts at the recreation of classical styles and may more accurately be called neoclassical.

This trend continued well into the 1950s and 1960s. Orissi is a good example of a style that acquired a new neoclassical form only in the 1950s. Drawing inspiration from the ancient sculpture of the 2nd century B.C., it reformatted the vocabulary of movement as extant in the *maharis* and *gotipuas* and arrived at a consensus to re-create a style called Orissi. It was as ancient as it was modern. Today there are other examples of this trend, such as Kuchipudi and Mohiniattam. Each is the result of careful selection and reassembly of elements of a long tradition, accomplished with a contemporary sensibility.

In the 1930s, Uday Shankar, known as the father of Indian modern dance, evolved a personal movement vocabulary that initiated a new movement called modern dance. However, there is little parallel between Uday Shankar's work and that of Isadora Duncan or Martha Graham in Europe and the United States. Modern dance in India did not develop against so-called classical dance. Modern dance, or more specifically Uday Shankar's style, initially arose from an interaction between Shankar and Anna Pavlova. After his successful tours of Europe and the United States, he established the Almora Centre, where great traditional masters of music and dance also taught.

On the eve of independence, major centers of dance had been established: Shantiniketan in Bengal, the Kerala Kala Mandalam in Kerala, the Kalakshetra in Madras, the Schools of Menaka in Bombay, the Uday Shankar School in Almora, and some others in Ahmedabad, and Delhi. In number they were few, and yet these pioneers succeeded in rehabilitating dance in an urban milieu. Their inspiration was age-old Indian myth and legend; their formal technique, their regional and local focus, and their repertoire were tailored to new nationalistic aspirations.

By the 1960s, there was a phenomenal rise in the popularity of the performing arts, especially in music and dance. At present, a new generation of young artists from the urban centers has arisen. Some have received institutional training while others have studied with the gurus of the family traditions. Indeed, the traditional masters known as gurus and *ustads* (teachers) have migrated from the temples and courts not only to city centers but also settled abroad. There is a Balasaraswati School in the United States with many distinguished students and the Maihar School of Hindustani Music flourishes in California. Among members of the Indian diaspora there are many musicians and dancers. Indian music and dance have found votaries and students in the West: there is a new generation of American, British, Dutch, French, Italian, Japanese, Malaysian musicians and dancers who have devoted their lives to traditional schools of Indian music and dance. This is another instance of the resilience of tradition to maintain continuity and sustain change.

The 1980s and 1990s have witnessed another dance phenomenon. Some exponents of classical dance have experimented with large ensembles, created new themes, and incorporated movements from other styles, both Indian and foreign. The latest dialogue is between Kathak and Flamenco. Equally significant have been the bold departures taken by some leading dancers who have utilized the fundamental body language of particular styles of Indian dancers, such as Bharatanatyam and Kathakali, but have shed the content. They have discarded the mime (*abhinaya*) portions of Indian dance. The geometrical forms germane to these styles emerge on the stage as a modern or even postmodern concern with pure form. Chandralekha's work is the most characteristic example of this phenomenon. There are others like her who have woven the techniques of the martial arts of Kerala and Manipur into their choreography. Social milieu and period literary content are shed but the technique remains.

Visual Arts

Although India's cultural heritage includes great monuments such as Ajanta and Ellora, the temples of the southern, central, and eastern India, and the arts of the Himalayas, the urban educated long had little or no awareness of this wealth. The British had begun schools of art in Madras, Calcutta, and Bombay in the erroneous belief that India lacked or had lost a tradition in the visual arts. Not until the early 20th century did educated Indians pay attention to native artistic schools and styles. The Bengal School, motivated by a search for Indian identity, looked to these for inspiration. Its exponents re-created a tradition, although it was not without discontinuities and lack of comprehension of the inner dynamics of the mural paintings and styles. Some prominent art historians, such as E.B. Havell and A.K. Coomaraswamy, drew attention to the need for serious study of the distinctive Indian traditions. They wrote books on the subject and zealously defended Indian art from its detractors.

Artists such as Abindranath and Nandlal Bose pioneered new eclectic movements, each with a distinctive personal style. Village traditions were given a new formalism; Jamini Roy's work represents this trend. The coming together of European training and sensitivity to Indian themes is evident in the works of Amrita Shergil. Unlike the cases of music and dance, there was no attempt at the reassembly of fragments in the visual arts. Rather, many styles and techniques were churned to make individual visual statements. By the 1940s and early 1950s, new schools of modern Indian art had evolved. While the exponents of these schools rejected the immediate legacy of the Bengal School in content, form, and technique, they, too, were searching not only for a national identity but also for individual identities. Many more choices were available. Some artists followed European trends, while others used Western techniques but incorporated local content. Yet others found themselves suddenly discovering the power of local genres and ancient and medieval traditions. Geometric form attracted a few. Some understood the compositional structure of ancient and medieval painting; others did not, but employed traditional motifs and patterns and color tonalities nonetheless.

The prolific output and the plurality of styles and individual expressions belie strict classification, although there is some assertion of clear categories in critical writing on modern Indian art. A debate goes on among the traditionalists, the modernists, and the postmodernists. A vast spectrum exists, from the purely derivative to the extraordinarily innovative and original, from the figurative to the abstract, from the formalistic to the minimalist. Skills and techniques have been refined. Galleries have sprung up, and attendance of art exhibitions is the norm.

The museum system in India has received support and encouragement, not only through program grants for maintenance and development, but also through the organization of several workshops for particular purposes and through the active help and cooperation of the

International Council of Museums and its regional agencies. An important event in the museum movement was the launching of a new national institution called the National Research Laboratory for Conservation of Cultural Property, which was set up in Lucknow. This laboratory, which presently serves as the center for the Asian region, has evolved many indigenous techniques for conservation of cultural property along with the use of the most sophisticated modern equipment. The National Gallery of Modern Art and the Nehru Memorial Museum and Library have also grown into unique national institutions with distinctive personalities. The former has concentrated on the development of modern Indian art beginning with the late nineteenth and early twentieth centuries and ending with the most avant-garde artistic trends in the country. The latter is housed in the Teen Murti House, the former residence of the late Jawaharlal Nehru. In addition to a personalia museum and a wing dedicated to changing exhibitions relating to different facets of the freedom struggle, there are a library and a research program on modern India. This institution, which has fostered links with major institutions of higher learning in the field of contemporary history, has received wide acclaim for its microfilming library and its research programs.

Alas, the museum movement is also by and large dissociated from the educational mainstream, especially the university system. There are historical reasons for this. The British had purposely created one group of institutions to investigate and record the Oriental past and another to mold India into British contours. This trend continues, although there have been attempts to bridge the gap. Today, while a dozen or so universities do have departments of museology, much more needs to be done to integrate the museums as institutions with the teaching and research that takes place in the university system. Art history departments are few. Understandably, research in Indian art has suffered. While there have been great art historians, and many of them have been directors of museums—such as the late C. Sivaramamurti, Moti Chandra, and the late Rai Krishnadasa—art history remains by and large a matter of individual pursuit in isolated pockets. Despite these limitations, valuable work has been done by several art historians with varying backgrounds, including Karl Khandalavala in law, B.N. Goswamy in administration, and M.A. Dhaky and R. Nagaswamy in archaeology. Many specialists in Indian art have emerged from art history departments and museums in Europe and the United States.

Stella Kramrisch, Pratapaditya Pal, Michael Meister, and Frederick Asher come to mind in this connection.

A small but significant global community has developed. It has shed the predilections of the Orientalist discourse and is looking at the material afresh. From the preoccupation with dating the establishment of schools and styles, the discipline has moved on to issues of patrons, sculptors, painters, mobility patterns, narratives, and interpretations of both sociocultural milieu and the deeper significance of symbolic form, imagery, and philosophic meaning. One group of art historians continues to discover new material and published these findings in major magazines such as *Lalit Kala, Marg,* and the *Journal of Oriental Society.* Another group has focused attention on the relationship of text, image, and monument. A refreshing trend is the attempt to reestablish or reveal the intrinsic interrelationship of the arts, poetry, architecture, sculpture, painting, music, and dance. Institutionally, all these activities—research, documentation, curating of exhibitions, and art historical writing—are in the sphere of museums, departments of art history, and the national academy of the visual arts, the Lalit Kala Akademi.

Museums and institutions have long been the repositories of fragments of art, individual art objects, and parts of archaeological monuments. Some of these were taken abroad and adorn the many museums of Europe and the United States. Other objects remained in institutions in India, and many more continue to be in the hands of private collectors. At independence, the Indian Museum in Calcutta and the Madras Museum were the most important repositories. The central government established the National Museum and nationalized other museums, such as the Victoria Museum in Calcutta, and the Salarjung Museum in Hyderabad. The collections of the Bharat Kala Bhavan were given a new institutional identity within the Banaras Hindu University, as was the Ashutosh Museum at the University of Calcutta. Over recent years, each of these institutions has developed remarkably, adding to their respective collections, bringing out guide books, catalogs, and some fine publications, and mounting significant national and international exhibitions.

The National Museum has compiled major exhibitions, such as "Five Thousand Years of Indian Art" (a stone sculpture exhibit) in the 1960s, and "Image of Man" and many others in the 1980s. This museum also runs an institute of art history, and as the richest repository of art objects in India, it draws scholars and lay public from the entire country and abroad. The chain of museums is linked to each other through the All-India Museums Association and the Indian Committee of the International Council of Museums. In addition, the government has set up an All-India Advisory Committee for Museums. These agencies have contributed significantly to India's museum system by upgrading skills, conservation techniques, and display methods.

Theater

Indian theater fared much as the visual arts did until the late 1940s and early 1950s: 20th-century urban Indians were largely not open or sensitive to its roots. However, Shakespeare and Ibsen continued to be favorites, and the plays of Albert Camus and Christopher Fry were enacted by amateur theater groups in universities. Then, the Indian People's Theater Movement and Prithviraj Kapoor, with his powerful realistic plays on partition, catalyzed a new movement. These nationalist efforts sparked new developments in theater movements. As in the case of the visual arts, sources of inspiration varied. Some followed modern European trends; others tried to re-create ancient Greek theater; some attempted to reconstruct ancient Sanskrit theater; and others turned to traditional regional forms. None of these productions consisted of reassembly, as in the case of dance. Instead, local and regional forms were employed to make a contemporary statement. Once the constraints of the proscenium and the preoccupation with the unity of time and place were broken, the spoken word was no longer the only instrument of expression. Chorus, recitation, mime, and movement entered urban Indian theater. Significantly, Brecht and Ionesco played important roles in this journey home.

Ultimately, producers and directors moved not only from English to regional languages but also to the rich and varied storehouse of oral literature. A variety of approaches and a diversity of theatrical forms have emerged. After experiments with realistic forms, the theater of the absurd, and a revival of Sanskrit theater, Indian theater manifests a dynamic stability. Styles range from the street theater of Badal Sircar to the high *yatra* style of Utpal Dutt; the declamatory chorus forms of Jabbar Patel to the musical of B.V. Karanth; the neoritualistic forms of Kovalam Panikkar to the powerful kinetic style of Rattan Teyyam and the sophisticated understatement of G. Shankara Pillai, to mention only a few. Each of these directors has delved into regional languages and employed the modes of traditional theater. These new forms, too, belie categorization, and experimentation and vibrancy are apparent. While there is a powerful movement of regional theater, there is also a real threat from the mass media and television serials. Will the small screen gradually supplant real theater? It remains to be seen.

Film and Television

While television has encouraged popular exposure to many art forms, it has in turn obliged artists to tailor their performances to the specifications of the medium. Complex forms and layers of meaning are sacrificed. Age-old myths become subject to black-and-white interpretation through stock characters of heroes and villains, gods and demons. The power of Indian myth lies in its structured ambiguity, multilayered meaning, openness to interpretation, and articulaton in a variety of media. In its flexibility lies its power to be perennial and pertinent. Television interpretations give these myths fixity of stock types. The possibilities for multiple articulations shrink, thereby diminishing the power of myth and threatening its very survival. This is no more than popular culture masquerading as ancient classicism. The danger is that instead of rejuvenating the myths, television simplifies and distorts them. Another popular television format is the musical, with songs devoid of art and body language without sophistication. This indeed is part of an India of many hues and colors, but this element is motivated by the urge for new stimuli rather than by a unifying civilization.

Since the 1950s, Indian cinema has taken strides in numerous and diverse directions. Its themes have included migration from the country to the city, the rootlessness of industrialized living, retold stories of the struggle for freedom, lonely perennial journeys, and confrontation between heroes and villains in high society and mythology. In style, the spectrum ranges from glitziness to melodrama to spartan intellectualism.

A serious cinematic movement emerged in the 1960s and 1970s. Satyajit Ray changed the course of Indian cinema. His film *Pather Panchali* was a monumental milestone. Today, the "parallel cinema" flourishes along with the popular cinema. Many of its directors are acclaimed not only in India but also abroad. Each tackles the human predicament of our times in his or her individual style. Some have adopted a narrative mode, others a nonnarrative one. As is true of the other artistic fields, plurality and diversity characterize Indian cinema.

Indira Gandhi National Centre for the Arts

The youngest of the institutions concerned with culture is the Indira Gandhi National Centre for the Arts in New Delhi. Through its conceptual plan and its interdisciplinary and multidisciplinary programs, it has, over the ten years of its existence, unambiguously established a new theoretical model for comprehending, assessing, and disseminating the Indian cultural phenomenon. It has transcended the boundaries of the disciplines of archaeology and anthropology, broken the false hierarchies of the textual and the oral, and eschewed the notions of dominant and subordinate, mainstream and substreams, great and little traditions, and tradition and modernity. The center has succeeded in establishing a meaningful, sustained dialogue between the field of science and technology, and that of the humanities and the arts.

The Indira Gandhi Centre has also made a heroic effort to retrieve, conserve, and reassemble the fragmented material spread all over the world through an extensive program of reprography and duplication. The institution has been able to make or collect over 15 million folios of unpublished manuscripts and 100,000 slides of Indian art dispersed in Indian and foreign collections. All this material is gradually being digitized for easy accessibility and long-term preservation. This is much more than deconstruction and assembly of parts; it is an effort at reconstruction and reassembly, albeit through replication of the whole.

Based on the material, an ambitious program of collecting and publishing seminal fundamental texts on the arts has been launched. Twenty-two major texts, from the 2nd century B.C. to the 17th century, on music, architecture, theater, dance, and rituals have been published, and another eighty are envisaged. Scholars from all parts of the world have been involved in this effort to publish these multilingual texts—Bengali, Hindi, Orissa, Persian, and Sanskrit—with English translations. Another unique program has been the investigation of key concepts and terms of the Indian tradition through primary works in various disciplines. The endeavor here is to reveal explicitly the holistic worldview of the multidisciplinary system intrinsic to the Indian intellectual tradition.

The programs that focus on the oral traditions, regional and local cultures, and the people are complementary and closely interlocked. Through field studies conducted by multidisciplinary teams, cultural areas and ecocultural zones have been studied with the full participation of the specific groups involved. The results are expressed in the form of both monographs and films. The documentation of the Meitheis of Manipur, the Garos of Meghalaya, and the Todas of Nilgiri Hills have culminated in aesthetically pleasing films that have won national awards.

A distinguishing feature of the Indira Gandhi Centre has been its multidisciplinary, cross-cultural, multimedia exhibitions, seminars, and publications. The efficacy of the holistic global view is evident from five major conferences and exhibitions held at the institution on the themes of Space, Time, Letterform, Primal Elements, and Chaos and Order. Here scientists, astrophysicists, microbiologists, metaphysicians, philosophers, archaeologists, anthropologists, and artists have all been brought together to reflect and to communicate with each other on some perennials that have encompassed and continue to encompass all of humanity, past and present.

Lastly, the Centre has established a state-of-the-art multimedia computer laboratory, where a serious effort is being made to establish a meaningful dialogue between tradition and technology, between the creativity of the artist and the expertise of the software specialist. Programs based on prehistoric rock art and on the three-dimensional modeling of an Indian temple are planned, and the laboratory has recently made a multimedia presentation of a 12th century Sanskrit poem, the *Gita Govinda*. Six verses of the poem have been captured in forty gigabytes through a variety of interpretations using contemporary Indian music, dance, congregational singing, and the many schools of Indian miniature painting. Perhaps there could be no better way of demonstrating and communicating the phenomenon of diversity and unity of continuity and change and the innate holistic view of a live tradition.

And yet, while this institution, like others, has miles to go in its journey of exploring outside space (India's dialogues with other cultures—Central Asian, Southeast Asian, and European) and inside space in greater and greater depth, a beginning has been made.

Conclusion

Although limited in scope, the above discussion should make obvious that political freedom and developments in cultural lifestyle and artistic expression are not necessarily coterminous. Also obvious is the fact that many diverse movements coexist. While one part of the Indian psyche moves in the calendar time of the world of work and organizations, the other follows the lunar cycle, punctuated by the life-cycle ceremonies of the family and the annual cycle of fairs and festivals of the community. Indian artists, consciously or unconsciously, carry within themselves varying senses of space and time. They adjust, accommodate, and manipulate these perceptions, but the flow of life simultaneously changes their perceptions according to either seasonal continuity or more contemporary demands. Nonetheless, the dangers of homogenization of these multiple identities into a single mass culture at the cost of the rich plurality are real and cannot be discounted.

So in fifty years—both too long and too short a period—India's culture has taken many inward and outward journeys, directly and via detours, which have been both complex and lucid but never one-dimensional or uniform. No linear graph can be drawn to represent India's path; it has been a mobile, multilayered system that has been facilitated and on occasion has even created obstacles to mobility, vertical and horizontal. Flux, change, inversion, reversion, and recoil are concepts more germane to this process than linear progression. Viewed from the standpoint of fixed categories, the phenomenon is staggeringly complex. It is fascinating and understandable only if looked at with a flexibility that allows acceptance of the perennial flow of continuity and change as its dynamics of movement.

History and Politics

Vinay Lal

The Emergence of a Historical Sensibility
in 19th-Century India

In the fifty years since independence, Indian historians have undoubtedly assumed charge of their own history. Although historians—more than archaeologists, anthropologists, professional philosophers, or linguists—can be public figures everywhere, in few countries have they acquired such a prominent public presence as they have in India. In the controversy surrounding the Babri Masjid, a 16th-century mosque that Hindu militants claim was built after the destruction of a temple on the same site dedicated to Lord Rama, historians found that they had become ascendant among the class of intellectuals, called upon to verify or dispute the claims of both the militants and their opponents; and in the aftermath of the destruction of the mosque in December 1992, they were transformed into editorialists, pamphleteers, and activists.[1] At issue was the "authentic" history not only of the mosque but of its representations over five centuries and of Hindu-Muslim relations in India and the rest of South Asia. In the meantime, the advent of the "subaltern school" of Indian history, comprised mainly of Indian historians clustered at a few universities and research centers in Delhi, Calcutta, and elsewhere, was to give Indian historical study not only an unprecedented international respectability, such as has ordinarily been reserved for developments in French or English historiography,[2] but

---

1. For a discussion of this phenomenon, see Vinay Lal, "The Discourse of History and the Crisis at Ayodhya: Reflections on the Production of Knowledge, Freedom, and the Future of India," *Emergences,* nos. 5–6 (1993–94):4–44. I am grateful to my research assistant, Ben Marschke, for his help with library work.

2. The obvious reference here is to the work of Le Roy Ladurie, Braudel, and others of the Annales school, and to the "history from below" associated with English social historians such as E.P. Thompson.

also an important place in various debates in postcolonial theory, postmodernism, and what is termed "cultural studies." Historians and scholars around the world have looked to the writings of the subaltern historians to pose questions about the politics of knowledge, the nature of "elitist" history, the apparently frequent congruence between nationalist and imperialist models of history writing, and the various voices through which history is interpreted.

These developments in Indian historiography must appear all the more remarkable when we consider that as late as 1925, the English historian and "friend of India" Edward Thompson was able to write, with all the supreme arrogance that the ruling class everywhere is capable of, "Indians are not historians, and they rarely show any critical ability. Even their most useful books, books full of research and information, exasperate with their repetitions and diffuseness, and lose effect by their uncritical enthusiasms. . . . So they are not likely to displace our account of our connection with India."[3] This argument was scarcely original to Thompson, as by the first half of the 19th century modernizing Indians had themselves come to accept as axiomatic the argument that, being acutely deficient in historical sensibility, they were a people without analytical and rational faculties. James Mill, in his highly influential *History of British India* (1817), had set the tone for this argument when he contended that the Hindus were "perfectly destitute of historical records," supremely indifferent to chronology, and contemptuous of geography; and as he further averred, "all rude nations neglect history, and are gratified with the productions of the mythologists and poets."[4] The seriousness with which Mill's critique was received can be gauged by the fact that when a group of progressive Bengalis met for the first time in Calcutta in 1838 as members of the newly constituted "Society for the Acquisition of General Knowledge," they listened to one Reverend Krishna Mohun Banerjea present a speech entitled, "Discourse on the Nature and Importance of Historical Studies." Banerjea took the view that the modern nations of the West, which not long before had been living in "wretched degradation," had ascended to preeminence by attending closely "to the lessons of history." Among the Hindus, by contrast,

---

3. Edward Thompson, *The Other Side of the Medal* (London: Hogarth Press, 1925), 27–28.

4. James Mill, *History of British India*, ed. with notes by Horace Hayman Wilson, 10 vols (5th ed., London: James Madden, 1840–48), 2:46–48; 1:114–15.

there was a tendency "to confound in one mass history and mythology—facts and fables—truth and fiction—receiving them all indifferently as true or else rejecting them all as wholly false—sweeping the gold away from the dross." No progress could be hoped for until Indians learned to appreciate "historical compositions," and themselves commenced to undertake their execution.[5]

In 1835, Thomas Babington Macaulay, who had been appointed Law Member in the Viceroy's Council, decreed that henceforth public funds were to be expended on Western education conducted through the medium of English. Since Macaulay himself was partial toward the study of history, acquiring later in life a considerable reputation as a historian, he doubtless encouraged the introduction of "scientific history" in Indian schools. Indeed, from the middle part of the 19th century, history came to occupy, along with science, the chief part of the syllabus of Indian schools.[6] Historical analysis was valorized as akin to the scientific method, with the proper use and aid of which one coaxed the truth out of one's materials. With the establishment of universities at Calcutta and elsewhere in 1857, the study of history was further consolidated; and while much of northern India simmered in revolt, Bengali translations of histories of Bengal and India by British historians were undertaken. Both the manner of the British victory at Plassey in 1757, where bribes rather than arms had enabled the British to gain the upper hand, and their more recent resort to brutality and naked force in their endeavor to suppress the Rebellion of 1857–58, had moved Indian writers to the consideration that "the criteria of divine intervention, religious value and the norms of right conduct in judging the rise and fall of kingdoms" were of little use in understanding history.[7] The success of the British in India was now likely to be portrayed as the conse-

5. Rev. Krishna Mohun Banerjea, "Discourse on the Nature and Importance of Historical Studies" (1840), reprinted in *Awakening in Early Nineteenth Century (Selected Documents)*, ed. Gautam Chattopadhyay (Calcutta: Progressive Publishers, 1965), 1:1–23 esp. 4, 7–8, 22–23.

6. See Gauri Viswanathan, *Masks of Conquest: Literary Study and British Rule in India* (New York: Columbia University Press, 1989), 100–101.

7. Partha Chatterjee, "Claims on the Past: The Genealogy of Modern Historiography in Bengal," in *Subaltern Studies VIII: Essays in Honour of Ranajit Guha*, eds. David Arnold and David Hardiman (Delhi: Oxford University Press, 1996), pp. 1–50 at p. 20. Chatterjee's article is an expanded version, although not so mentioned, of an essay first published as "History and the Nationalization of Hinduism," *Social Research* 59, no. 1 (Spring 1992): 111–49.

quence of a relentless and ruthless pursuit of power, and as Partha Chatterjee has noted, the "modern historiography seemed to validate a view of political history as simply the amoral pursuit of *raison d'état*."[8] Indian writers were beginning to understand that history might have less to do with destiny, ethical conduct, and the movement of large intractable forces than with greed, nefarious political schemes, and those innumerable frailties to which the human race is susceptible.

It was a novelist rather than a historian, however, who was to give shape to the principal concerns of Indian historians for some time. The Bengali writer Bankim Chandra Chatterji (1838–94) populated his novels with historical characters. In the later years of his life, he turned his attention to pondering why India had been a subject nation for most of its history. Might that have something to do, he asked, with the profound and deeply disturbing indifference of Indians toward history? He encapsulated his observations most poignantly in his essays on Krishna and the *Bhagavad Gita*, in which he delineated the two modalities, broadly speaking, of apprehending Krishna in Indian traditions. There was the Krishna of art, religious legends, and devotional literature, who appeared as a loving, playful, and mischievous god and whose very historicity was doubtful; there was also the Krishna of the *Bhagavad Gita*, "who by the strength of his arms suppressed the enemy, who by the strength of his intellect united the country of the Bharatas, and who in his unique, selfless wisdom promulgated dharma."[9] This was a Krishna worthy, so Bankim and many of his contemporaries imagined, of the monotheistic faiths, one who could offer leadership and guidance and who could motivate men to acts of courage, resistance, and patriotism. The tragedy of Indian history, Bankim was to argue, was that Indians had largely abandoned the "historical Krishna" for a "mythical Krishna": partly in this circumstance were to be found the grounds for their effeminacy, passivity, and subjugation. Bankim went on to distill his wisdom in a precise formulation, "'Knowledge is power': that is the slogan of Western civilization. 'Knowledge is salvation' is the slogan of Hindu civili-

---

8. Ibid.

9. Bankim, Chandra Chatterji, *Dharmatattva* (*The Essence of Dharma*), in *Bankim Racnabali*, ed. Yogesh Chandra Bagal, 2 vols. (Calcutta: Sahitya Samsad, 1965), Vol. 2. It is conventional to refer to most Bengali figures by their first names, even in formal writing; hence, reference is made to Bankim throughout.

zation."[10] Perhaps Indians, especially Hindus, would do well to worship at the altar of power.

Bankim was giving expression to the sentiments of many nationalists and modernizers who agonized over India's enslavement and lack of a historical literature, and who saw in those twin deficiencies an inescapable connection. His near contemporary, the revered Punjabi nationalist Lala Lajpat Rai (1865–1928), similarly deplored his countrymen's want of "love of history": "They read Shakespeare, Milton and Dante and obtain degrees. But they do not know anything about even important things relating to their country. They have no idea of the deeds of their forefathers."[11] Bankim's clarion call was not issued in vain: Within a little over a generation after his death, the study of history had acquired respectability to the point that at a professional gathering of historians in 1939, it was admitted that "no subject is perhaps studied in Indian universities of the present day with the same assiduity as the history of India."[12] Taking their cue from Bankim, the nationalists were to mine the past for heroes and otherwise seek to historicize legendary figures from Indian mythology; at least the first generation of historians such as R.C. Dutt (1848–1909) and R.G. Bhandarkar (1837–1925) was to devote its labors largely to the study of ancient India, which was already being envisioned as the high point of Indian civilization. With the knowledge gleaned of what was unreflectively construed as India's "glorious past," the degradation of the present was more acutely perceived. As nationalists engaged in the social reconstruction of Indian society, so the reconstruction of Indian history would be attempted, acquiring, with the rapid political changes leading to the end of colonial rule, a degree of urgency.

Independence and Historical Projects of the State

With the advent of independence in 1947, the creation of an Indian history, for and by Indians, became something of a national imperative.

10. Idem, "Sankhyadarsan," in *Bankim Racnabali*, 2:222–26, cited by Partha Chatterjee, *Nationalist Thought and the Colonial World: A Derivative Discourse?* (London: Zed Books, 1986), 56–57.

11. Cited by J.C. Srivastava, "Lala Lajpatrai's Urdu Biography of Shivaji," in *Chhatrapati Shivaji: Architect of Freedom*, ed. Narayan H. Kulkarnee (Delhi: Chhatrapati Shivaji Smarak Samiti, 1975), 73.

12. Subodhkumar Mukherji, "The Cultural History of India—An Apology," *Proceedings of the Indian History Congress*, 3rd Session (Calcutta: Calcutta University Press, 1939), 107.

Since at least the time of Bankim, nationalist Indians were firmly of the opinion that imperialist history was irredeemably contaminated. In their view, British accounts of the Indian past existed for no other reason than to serve colonial interests, establish the purported superiority of Western civilization, and create rifts between various Indian communities, whether constituted on grounds of religion and caste (as was most common), ethnicity, or linguistic affiliation. British histories of India, in the unabashedly expressed expectation of one practitioner, would "make the native subjects of British India more sensible of the immense advantages accruing to them under the mildness and equity of [our] rule."[13] Nationalists argued that in such histories Indians were invariably represented as a supine people who had never offered resistance and whose destiny (until the enlightened British came along) condemned them to the eternal acceptance of a merciless Oriental despotism. By a perverse twist of logic, the genius of Indians (by this was meant Hindus) was construed as residing in their capacity to submit, almost without distinction, to all invaders and to absorb them in turn. Bankim had argued that India's indifference to history had created the grounds for its repeated conquest by foreign powers, as Indians had become oblivious of the greatness of their own past, the valor of their soldiers, and the eminent justness of their kings. It was entirely unreasonable to suppose that anyone else would sing of the glories of Bengal or India; perforce Indians must accomplish this task themselves. As Bankim explained, in a text where Bengal stood for India as well, "Bengal must have her own history. Otherwise there is no hope for Bengal. Who is to write it? You have to write it. I have to write it. . . ."[14] So long as India remained under colonial rule, however, its aspirations to represent its own history and acquire something of an intellectual autonomy would be thwarted.

Thus, on the attainment of independence, no intellectual task, other than that of ushering India into the scientific era and ensuring that the

---

13. Sir H.M. Elliot, *The History of India as Told by Its Own Historians: The Muhammadan Period*, ed. (and continued) by John Dowson, 8 vols. (1st ed., 1867–77; reprint ed., Allahabad: Kitab Mahal, 1963–64), 1:xxii.

14. Cited by Ranajit Guha, *An Indian Historiography of India: A Nineteenth-Century Agenda and Its Implications* (Calcutta: K.P. Bagchi & Co., 1988), 1. For a discussion of Bankim's enchantment with historical discourses, see Vinay Lal, "History and the Possibilities of Emancipation: Some Lessons from India," *Journal of the Indian Council of Philosophical Research*, Special Issue: Historiography of Civilizations (June 1996), pp. 95–137 at pp. 106–113. See also Chatterjee, "Claims on the Past," 2–4.

country acquired a pool of scientific talent, acquired a greater sanctity and urgency than creating new histories of India. In a speech given shortly after his inauguration as the first president of the Republic of India, Rajendra Prasad underscored the importance of the role of history in nation building. In his address to the All-India History Congress, Prasad emphasized that "India needs a true and exhaustive history of its distant and glorious past, no less than of its unique and unprecedented struggle which has succeeded in placing it, once again, on the map of the world."[15] Prasad did not doubt that history is taught by example, and provided "guidance for the future": the historian was most certainly bound to the highest standards of "truth." Had Prasad said no more, he would have been confined to the conventional pieties about the lessons of history, but rather uncommonly, he advanced the argument that history would be inadequate if it did not go beyond "an account of kings and nobles" to a consideration of the achievements of the "common man." More particularly, pointing to the apotheosization of the warrior in European culture, as manifested in war memorials and monuments of conquerors and soldiers, Prasad hoped that historians of India would be cognizant of the unique importance of the new technique of resistance forged by Gandhi and attentive to the history of the nonviolent armies raised by him. Here, the task of the historian, Prasad appeared to imply, was to demonstrate that "non-violence has victories more glorious than war."[16]

Fortuitously for those who wished to advance the study of history in India, the mantle of political and intellectual leadership had fallen upon Jawaharlal Nehru, who not only possessed a fine historical imagination but had also made a considerable name for himself as the author of historical works. Being openly partial to the enterprise of history was only one manner in which Nehru displayed a sensibility quite at odds with that of his political mentor Gandhi, who in a characteristic moment had written, "I believe that a nation is happy that has no history."[17] In a remarkable and extended series of letters to his daughter

---

15. Rajendra Prasad, "The Role of History," in *Speeches of Rajendra Prasad 1952–1956* (New Delhi: Government of India, Ministry of Information and Broadcasting, Publications Division, 1958), 103.

16. Ibid., 104–8.

17. M.K. Gandhi, "My Jail Experiences—XI," *Young India* (11 September 1924), reprinted in *The Collected Works of Mahatma Gandhi* (hereafter *CWMG*), 100 vols. (New Delhi: Government of India, Ministry of Information and Broadcasting, Publications Division, 1958–94), 25:128.

Indira collected in *Glimpses of World History* (1934), Nehru confessed, "I do not claim to be a historian," but nonetheless he hoped that these letters would offer her glimpses of the past and awaken her curiosity.[18] Quite unlike most world histories, which were scarcely more than accounts of the development of Western civilization, the narrative of Nehru displayed an exemplary ecumenism and a genuine attempt to give a parity to all the principal civilizations. In this respect, *Glimpses of World History* foreshadowed Nehru's propensity toward nonalignment, and his stated policy of cultivating South-South relations and paying close attention to India's relations with other colonized parts of the world. Nehru was not inclined to the view that as the West had been preeminent in world affairs since the late 15th century, it ought to command center stage in history books. He sought even his daughter's indulgence in being, perhaps, somewhat more attentive to India. As an Indian, he was more fully conversant with Indian history and culture; moreover, as he wrote to her, "If we are to understand India as she is, we must know something of the forces that went to make her or mar her. Only so can we serve her intelligently, and know what we should do and what path we should take."[19]

Nehru continued his exploration of Indian history in his autobiography (1941), which purported to trace his own mental development rather than offer a survey of recent Indian history,[20] and in *The Discovery of India* (1946), in which he painted a broad canvas of India's multifarious and tumultuous past. India appeared to him as akin to some "ancient palimpsest on which layer upon layer of thought and reverie had been inscribed, and yet no succeeding layer had completely hidden or erased what had been written previously." While Nehru may even have accepted many of the assumptions of colonialist histories, he rejected the narrative that sought to render India's past as little more than a tale of invasion, conquest, bloody warfare, Oriental despotism, and fratricide. Most of all he strenuously repudiated the view that there was never an India, or Indian civilization, until the British came along

---

18. Jawaharlal Nehru, *Glimpses of World History: Being Further Letters to his Daughter, Written in Prison, and Containing a Rambling Account of History for Young People* (London, 1934; reprint ed., Delhi: Oxford University Press, 1982), viii, 94. For an extended discussion of this work, see Vinay Lal, "Nehru as a Writer," *Indian Literature*, no. 135 (Jan–Feb 1990), 20–46.

19. Nehru, *Glimpses of World History*, 429.

20. *Toward Freedom: The Autobiography of Jawaharlal Nehru* (Boston: Beacon Press, 1958), preface.

and welded together disparate and quarrelsome communities into one people. "Though outwardly there was diversity and infinite variety among our people," wrote Nehru, "everywhere there was that tremendous impress of oneness, which had held all of us together for ages past, whatever political fate or misfortune had befallen us." The "essential unity" of India, which he had comprehended through his extensive travels in India in 1936–37 not only as an "intellectual conception" but as an "emotional experience," had been "so powerful that no political division, no disaster or catastrophe, had been able to overcome it."[21]

Having gone far beyond the commonplace nationalist view that India had been united under the reign of powerful monarchs such as Ashoka, Chandragupta Maurya, Harsha, and Akbar, Nehru was also prepared to undertake a postmortem on India's inability to preserve its political integrity. In a clear demonstration of his readiness to give his historical sensibility a public face and allow his historical understanding to pervade the contours of his political thought and economic policies, Nehru embraced the view that the cultural and emotional unity of India would not suffice in the age of the modern nation-state to furnish India with secure borders and political integrity. India had almost fatally succumbed to British rule, and modern political arrangements had an intractability that even the most resilient civilizations might find taxing. The decentralization that had been the strength of India as a civilization was disempowering to India as a nation-state, and while tempted to experiment with federalism, Nehru resolved that India would now be governed from a strong center. Just as his view of center-state relations was historically informed, so Nehru looked to the contemporary history of the Soviet Union, whose practical achievements he was to describe as tremendously impressive, in formulating plans for India's economic development. If the "Soviet Revolution had advanced human society by a great leap . . . and had laid the foundations for that new civilization toward which the world could advance,"[22] then there could be no doubt that India's future likewise lay in centralized economic planning and investment in industrial infrastructure.

In an analogue to the dams and steel mills that Nehru had character-

---

21. Jawaharlal Nehru, *The Discovery of India* (1946; reprint ed., Delhi: Oxford University Press, 1988), 59.
22. Ibid., 29.

ized as the future "temples" of India, the new nation-state proceeded to initiate, with his apparent blessing, large projects of historical scholarship and narrative. These were designed to edify and instruct the public just as industrial schemes were intended to develop the country: history was to be the handmaiden of industrial progress, as in the 19th century it had been construed as eminently worthy of producing "improvement."

At the very first meeting of the Indian Historical Records Commission held after the end of colonial rule, it was resolved to prepare an "authentic and comprehensive" history of the "freedom struggle."[23] As a consequence, a committee was appointed in 1950, at the behest of the government of India, to supervise the collection of material "throwing light on the various phases and technique" of the "freedom struggle" around the country, and so highlight its "unique" character.[24] India had not merely achieved its "independence": as the chairman of the committee, the distinguished historian and educational advisor Tara Chand put it, "Independence is a negative concept. Its implication is absence of dependence; it has no positive connotation; it does not indicate the quality and character of the society which achieves political sovereignty after throwing off alien domination."[25] A free people must have a history of which they can be proud, and Tara Chand could not have been unaware of the fact that in some circles India's attainment of freedom was prone to being characterized as a gift from the British; moreover, the largely nonviolent nature of the engagement, owing to Gandhi's leadership of the movement, had created the illusion that British rule in India had been, on the whole, a mild and gentlemanly affair. It was, perforce, necessary to inject into the understanding of India's resistance to colonial domination the sense that Indians had had to wage a struggle, that they had striven to be free: nonviolent resistance can be active and aggressive, and so, too, violence is often the resort of the weak and the passive. "Freedom is more than the mere absence of foreign control," Tara Chand noted, "for it implies a society

---

23. Foreword by Humayun Kabir to Tara Chand, *History of the Freedom Movement in India*, 4 vols. (New Delhi: Government of India, Ministry of Information and Broadcasting, Publications Division, 1961–72), 1:vii.

24. Foreword by Jugal Kishore, Minister of Information (1961), to *Freedom Struggle in Uttar Pradesh*, ed. S.A.A. Rizvi, 6 vols. (Lucknow: Government of Uttar Pradesh, Information Department, Publications Bureau), 6:vii; see also Preface by Kamalapati Tripathi, Minister of Information (1957), to Vol. 1, iii.

25. Tara Chand, *History of the Freedom Movement*, 1:xi.

possessing certain positive attributes—a capacity to order its affairs in accordance with the will of the people, and a democratic way of life guaranteeing liberty and equality to all its members."[26] It was as a freedom struggle rather than an independence movement that the Indian state sought to enshrine the resistance to British rule in official histories, and it is as freedom fighters that opponents of British rule are still celebrated in Indian histories.

Over the next three decades, numerous state-sponsored histories of the freedom struggle, which were often little more than compilations of source material, were to make their appearance.[27] Not unexpectedly, the official histories took on a largely hagiographic tone, with homage being rendered in reverential language to the martyrs of the revolution. This endeavor was, on occasion, no easy task, considering that in some parts of India the "freedom struggle" had not been received with enthusiasm by Indians, while in others native rulers had even worked to suppress the nationalist movement. Hyderabad, which under the Nizam had offered unstinting support to the British both during the Rebellion of 1857–58 and throughout the years of the nationalist movement, was implausibly represented by an Andhra patriot as a hotbed of sedition, and Andhra was described as having contributed, "next to Uttar Pradesh," "the largest contingent of women Satyagrahis who willingly entered jails braving great hardships."[28] More belabored still was the attempt of the author of the official history of the nationalist movement in Orissa, who was to note that the "freedom struggle in Orissa began as far back as 3rd century B.C. when the Maurya Emperor Asoka invaded Kalinga in 261 B.C."[29] It was scarcely necessary, on this logic, to examine what (if any) place the idea of freedom occupied in Indian political philosophy, and whether the political structures were hospita-

---

26. Ibid.

27. See K.K. Datta, ed., *History of the Freedom Movement in Bihar*, 3 vols. (Patna: Government of Bihar, 1957–58); *The History of the Freedom Movement in Madhya Pradesh* (Nagpur: Government Printing, 1956); Mamidipudi Venkatarangaiya, ed., *The Freedom Struggle in Andhra Pradesh* (Hyderabad: Andhra Pradesh Committee Appointed for the Compilation of a History of the Freedom Struggle in Andhra Pradesh, 1965–74); K.K. Choudhari, *Maharashtra and Indian Freedom Struggle* (Bombay: Government of Maharashtra, 1985).

28. See Sarojini Regani, ed., *Who's Who of Freedom Struggle in Andhra Pradesh* (Hyderabad: Ministry of Education and Cultural Affairs, Government of Andhra Pradesh, 1978), 1:v.

29. Sushil Chandra De, *Story of Freedom Struggle in Orissa* (Bhubaneswar: Orissa Sahitya Akademi, 1990), 1.

ble to the idea of freedom. The history of Orissa was, consequently, none other than the story of the Oriyas' continuing attempts, in true Enlightenment fashion, to retain their freedom: "That sense of freedom has been all along with the Oriyas and Orissa was the last province in the country to come under the Mughal subjugation. It was, therefore, not unusual that these people should be fighting hand in hand and shoulder to shoulder with their brothers in other parts of the Country to free India from the British."[30] The States' Reorganization Commission had already created "linguistic states," and the task of the state historians was to consolidate further the idea of provincial integrity and autonomy. While it was critical that a "unified history" of the nationalist movement should encourage Indians to think of the nation, the states were eager that the people should be equipped to take pride in their local pasts.

The nationalist tone of these undertakings is signified by the fact that six volumes of the *Freedom Struggle in Uttar Pradesh*, published between 1957 and 1961, all appeared on August 15 (Independence Day), January 26 (Republic Day), or October 2 (Mahatma Gandhi's Birthday). The intellectual agenda of the compilers and authors was nonetheless more complex, as the ambition was to dispel the notion that the Rebellion of 1857–58 was merely the aggregate of sporadic and spontaneous uprisings, lacking any coherence, direction, or potential to be transformative. Indeed, the entire set was to be devoted to making available material pertaining to that rebellion. The author of the foreword to Volume 1 gave it as his considered opinion that "to those who have been prone to belittle the 1857 struggle as a mere sporadic mutiny of sepoys and a few disgruntled princes this material is bound to prove an eye-opener." It was Uttar Pradesh, then the United Provinces, that "constituted the principal theatre of the Struggle," and "the emotions and aspirations that inspired her fighters" were the mainstay of the "entire process of revolt and its organisation."[31] While it was understandable that European historians had not been overly keen on recording the achievements of Indians, the editor thought that "contemporary Indian scholars" had, in the matter of the Rebellion of 1857–58, "done greater injustice to the historical truth" and "intentionally suppressed the national character of the movement."

---

30. Ibid., introductory note by Surendranath Satapathy, i–ii.
31. Foreword by Sampurananda to *Freedom Struggle in Uttar Pradesh*, i.

By striving to prove that the movement was the handiwork of "a limited number of disloyal and mean wretches," they had succeeded even in contradicting the work of those English scholars "who believed willingly or unwillingly that the upsurge was a national one."[32] Although refraining from the observation that Indian historiography was, at this time, wholly derivative, the editor meant to imply all too clearly that Indian historians were themselves profoundly colonized.

While work on compilation of regional histories of the freedom struggle continued unabated, the government of India sought to fulfill a more sacred task when it established an office to collect all the known works and speeches of the "Father of the Nation." This was doubtless a way of rendering homage to Gandhi, preserving the records of a large chunk of the history of the independence movement (at the helm of which Gandhi had stood for over two decades), and perhaps even keeping alive his name when he already appeared as something of an embarrassment and anachronism to those elites who rendered craven submission to the West. More pointedly, it was also a way of asserting that Gandhi ought to occupy in the Indian imagination the place reserved in the Soviet Union for Marx and Lenin, the publication of whose collected writings in uniform volumes had become not only a matter of great state prestige but also a way of continuing to foment communist revolutions around the world.

The first volume of the *Collected Works of Mahatma Gandhi*, published with a massive state subsidy, made its appearance in 1958; although it had been presumed that Gandhi's writings would run to some sixty volumes, it was only in 1994 that the project was brought to a close with the publication of Volume 100 of the series.[33] Nothing as ambitious as this enterprise was to be attempted in respect to other principal figures of the nationalist movement, although many historians would be employed, as they still are today, in preparing volumes of selected writings, usually sponsored by regional governments, of numerous national heroes. Among those so honored were Vallabhai Patel, one of Gandhi's principal associates and the man chiefly responsible for the integration of Indian

---

32. *Freedom Struggle in Uttar Pradesh*, vii, xiv.

33. Vols. 91–97 are supplementary volumes; Vols. 98–99 provide a comprehensive index of subjects and persons; and Vol. 100 reprints the introductions to the previous 99 volumes, thereby providing a resume of the entire series. A Hindi edition, although not of the entire set at this time, is available; there are also editions in other Indian languages.

states after partition; B.R. Ambedkar, the chief architect of the Indian
Constitution; and G.B. Pant, a principal leader of the nationalist movement in Uttar Pradesh.

Nation Building and the
Making of Indian History

Histories of the freedom struggle were to instill in Indians a sense of
pride in those of their countrymen and women who had devoted their
lives to the attainment of freedom and make them aware of the unique
nature of the struggle under the leadership of Gandhi and his associates. However, the pressing task of presenting a comprehensive account of Indian civilization, from remote antiquity to the end of British
rule, remained. Until the early part of the 20th century, Mill's eight-
volume *History of British India,* which Macaulay had described as the
"greatest historical work which has appeared in our language since that
of Gibbon," had retained its paramount importance as a textbook in
Indian universities and as a tool for training civil servants.[34] The
consensus of nationalist historians was that the work of other British
historians was only slightly less offensive to the sentiments of Indians, being just as rooted in palpable falsehoods. If Mill was animated by anti-Hindu feeling, other histories were inclined to view
Muslims as, in the words of John Malcolm, the "scourge of the
human race."[35]

To a very considerable extent, the energies of the two generations of
Indian historians before 1950 were expended either on merely combat-
ing the British view of India or on staking various political positions.
Thus, for example, the supposition that India before the advent of
British rule was altogether lacking in democratic institutions, or that
Hindu polity was irredeemably despotic, was keenly contested. The
early nationalist historian K.P. Jayaswal (1881–1937), in his *Hindu
Polity* (1924), advanced the view that "democratic and republican

34. Cited by G.P. Gooch, *History and Historians of the Nineteenth Century* (1913),
306. The importance of Mill's history is underscored by Ronald Inden, *Imagining India*
(Oxford: Basil Blackwell, 1990), 45–46.

35. Cited by R.C. Majumdar, *Historiography in Modern India* (London: Asia Publishing
House, 1970), 15. Sir John Malcolm rose to high office in India, becoming the governor of
Bombay. He is one of the four early administrators described as having a "romantic" view
of India: see Eric Stokes, *The English Utilitarians and India* (Oxford: Clarendon Press,
1959).

states were experiments of the Hindus themselves."[36] Many Indian historians were drawn to the study of ancient Indian culture: here, it was supposed, Hindu India was to be witnessed in its pristine glory, and here indubitably the essence of Indian civilization was to be discerned. The lives of Indian emperors began to appear as exemplary in their policy and conduct, and it required little encouragement to depict Ashoka, Chandragupta, and Harsha as paragons of wisdom, patrons of learning, and—most significantly—architects of Indian unity. As Radha Kumud Mookerji (1880–1964), who wrote monographs on all these figures in addition to his more general accounts of *Nationalism in Hindu Culture* (1921) and *Hindu Civilization* (1957), put it in his study of Harsha, that monarch provided "one of the few examples in our ancient annals of a king who by his conquests made himself a king of kings and achieved the political unification of a large part of India as its paramount sovereign."[37] In the lives of these early "nationalists," as they had now become, there was inspiration enough for the present generation of nationalists laboring to achieve and retain the sovereignty of India under Indian hands: this was history most evidently taught by example.

At the dawn of independence, then, although Indian historians appeared to have made considerable strides, particularly in the interpretation of ancient India, the prospect of a comprehensive history of India appeared rather unpromising. Yet it was altogether an intolerable thought that such a project should not be attempted, since it is incumbent upon a nation-state in our times to produce a master narrative that documents the people's triumph over adversity, the nation-state coming into its own, and the fulfillment of destiny. It is through history that a nation proudly occupies its place among the pantheon of nations. In addition, there remained the vexatious problem that no history could be construed as comprehensive or complete until it contested the British interpretation of the history of Islam in India, the logical outcome of which, at least on the nationalist reading, had been India's partition and the creation of Pakistan. As British writers had, following the example of European history itself, parceled the history of India into three periods—ancient, medieval, and modern, which by sleight of hand became transformed, respectively, into Hindu, Muslim, and British (rather than

36. Kashi Prasad Jayaswal, *Hindu Polity: A Constitutional History of India in Hindu Times* (Calcutta: Butterworth, 1924), 1:189, cited by Inden, *Imagining India*, 189.

37. Radha Kumud Mookerji, *Harsha* (1925; 3rd ed., Delhi: Motilal Banarsidass, 1965), 1.

Christian)—it remained to subject "medieval" history to a thorough reinterpretation. Finally, there was also the consideration that, with the publication of the multivolume *Cambridge History of India* (1922–32), whose contributors with few exceptions were British, a nationalist rejoinder to that enterprise, which bore all the marks of authority and imperial fervor that Cambridge histories carry, seemed unavoidable.

At the 1940 annual session of the Indian History Congress, a national association of Indian historians, it was resolved to produce a twelve-volume comprehensive history of India. Yet the enterprise was soon stalled: the first volume was not released until 1957, and another volume made its appearance only in 1970.[38] Meanwhile, the novelist, dramatist, and scholar of Gujarati culture K.M. Munshi had founded the Bharatiya Vidya Bhavan, an educational institution dedicated to the promotion of Indian, and particularly Hindu, spiritual, and cultural history. As Munshi was to write some years later, he had "long felt the inadequacy of our so-called Indian histories" and had dreamed of commissioning an "elaborate history of India."[39] When the wealthy industrialist G.D. Birla promised his financial support, Munshi secured the services of the historian R.C. Majumdar as general editor of the series. By 1951 the first of eleven projected volumes of *The History and Culture of the Indian People* had been released; subsequent volumes, published by the Bhavan itself, appeared in relatively quick succession, and with the publication in 1969 of the ninth volume, the *Struggle for Freedom*, Munshi could declare with satisfaction that his "long-cherished ambition of preparing and publishing a comprehensive history and culture of the Indian people by Indians" had been nearly realized.[40]

As *The History and Culture of the Indian People* remains the most ambitious history of India by Indians ever attempted, it merits some critical attention. Munshi, who was to write a foreword to every volume, defined the political contours of the study at the outset. He noted that generations of Indians "were told about the successive foreign invasions of the country, but little about how we resisted them and less

---

38. K.A. Nilakanta Sastri, ed., *A Comprehensive History of India*, Vol. 2: *The Mauryas and Satavahanas, 325 b.c.–a.d. 300* (Bombay: Orient Longmans, 1957), see "Note on the Volume." Vol. 5, on the Delhi Sultanate, appeared in 1970. Another four volumes have since been published.

39. Foreword to *The Vedic Age*, Vol. 1 of *The History and Culture of the Indian People* (hereafter *HCIP*), ed. R.C. Majumdar, 11 vols. (London: George Allen & Unwin, 1951), 7.

40. Foreword to *Struggle for Freedom*, Vol. 11 of *HCIP*, ed. R.C. Majumdar (Bombay: Bharatiya Vidya Bhavan, 1969), p. vii. Vols. 9 and 10 would appear later.

about our victories." Indeed, Munshi was inclined to the view that the role of alien invasions in the history of India had been greatly exaggerated: the Aryan and Turko-Afghan conquests had, over time, "lost their character of foreign military occupation," and only during the British period was the country "governed essentially by foreigners from a foreign country and in foreign interests." Although the "Hindu social system" had been loudly decried as an execrable remnant of India's past, Munshi pointed to its role in protecting life and culture "in times of difficulty by its conservative strength," and its vitality in enabling "the national culture to adjust its central ideas to new conditions."[41] During the entire period of India's occupation by conquering forces, the "vitality of the race and culture" expressed itself "with unabated vigour in resistance movements, military, political, and cultural."[42] It was a canard to suggest that Indians had been a supine people; equally, if the Hindu social system had served the country well in the past, might it not be supposed that the system would be able to withstand the onslaught upon it by lower-caste Hindus?

It is striking that Munshi took it as axiomatic that national culture is nothing other than Hindu culture. While sharing Munshi's worldview, Majumdar was to delineate yet more sharply the specific tenor of the arguments. One had perforce to "adopt a different scale of values in order to appraise her [India's] culture and civilization," since in India it was not the rise and fall of empires or the development of political ideas and institutions that mattered, but rather "philosophy, religion, art, and letters, [and] the development of social and moral ideas."[43] However, while purporting to critique the Orientalist framework of knowledge, which had made impossible any "authentic" history of India, Majumdar was himself replicating a cardinal feature of the Orientalists' epistemology, namely the distinction between a "materialist West" and "spiritual East." He also agreed with Munshi that the shape and texture of Indian civilization had been set by the ancient Hindus, long before civilization emerged elsewhere in the world, and

---

41. This point is reinforced by Munshi in subsequent volumes: In his foreword to *The Age of Imperial Unity*, Vol. 2 of *HCIP*, Munshi wrote that the *sanatan dharma* (eternal religion) of the Hindus, as represented in the *Manu Smriti* and other law books, "laid down a code of social conduct; while it made society slow-moving, it prevented chaos; while foreigners were after some time absorbed and their ways adopted, it provided a firm foundation to social institutions and ensured the continuity of cultural values" (xxi).

42. Foreword to *The Vedic Age*, Vol. 1 of *HCIP*, 7–12.

43. *HCIP*, 1:38–39, 43.

most certainly before Islam came to disturb the social fabric of Indian life.[44] After the capture of the Delhi Sultanate in 1296 by Allaudin Khilji followed "the darkness of the long night, so far as Hindu civilization is concerned, a darkness which envelops it even now."[45] As Majumdar was to write, in obvious contradiction to the view he had espoused about the *sui generis* nature of Indian history, and in just as obvious emulation of European categories of experience, "the onslaught of Islam, accompanied by a marked decadence of culture and the disappearance of the creative spirit in art and literature, seems to mark A.D. 1000 as the beginning of the Medieval Age."[46] Transposing the equation, common among European scholars, that links the European middle or dark ages with superstition, magic, and religious bigotry to the Indian scene, he arrived at the reading that the medieval or Islamic period represented the dark side of Indian history.

If darkness appeared to Majumdar to envelop Hindu civilization even after independence, it is worthwhile probing how, in the latter volumes, Majumdar represented the quest for freedom from British rule. In his earlier *History of the Freedom Movement in India* (three volumes, 1962–63), he had suggested that Hindus lost their freedom, long before the arrival of the Europeans, when they submitted to Muslim rule; and that although Hindus and Muslims had lived together, they did so as separate nations.[47] Elsewhere he openly decried, as an offense against canons of historical truth, the "distinct and conscious attempt to rewrite the whole chapter of the bigotry and intolerance of the Muslim rulers toward Hindu religion."[48] This, in turn,

---

44. Foreword to *HCIP*, 2:xii.

45. *HCIP*, 1:29.

46. Ibid., 24.

47. Majumdar appears to be a proponent of the two-nation theory, but this should not be construed to imply that he was agreeable to the partition of India. Quite to the contrary, he held to the view that the essential features of Indian civilization were Hindu, and that Muslims would reside in undivided India as a separate race. Throughout, he insisted that Hindus and Muslims had not forged common bonds of culture; as he wrote in one of his lesser-known books, "There is a general impression, deliberately created by the politicians of the early twentieth century, that the close contact between the Hindus and Muslims during the long period of six or seven centuries resulted in such a transformation of both that each lost its individual character and a new culture was formed by the fusion of both, which was neither exclusively Hindu nor purely Muslim. This is not, however, borne out by the actual state of things in India. A fundamental and basic difference between the two communities was apparent even to a casual observer." See his *Glimpses of Bengal in the Nineteenth Century* (Calcutta: Firma K.L. Mukhopadhyay, 1960), 5.

48. Majumdar, *Historiography in Modern India*, 48.

bound Majumdar to the view that the events of 1857–58 could in no manner be construed as a nationalist uprising in which Hindus and Muslims joined forces to evict the British, and the attempt to argue otherwise, from the expedient political motive of creating communal harmony, seemed reprehensible to him.

In the *Struggle for Freedom*, which carries the history of India from the partition of Bengal in 1905 to the attainment of independence, Majumdar was to press these points further. The history of Islam is represented as forming only an incidental and unfortunate part of the history of India.[49] Majumdar insisted on taking the "realistic," rather than "idealistic,"[50] approach to Hindu-Muslim relations, and it is in the application of this criterion that he found Gandhi truly wanting, deficient in political realism. Gandhi's controversial support of the Khilafat movement,[51] Majumdar maintained, was to be explained principally on the "grounds of expediency."[52] He seems, however, to have little understood that Gandhi did not cave in to repeated offers from Muslim leaders that Muslim abnegation from cow slaughter would be the reward for support of the Khilafat movement: rather, his support was given unreservedly in an attempt to endow the Muslim community with political meaning and intent. Majumdar's account of the political negotiations leading to independence and the partition of India ends with the observation that Gandhi and other Hindu leaders allowed themselves to believe that the slogan of "Hindu-Muslim Brotherhood" was a reality, something more than merely an empty vessel that Muslim communalists would exploit to their own ends.[53]

Majumdar was, in effect, predisposed to the view that Gandhi was to be held responsible for India's partition. In the acceptance of his verdict by some other historians associated with the revival of Hinduism, as well as by considerable elements of the middle-class elite who have always disowned Gandhi for his supposed effeminacy and friendliness toward Muslims, lies the most compelling demonstration of the

---

49. See Majumdar, *Struggle for Freedom*, Vol. 11 of *HCIP*, 981–92, 1069–73.

50. Ibid., 792.

51. The Khilafat movement was designed to persuade the British government not to dismember the Ottoman Empire, so that the Ottoman sultan would continue to exercise spiritual and temporal authority as the chief custodian of Islam. See Gail Minault, *The Khilafat Movement: Religious Symbolism and Political Mobilization in India* (New York: Columbia University Press, 1982).

52. Majumdar, *Struggle for Freedom*, Vol. 11 of *HCIP*, 318–9.

53. Ibid., 792.

interface between history and public life in modern India. Whatever the authority that historians wield in other societies may be, in India the views espoused by Majumdar and other like-minded historians have exercised an incalculable influence.

Aryans as Beef Eaters, Mughals as Foreigners: Communalism and Iconic Debates in Indian History

Throughout the 1950s and 1960s, Majumdar was the most prolific of all Indian historians, and certainly among the most influential in India. In his pedestrian attachment to "facts," and warm-hearted embrace of the dictum that the task of the historian is "simply to show how it really was,"[54] Majumdar most came to represent the dominant strand of Indian historiography from 1947 until at least the mid-1970s. Few historians anywhere in the world have been active for as long as six to seven decades, as Majumdar was. Yet his readings of Indian history have little to commend for themselves, and not only because they are characterized by virulent anti-Muslim sentiment. Although he was critical of the British historiography of India and was a fervent nationalist in his own right, Majumdar never disguised his admiration for the British for having ushered India, as he thought, into the era of modernity. It is for this reason also that Gandhi, who appeared to be repudiating all the achievements of the "Bengal Renaissance" with his critique of science and modernity, was unpalatable to him. As Majumdar's works continued to be used (until at least the early 1980s) widely in schools and colleges as textbooks, it can reasonably be surmised that his insistence on India's essential "Hinduness" and on the desirability of embracing a "rational," "scientific," and "modern" outlook greatly appealed to those Indians who were eager to see India's emergence as a strong nation-state molded in the image of the Christian powers of the West.

With Nehru's death in 1964 came the first signs of the diminishing appeal of the nationalist consensus. By the early 1970s, the focus of contemporary Indian historians was beginning to shift from obsessive

---

54. The aphorism is associated with the German historian Leopold von Ranke. For an interesting discussion, see Peter Novick, *That Noble Dream: The "Objectivity Question" and the American Historical Profession* (Cambridge: Cambridge University Press, 1988), esp. 26–31.

concern with the "freedom struggle" to a wider array of questions in political, cultural, and social history. The 1971 war with Pakistan brought to the fore questions of ethnicity, language, and nation formation, just as the Pakistani army's massacre of Bengali intellectuals brought an awareness of the precariousness of intellectual life in South Asia. The unrest of the mid-1970s, which led to the declaration of an internal emergency in India in 1975, the arrest of thousands of political figures, and the regime of censorship (some of it self-imposed), politicized many teachers and researchers, many of whom had hitherto been content to practice what they considered to be "objective" scholarship. The previously virtually unchallenged supremacy of the Congress Party had been seriously fractured, but the ascendancy of numerous other parties, including what was then the Jana Sangh, which championed the interests of Hindus, was to introduce new factors into Indian politics. The state's commitment to secularism no longer seemed so secure. India's special relationship, as it was imagined, with the Soviet Union had no doubt served to strengthen ties to Marxist scholars in the Soviet bloc, and a very considerable strand of "Left scholarship" would continue to leave its imprint upon the study of Indian history. The establishment of Jawaharlal Nehru University (JNU), an institution where the majority of the faculty was reputed to have a pronounced inclination to the Left, certainly gave Marxist historians a boost, and it is from JNU that nationalist and communalist historians alike have since received some of the most concerted resistance.

At the same time, communalism was to assume a heightened importance in historical scholarship and public discourse alike. The communal narrative depicts India as comprised essentially of religious communities that, however attenuated the hostilities may be at any one time, have always been at war with each other. As one British official had earlier put it in his book, *Dawn in India*, "the animosities of centuries are always smouldering beneath the surface."[55] Communalist historians adhere to the view that Muslims and Hindus in India have lived largely separate existences; on the other hand, those historians who subscribe to the view that India has always had a largely syncretistic past emphasize the customs in common between Hindus and Muslims, the various forms of composite culture—from cuisine and everyday practices to architecture and music—that emerged from their

---

55. Francis Younghusband, *Dawn in India* (London: 1930), 144.

proximity to each other, and even the forms of religious worship
shared by them, such as the devotion offered at the *dargahs* (tombs) of
Sufi *pirs* (religious teachers).

In Indian history, the syncretistic and communalist viewpoints have
been represented in numerous iconic debates, many revolving around
important historical figures. Communalist historians, insisting on the
bigotry and fanaticism of India's Islamic rulers, point accusingly to the
Mughal emperor Aurangzeb (reigned 1658–1707), who is said to have
destroyed Hindu temples, imposed a poll tax on Hindus, and attempted
to establish forcibly an Islamic state in India. Aurangzeb's defenders
note, on the other hand, that he conferred land grants (*jagirs*) upon
Hindu temples, and that more Hindus rose to levels of eminence under
him than during the reigns of his predecessors. The syncretists and
secularists adduce, moreover, the example of Akbar (reigned 1556–
1605), who is conventionally described as having had not merely toler-
ant but ecumenical religious policies (at a time when Europe had
scarcely any enlightened rulers), and who—despite being Muslim—
promoted Hindu learning just as he undermined the authority of the
ulama (Muslim clergy).[56] Similarly opposed views have been entertained about the Maratha leader Shivaji (1627–80). Nineteenth-century
Indian nationalists in search of martial heroes raised him to the eminence of a freedom fighter, and in the writings of his Hindu supporters,
he appears as the savior of Hindus, a staunch and brave antagonist of
Aurangzeb, even the architect of Indian unity.[57] But this view presup-
poses, as secular-minded historians argue, that Hindus were oppressed
by the tyranny of Muslim rulers, and they object to attempts to com-
munalize the past, that is, to transplant into a past where notions of
"Hindu" and "Muslim" were fuzzy in the modern notions of a supposed Hindu-Muslim enmity.[58]

---

56. For some views of Akbar and Aurangzeb, see Tara Chand, *History of the Freedom
Movement*, 1:111–12; Nehru, *The Discovery of India*, pp. 265–71; Satish Chandra, "Reas-
sessing Aurangzeb," *Seminar*, no. 364: *Mythifying History* (December 1989), 35–38; M.
Athar Ali, *The Mughal Nobility Under Aurangzeb* (Bombay: Asia Publishing House, 1968),
30–32; B.N. Pandey's comments in *Parliamentary Debates, Rajya Sabha*, Vol. 102 (July 29,
1977), col. 127; and Sita Ram Goel, "Some historical questions," *Indian Express* (April 16,
1989), 8.

57. Cited by J.C. Srivastava, "Lala Lajpatrai's Urdu Biography of Shivaji," 72–4.

58. For Hindu nationalist and communalist interpretations of Shivaji, see B.K. Apte,
ed., *Chhatrapati Shivaji: Coronation Tercentenary Commemoration Volume* (Bombay:
University of Bombay, 1974–75), introduction, vii–viii; R.C. Majumdar, "Shivaji's Relevance to Modern Times," in Kulkarnee, *Chhatrapati Shivaji*, 2–3; Jadunath Sarkar, *Shivaji*

That these debates on history are by no means academic can be gauged by any number of circumstances. With the creation in 1960 of the new state of Maharashtra, carved out of the old Bombay presidency, Shivaji became canonized as the creator of the "Marathi nation"; and when a Marathi historian at Marathwada University sought in 1974 to dispute the hagiographic view of Shivaji, he was summarily dismissed from his position.[59] More significant, just as under colonial rule Shivaji's name and courage were invoked by the nationalist Bal Gangadhar Tilak (1856–1920) to rouse Indians to resistance against the British, so he now continues to be flaunted by militant Hindus as an exemplary figure of resistance whose name supposedly resonates with fear among Muslims. The psychoanalyst Sudhir Kakar, in his study of the violent culture of communalism, found that among Hindu rioters, men who kill almost with nonchalance, Shivaji is held in the highest esteem: as one man told him, "First, I talk like Gandhiji. Only when talk fails, I use force like Shivaji or Bose."[60] It is no surprise that the effeteness of Gandhi is contrasted with the masculinity of Shivaji, and that Gandhi's assassin and his associates, largely Marathi Brahmins, had almost divinized Shivaji. Sadhvi Rithambra, a leading advocate of militant Hinduism, has publicly warned Muslims that if they do not live peacefully among Hindus, "then the Hindu youth will deal with you as Rana Pratap and Chhatrapati Shivaji dealt with your forefathers."[61] Rana Pratap, a Rajput ruler who offered resistance to Muslim rulers, is now being widely celebrated: the massive Interstate Bus Terminal in Delhi was recently renamed after him. Numerous other historical personages, such as the Muslim ruler Tipu Sultan, have been the subjects of controversial television serials, and in still more unexpected ways the fruits of historical debate and memory are to be seen in the public realm. When a few years ago India developed a surface-to-air

---

and His Times (Calcutta: M.C. Sarkar and Sons, 1919); for an opposed view, see Nehru, *Discovery of India*, 272, and Kulkarnee, *Chhatrapati Shivaji*, introduction.

59. See Vijay Chandra Prasad Chaudhary, *Secularism Versus Communalism: An Anatomy of the National Debate on Five Controversial History Books* (Patna: Navdhara Samiti, 1977), 104.

60. Sudhir Kakar, *The Colours of Violence* (New Delhi: Viking, 1995), 94, 96, 102. Subhas Chandra Bose, whose name is revered in Bengal, led the Indian National Army (INA), an independent armed force that waged war against the British during the later stages of World War II.

61. Quoted in ibid., 205; see also Tapan Basu, et al., *Khaki Shorts and Saffron Flags: A Critique of the Hindu Right* (Delhi: Orient Longman, 1993), esp. 92–102.

missile capable of hitting Pakistani cities, it was named Prithvi, which, although it means "earth," also evokes the name of Prithviraj Chauhan, another Rajput raised to iconic status by Hindu nationalist historians. Now Pakistan, which has just tested its own comparable missile, has given it the name of Ghori, after the Muslim ruler Muhammad Ghori who inflicted a decisive defeat on Prithviraj in A.D. 1192.

One of the terrains on which fiercely competing versions of history are propagated is history textbooks, which in India come under the purview of the National Council for Educational and Research Training (NCERT), an autonomous institution that nonetheless owes its existence to government funding. In 1977, the government proposed to withdraw from circulation several books, including two published by NCERT for use in high schools, Bipan Chandra's *Modern India* (1971) and R.S. Sharma's *Ancient India* (1977). Unlike his fellow Marxist scholars, who were prone to dismiss the "freedom struggle" under the Congress as a bourgeois enterprise, the JNU historian Bipan Chandra submitted that the nationalist movement was critical for the "nation-in-the-making." While embracing Marx's theory of social relations, he found that Marx himself subscribed to a largely colonialist interpretation of India. Chandra objected forcefully, moreover, to the communalist view of Indian history; he saw communalism as a divisive force, which the British did everything to promote, that tunneled the energies of the nationalists into unproductive and ultimately disastrous channels. "To declare Akbar or Aurangzeb a 'foreigner' and [Rana] Pratap or Shivaji a 'national' hero," he wrote in obvious rejection of communalist history, "was to project into past history the communal outlook of 20th century India. This was not only bad history; but was also a blow to national unity."[62] Not surprisingly, Chandra was accused of pandering to Muslim sentiments, overlooking the history of Muslim oppression, and suggesting by his reference to the "communal outlook of 20th century India" that Hindus and Muslims had in the past forged a common culture.

More strenuous still were the objections to the textbook on ancient India by Sharma, a prominent Marxist historian then on the faculty at Delhi University. An anonymous note submitted to the government claimed that "communist" intellectuals had infiltrated "important national building Ministries and allied organisations," and were promoting, with grants to "fellow travellers," their "own way of thinking on

---

62. Bipan Chandra, *Modern India* (New Delhi: NCERT, 1971), 253.

their favourite subjects which presented a completely different view of the image of the country far removed from our traditional and cultural and scientific values." Referring to NCERT's vital role in building up the character of youth through their textbooks, the author(s) of the note expressed concern that "the greatest casualty" of the alien way of thinking represented by Bipan Chandra, R.S. Sharma, Romila Thapar (another prominent JNU historian), and others was "in the highly important subject of history."[63] The attack upon Sharma was stepped up with printed Hindi pamphlets, denunciations of his scholarship by the archaeologist S.P. Gupta, and public meetings convened by Hindu communal organizations such as the Arya Samaj and the Rashtriya Swayamsevak Sangh (RSS), in which calls were issued for banning his book.

Of the numerous objections voiced against Sharma's book, two might be considered briefly for the light they shed on the politics of historical knowledge and the public uses of history in contemporary India. Sharma stated in *Ancient India* that the ancient Aryans were beef eaters; as he was to explain in his defense of the book, "it is because of the prominence of pastoral life that beef-eating prevailed in Vedic times."[64] Sharma had said nothing exceptional and had the weight of much Indological scholarship behind his work; even K.M. Munshi had noted, without a trace of embarrassment, that "in spite of Jainism and Buddhism, fish and meat, not excluding beef, were consumed extensively by the people."[65] Yet Sharma's remarks were construed as conveying his advocacy of nonvegetarianism, and particularly beef eating, and so Sharma was charged with deliberately offending the sentiments of Hindus, among whom the consumption of beef is strictly prohibited. A local Hindu leader demanded the "immediate banning of Prof. R.S. Sharma's *Ancient India*" for his references to beef eating in Vedic India. His supporters, in a foreshadowing of the later debates on Ayodhya, insisted principally that scientific and objective history was not to be sacrificed to political and much less communal ends, and that the objections of Sharma's critics were "completely baseless on historical grounds."[66]

---

63. Cited by Chaudhary, *Secularism Versus Communalism*, 4–5.

64. R.S. Sharma, *In Defence of "Ancient India"* (New Delhi: People's Publishing House, 1978), 20–21.

65. Foreword to *HCIP*, 2:xxiv–xxv.

66. The controversy surrounding Sharma's book is discussed, although with shocking shoddiness, in Chaudhary, *Secularism Versus Communalism*, 47, 67–110, passim; for references to beef eating, see 83, 91, 110.

It was scarcely recognized that the strenuous objections to Sharma's argument quite likely disguised a profound anxiety among communalists about the thin line that divides Hindus from Indian Muslims, for a beef-eating Hindu, by virtue of the transgression that is implied in that act, might be inferred as becoming akin to a Muslim. If a circumcised penis remained one of the few ways to distinguish Hindu and Muslim men during the horrendous killings accompanying the partition, the all-consuming anxiety over beef eating is better understood. Where substantive differences are minimal, and certainly subservient to common cultural practices, symbols are the preeminent way in which differences are exaggerated in order to permit the drawing of boundaries.

Sharma also reasonably maintained, following the almost overwhelming international scholarly consensus on this question, that the Aryans had come to India from outside. He was consequently attacked for supposing that so glorious a civilization as that of Vedic India had emanated from a foreign soil; in recent years, moreover, the argument that there never was any Aryan migration to India has been energetically revived. As one vocal proponent of the India-as-Aryan-homeland thesis asks: If the "invading" Aryans are supposed to have been barbarians, while the Harappans, whom the Aryans in the conventional view are supposed to have displaced, are represented as a people who were literate, then why is it that the Aryans alone bequeathed a great literature to the world?[67] And if the Aryans of India did originate elsewhere, asks the historical novelist Bhagwan S. Gidwani, why is it that the region that was their supposed homeland "itself showed no evidence of such philosophic development or artistic achievement or spiritual heritage" as is commonly associated with ancient India?[68] It is suggested, rather, that the Harappans and the Aryans were one people, and that India furnishes evidence of one continuous civilization from remote antiquity.

The invasion theory is, in any case, something of a red herring, since most historians, while they firmly adhere to the idea that the

---

67. The argument is summed up in Navaratna S. Rajaram, *The Politics of History: Aryan Invasion Theory and the Subversion of Scholarship* (New Delhi: The Voice of India, 1995), 28–29. The same author's *Aryan Invasion of India: The Myth and the Truth* (New Delhi: Voice of India, 1993) offers a briefer account of the Aryan invasion theory and its purported refutation. See also Srikant G. Telageri, *Aryan Invasion Theory and Indian Nationalism* (New Delhi: Voice of India, 1993), and Girilal Jain, *The Hindu Phenomenon* (New Delhi: UBS Publishers' Distributors, 1994), 21–22, 121–28.

68. Bhagwan S. Gidwani, *Return of the Aryans* (Delhi: Penguin Books, 1994), xiii.

Aryans emigrated to India, reject the idea of an invasion. Merely because there were invasions of India by Turks or Afghans, or because
the characteristic pattern of European interaction with much of the rest
of the world has been one of invasion and conquest, is no reason to
assume that the Aryans came into India as plundering or invading
hordes. While those who insist on inverting the Aryan invasion theory
are easily answered,[69] the question that remains is why so much has
been invested in attempting to establish that India is the original Aryan
homeland, and why there should be so much umbrage at the thought
that Aryans were at one point "foreigners" in India.

When one understands that the revival of the India-as-Aryan-homeland theory has occurred at a time of heightened communal tension,
the true subtext of the dispute begins to emerge. For militant Hindus
and their xenophobic supporters among the ranks of historians and
other scholars, the argument that the Muslim in India is a foreigner,
whose loyalty to India is consequently suspect and who did nothing to
contribute to the essential features of Indian civilization, remains decisive in their endeavor to draw the boundaries of an "authentic" Indian
civilization and even to give birth to a Hindu state. Yet there is an
apprehension that the argument cannot be sustained if their own (real
or imagined) ancestors themselves came to India from somewhere else
and displaced the original inhabitants. Any such concession, militant
Hindus believe, renders the meaning of "home" or homeland unacceptably flexible and deflates the possibility of construing Indian civilization as a civilization that is Hindu in its most essential and fundamental
aspects. On the one hand, the two-nation theory that led to the creation
of Pakistan is accorded credence, since the idea of a homeland to
which they must eventually repair is held out before Indian Muslims as
their ultimate destiny (unless they should wish to live by Hindu norms
in a Hindu state); on the other hand, the dream of a united India is
intrinsic to the concept of India as the original Aryan homeland
(*Aryavarta*), and the vivisection of India is attributed to the malicious
designs of India's colonial rulers and the cowardice and effeteness of

---

69. For a devastating critique of Navaratna and his ilk (note 67), see Shereen Ratnagar,
"Revisionism at work: A chauvinistic inversion of the Aryan invasion theory," *Frontline*
(February 9, 1996):74–80. There is, on the whole, more scholarly consensus on the issue
of an Aryan migration to India than on any other subject. Among historians and archaeolo-
gists of India, one could consult the works of H.D. Sankalia, R.S. Sharma, F.R. Allchin,
Suvira Jaiswal, and Romila Thapar, not to mention the work of scores of scholars in
Indo-European studies.

much of the Hindu leadership. It is on the horns of this dilemma that "Hindu history," which is poor history to begin with, irreversibly falters.

Disputes over Monuments:
Historians in the Nation-State

On December 6, 1992, Hindu militants and their supporters reduced to rubble a 16th-century mosque, known as the Babri Masjid, in the venerable town of Ayodhya in central Uttar Pradesh. The Babri Masjid is thought to have been constructed from 1528 to 1559 at the orders of Babur (1483–1530), the founder of the Mughal Empire, although this is far from certain.[70] Militant Hindus claim that a temple was destroyed to make room for the mosque; however reprehensible that may be, the crime is said to have been infinitely compounded by the fact, as they call it, that the temple commemorated the birth of Lord Rama, who is alleged to have been born on that very spot several thousands of years ago. They maintain that Hindus have recognized Ayodhya's sacredness since remote antiquity. While Rama is worshiped as a deity by most of his devotees, to others he is the exemplar of the just and noble king, the hero of the epic *Ramayana*. He is in any case no ordinary deity-king, and the *Ramayana*, the text that narrates his triumph amidst hardship, is in its various regional variants and versions among the most revered of all religious texts. The militants demanded the removal or destruction of the mosque, on the grounds that as it stood as a perpetual reminder to Hindus of their enslavement under Muslim rulers, restitution was consequently due to them. They proposed to install a magnificent new temple to honor Rama, as in this manner the Rama Janmabhoomi (literally, "birthground of Rama") would receive its proper consecration. The latter objective has not so far been achieved.

The Babri Masjid is scarcely the first religious edifice over which Hindus and Muslims have fought, but it certainly furnishes the only example of a place of religious worship that has been willfully destroyed when it was placed under the protection of the government in a country whose constitution proclaims it to be a secular republic. While

---

70. Sushil Srivastava, *The Disputed Mosque: A Historical Inquiry* (New Delhi: Vistaar Publications, 1991), finds it probable that a Buddhist stupa stood at the site of the mosque (pp. 113–124). Arvind Das, "Cut-price Culture: VHP Digs Up Myth, Buries History," *Times of India* (December 11, 1990), 6, takes the same view in a favorable review of the book.

in the course of war or insurgencies the destruction of religious edifices is not unknown, the government was pledged to safeguard the Babri Masjid, yet a large police force stood by while a very large crowd demolished it with axes, shovels, and their bare hands. In the days leading to the events of December 6, people were trucked to Ayodhya from various parts of India: thus the destruction of the mosque bore all the marks of an orchestrated campaign to which the government remained indifferent. In the wake of its destruction, violence erupted in many of India's metropolitan centers with very considerable loss of life. If in these respects the Babri Masjid affair occupies an exceptional place in the annals of independent India, no less extraordinary, as we shall see, is the unusual part played by historians in the public debate surrounding the status of what the Indian government evasively called the "disputed structure."

By way of enlarging the context of claims by Hindu militants, it is imperative to recognize that they describe the Babri Masjid as one of many monuments, not all of them religious edifices, that are allegedly Hindu in origin when their outward appearance and history are often altogether to the contrary. That some mosques were built with the remnants of Hindu temples is, however, amply documented: such use of plunder no doubt signified to some the triumph of the believers over the infidel. But it is just as reasonable to infer that Muslim architects forged with Hindu materials a new style, and even that the use of such material was a testimony to their appreciation of Hindu aesthetics, such as was revealed in patterned pillars or geometrical designs. No less important a consideration is that places of worship, not unlike other monuments and institutions, change ownership when political power passes into other hands. Both Hindus and Muslims worship at the *dargahs* of Sufi *pirs*; yet, when Hindu kings were in power, some *dargahs* would take on signs more characteristic of the Hindu faith, just as they would assume a more Muslim ambiance under Muslim rule. The art historian Michael Meister has suggested also that broad (and loud) claims in Muslim sources about the leveling of temples and the punishment of idolaters "should be read with a sensitivity to the value of verbal virtue,"[71] to which one might add that the rhetorical claims may have been all the more exaggerated to disguise the degree

---

71. Michael W. Meister, "Mystifying Monuments," *Seminar*, no. 364: *Mythifying History* (December 1989), 24–27.

to which Muslim rulers desisted from the destruction and plunder of Hindu temples.

Such sensitivity as Meister asks for was not much on display as historians were brought to the fore to help resolve questions about the history and status of the Babri Masjid. The proponents of the "temple theory" considered it as "an undisputed *historical fact* that at Ramjanmabhumi there was an ancient mandir (temple)" [emphasis added], and "*authentic history books*" [emphasis added], which on closer examination turned out to be accounts by European writers and travelers who were otherwise decried as holding views highly prejudicial to India, were said to have established the destruction of an ancient Rama temple.[72] The first systematic rejoinder came in the form of a pamphlet, entitled "The Political Abuse of History," authored by twenty-five historians at JNU. While recognizing that behind the controversy lay issues of "faith, power and politics," they felt pressed, in view of the fact that "beliefs [laid] claim [to] the legitimacy of history," to demarcate "the limits of belief and historical evidence." The authors rejected the assumption as not warranted by "historical evidence" that "Muslim rulers were invariably and naturally opposed to the sacred places of Hindus." The brunt of the evidence indeed points to the generous patronage of Muslim nawabs, which not only led to the construction of new Hindu temples, but turned also Ayodhya into an important pilgrimage center.[73] On more specific questions of the ancient history of Ayodhya and the architectural features of the Babri Masjid, the JNU historians were to be joined by R.S. Sharma, whom we have encountered previously as the author of *Ancient India,* and other scholars. They argued that the Ayodhya of the *Ramayana,* assuming its historicity to begin with, is not the present-day Ayodhya; that Ayodhya was not particularly associated with the worship of Rama in antiquity; and that Ayodhya, contrary to the claims of the temple advocates, was not an important pilgrimage site for Hindus in the ancient or middle periods. Similarly, on the architectural points, the evidence did not permit any reasonable inference about the

---

72. Both citations are from Sarvepalli Gopal, ed., *Anatomy of a Confrontation: The Babri Masjid–Ram Janmabhumi Issue* (Delhi: Penguin Books, 1991), 138, notes 6–7. In the elucidation of the role played by historians in this affair, I draw heavily upon my earlier published paper, "The Discourse of History and the Crisis at Ayodhya."

73. Sarvepalli Gopal, et al., "The Political Abuse of History," as reprinted in *Social Scientist,* nos. 200–201 (Jan–Feb 1990), 76–81, esp. 76, 80. See also Ashis Nandy, et al., *Creating a Nationality: The Ramjanmabhumi Movement and Fear of the Self* (Delhi: Oxford University Press, 1995), 2–3.

presence, and subsequent destruction, of a temple on that spot. It is more likely, wrote Sharma and his associates, that there was a Buddhist stupa at the disputed spot.[74]

The overwhelming evidence was such as to render the arguments of the temple proponents altogether improbable. Nonetheless, as the dispute spilled over into major newspapers, the communalists and the secularists, as the two camps came to be known in India's urban centers and in the media, continued to marshal evidence in support of their positions. Archaeological evidence acquired increasing importance: the communalists asserted with supreme confidence that archaeological findings offered conclusive evidence of the existence of an 11th-century Rama temple at the site of the mosque; their opponents, the secular scholars, offered the view that their research "totally demolishes the theory of the mosque having been erected on the ruins of a large temple."[75] The only point of agreement among the secularists and communalists appeared to be their readiness to deploy the discourses of history, although the appropriate disclaimers were issued. The secular historians stated, quite rightly, that irrespective of the historical evidence, the proposed destruction of the mosque could never be justified. In their elegant language, "the destruction or conversion of places of worship, if and when they have occurred in the past, were specific to the political culture of those times," and they rejected attempts to re-create that political culture.[76] The extreme dedication of the communalists to their cause, on the other hand, suggested that they would be prepared to proceed toward the fulfillment of their designs, whatever the weight of the historical evidence. "To take first things first," one of them wrote, "the question whether Lord Ram was born at this spot, or was born at all, is irrelevant. Items of religious belief are essentially matters of faith and not of history, in Hinduism as much as in other religions of the world."[77]

---

74. I have drawn upon: Gopal, "The Political Abuse of History"; R.S. Sharma, M. Athar Ali, D.N. Jha, and Suraj Bhan, *Ramjanmabhumi–Baburi Masjid: A Historians' Report to the Nation* (New Delhi: People's Publishing House, 1991); and R.S. Sharma, *Communal History and Rama's Ayodhya* (New Delhi: People's Publishing House, 1990).

75. S.P. Gupta, "Ram Janmabhoomi–Babri Masjid: Archaeological Evidence," *Indian Express* (December 2, 1990), 3, and introduction by Shereen Ratnagar to D. Mandal, *Ayodhya: Archaeology after Demolition* (New Delhi: Orient Longman, 1993), 3.

76. S. Gopal, et al., "In the Name of History," *Indian Express*, Magazine section (April 1, 1990), 4.

77. Abhas Kumar Chatterjee, "Ram Janmabhoomi: More Evidence," *Indian Express* (March 26, 1990), 8.

Nonetheless, it is remarkable how, putting aside their religious beliefs, the communalists—and not merely communal historians—conducted their campaign predominantly in the language of history. The memorandum on the Babri Masjid–Rama Janmabhoomi issue presented by the Vishwa Hindu Parishad (VHP), an organization created to do the work of Hindu cultural nationalism in India and abroad, to the government of India on October 6, 1989, set aside questions of religious belief and referred to the "historical evidence" in support of its claim. No less remarkable is the fact that secular historians could issue a "Report to the Nation" as though they had a mandate to do so from the people. Never before had the services of professional historians and archaeologists been recruited in this manner; never before were they placed so directly under the gaze of the nation.

On December 6, 1992, the Babri Masjid came crumbling down. The historians had arrived on the proscenium of the nation-state, but sanity had departed from the belly of an ancient civilization. One is tempted to snatch those memorable words from Auden's testimony to Yeats, "Poetry makes nothing happen," and say, "History makes nothing happen." The battle had moved on to turf other than that occupied by the historian: perhaps history makes everything happen.

Babri Masjid: The Ruin(s) of History

As violence engulfed some of India's urban centers after the destruction of the mosque, India's historians and intellectuals began to ponder the nature of Hindu-Muslim relations, the soundness of the political arrangements, and the future of the country. They deplored the fact that "myth," which is how they understood communalist history, had triumphed over (real) history; in the clichéd phrase, history was the greatest casualty. The other notable lament was about the passing of an age, the end of Nehruvian secularism. This was no mere affectation, as many Indians had been strongly committed to the principles of secularism. The ideals for which Gandhi and the "freedom fighters" stood had been betrayed, and even the Communists, who since the 1930s had derived immeasurable pleasure from deriding Gandhi as a bourgeois leader who placed too excessive a reliance upon Hindu religious idioms, suddenly found in the Mahatma the model of sanity, toleration, and religious ecumenism. In comparison with the Hinduism of VHP and RSS stalwarts, the Hinduism of Gandhi now seemed positively healthy and inspiring, a mild affair of the soul and a balm for the wounded.[78]

Yet there was almost no reflection on how it transpired that historians had become involved in the dispute, what their proposed solutions portended for the future of India, and what it meant for them to accept the call to offer testimony. Almost the sole voice of dissent from among the secular historians, and perhaps all the more poignant considering its source, was that of Majid Siddiqi, a Muslim intellectual at JNU who did not append his name to the document titled "The Political Abuse of History" released by his colleagues. Siddiqi asserted that it was not for historians to prove or disprove various claims made in the public realm: had they to enter the debate, they should have done so after "discard[ing] their personae as historians." As he advised his colleagues, historians "must exhibit intellectual self-confidence in their discipline and determine their own agenda in terms of their own questions and not allow the existence of communalism in this society . . . to force its agenda upon them."[79]

As one sifts through the writings of secular historians and intellectuals on the Babri Masjid affair, four considerations present themselves in trying to understand the uses and politics of history in India in recent years. First, their proposed solution to the problem had little to commend itself to the attention of Indians, having in it more than a faint touch of the otiose and the comic, before the destruction of the mosque altogether foreclosed the options. As the status of the mosque was "disputed," they proposed it be handed over to the Archaeological Survey of India (ASI) on the supposition that it would thereafter be in safe and neutral hands. Yet it is these very secularists who point to the indifference of Indians to their architectural and cultural heritage, the neglect of monuments, and even the ASI's poor handling and management of the monuments under its care.[80] The Babri Masjid would most likely have gone to seed under the ASI.

But the most objectionable aspect of the proposal is the manner in which it makes itself obeisant to the deadweight of colonial thinking

---

78. See, for example, A.B. Bardhan, *Sangh Parivar's Hindutva Versus the Real Hindu Ethos* (New Delhi: Communist Party of India, 1992), esp. 5–7.

79. Majid H. Siddiqi, "Ramjanmabhoomi–Babri Masjid Dispute: The Question of History," *Economic and Political Weekly* 25, no. 2 (January 13, 1990), 97–98.

80. See, for example, Arvind Das, "When History Causes Ennui," *Times of India* (July 11, 1993), 17.

and notions, widely prevalent in the Western world, of museumized cultures. Since religious worship has no attraction for secular intellectuals, it is of little consequence to them that religious edifices placed under the ASI's care generally are no longer used for worship; yet both Hindus and Muslims have at various times offered prayers at the Babri Masjid. Moreover, there are some who would like to see India develop, in the manner of the developed nations, a "heritage industry," which would no doubt be a source of employment for historians and "culture management specialists." But India, to our good fortune, is still far from reaching that stage in which its culture will be reduced to giant amusement parks, historic homes, national monuments, museums, and other sanitized and bracketed spaces. By turning over "disputed structures" to the ASI, we commit the much greater folly of substituting, for modes of cultural negotiation and social practices of pluralism, the authority of impersonal and transcendent institutions presumed to embody neutrality.

Second, secular historians sometimes seem to rely a little too excessively on the quid pro quo form of argument, and not only with reference to the Babri Masjid affair. They have often asserted that if Muslims are to be charged with destroying Hindu temples and idols, it should not be forgotten that both Jains and Buddhists were the victims of Hindu bigotry, and that Hindu temples were at times built with the remains of Buddhist stupas. "The large scale persecution of Buddhists by followers of Sankaracharya," one historian has written, has passed into "convenient oblivion," while the authors of a pamphlet (called "Black Sunday") published after the destruction of the Babri Masjid state that "destruction of places of worship was not done exclusively by Muslim rulers."[81] Insofar as it is true that no one culture or people has a monopoly on goodness, and that barbarism as well recognizes no cultural or religious boundaries, their argument can scarcely be faulted; and it is certainly just as reasonable to suggest that the destruction of religious edifices and places of worship was an activity in which the ruling classes engaged as an aspect of their quest for political power. Nonetheless, the attempt to establish equivalencies of evil has little ethical value, and a great deal more thought must be given to the

---

81. Ratnabali Chatterjee, "The Rulers and the Ruled in Medieval India and VHP's Myth," in *The Nation, the State and Indian Identity*, eds. Madhusree Dutta, Flavia Agnes, and Neera Adarkar (Delhi: Samya, 1996), p. 33; "Black Sunday," issue of *Manas* (Delhi: Sampradayikta Virodhi Andolan, 1992), 2.

political consequences and sociocultural effects of this mode of historicization. There is, in this form of argument, even a remarkable and uneasy similarity to the apologetics often encountered on behalf of Western imperialism, where the presumption is that Western powers did nothing to the people they conquered that they, the indigenes, had not previously done to themselves or others.

Third, secular historians, and indeed historians of every hue, must unravel the meaning of their relationship, and commitment, to modernity. The authors of "Black Sunday," the pamphlet released within days of the destruction of the mosque by the Movement Against Communalism, recognize that "the destruction of places in medieval and ancient times" was "an integral part of political power," and that, consequently, the destruction of such edifices should not invariably be construed as a sign of religious conflict.

Yet a great deal more is implicated in their analysis, for as they go on to say, the attack on the Babri Masjid "is reminiscent of the barbaric politics of ancient and medieval rulers that defies all modern, democratic, and civilised institutions of our society." The historian Neeladri Bhattacharya of JNU, in like fashion, has given it as his considered opinion that it was "medieval logic" that was "at work behind the struggle for the Ramjanmabhumi."[82] Considering that in Indian history the "medieval" period is itself taken to be congruent, however absurdly, with Islam, the argument has the wholly unintended effect of suggesting that in their present-day barbaric conduct, the Hindus are following the example set by Muslims. The equation of the medieval with the barbaric betokens an extraordinary faith in conventional narratives of the progress of history, while it ignores the remarkable plurality of premodern India. It is the "modern" Hinduism of Hindu militants that has insisted on homogenizing the faith, divesting it of the diverse, and often contradictory, strands of worship, conduct, belief, and thought. Although Indians in the "medieval" period were able to live comfortably with multiple versions of the *Ramayana*, the modern advocates of the temple theory decry this plurality. The Babri Masjid stood for nearly 500 years, through all the turmoil and "barbarism" of premodern India, until it fell on account of the enthusiasm of the modern advocates of Hinduism, the same zealots who are fixated on

---

82. "Black Sunday," 2; Neeladri Bhattacharya, "Myth, History and the Politics of Ramjanmabhumi," in Gopal, *Anatomy of a Confrontation*, 129.

historical evidence and on the desirability of establishing the historicity of Rama, Krishna, and other Indian deities and mythological figures. The premodern world, one gets the striking impression, may have been more modern than our own, although Indian historians are a long way from arriving at this recognition.

Fourth, secular historians are not only indisposed toward what they call myth, but appear to be wholly incapacitated in their ability to negotiate with discursive forms that are hostile, opposed, indifferent, or merely complementary to history. They have argued that the communalist writers engage in the "mythification of history," since the entire edifice of their argument appears to be constructed on myth. Thus various myths, such as "the myth of ancient Ayodhya, the myth of its loss and recovery, the myth of the destruction of the temple and the construction of the mosque," are sought by the communalists to be converted or transformed into history. In this reading, myths are false, distorted, or bad history; myths and history are in any case analytically separate. Myths are statements that "have no support in any historical evidence," but that is a scarcely helpful formulation, considering that the historical evidence is itself held to be in dispute. Another writer says of the VHP that it "digs up myth, buries history"; elsewhere, he rues that "the method Indians appear to have found to deal with their past is to mythologise it. Fact is at a discount. . . . Thus, while myths move millions, the actual and complex historical reality is ignored." The problem, to follow this logic, is not of the VHP alone: millions of Indians betray the same inability to confront the "complex historical reality" as do members of the VHP, so they too must harbor similarly communalist and fascist tendencies.[83] If we had better history, the people would not be led astray by myths; and so the historians must constitute the vanguard that will deliver us from the communal malaise. It is with this thought that Sharma concludes his brief study of the Babri Masjid dispute: "Only patient and sustained efforts of right thinking writers, researchers and educators can foil the communalist attempt to use the past as a wedge to divide the people into warring camps."[84]

Myth, in these formulations, is everything that history is not: as history is (or ought to be) fact, myth is not-fact. If this is the im-

---

83. Bhattacharya, "Myth, History and the Politics of Ramjanmabhumi," 132–37; "Black Sunday"; and Arvind Das, "Cut-price Culture."

84. Sharma, *Communal History and Rama's Ayodhya,* 32.

poverished reading of myth to which secular historians and intellectu-als hold, can their reading of history be substantially better? While secular historians view the debacle at Ayodhya as arising partly from attempts at the "mythification of history," we should perhaps wonder if it is not the historicization of myths that has contributed to the increas-ing communalization of Indian politics, the emphasis on the nation's Aryan "heritage," and the rise of aggressive nationalism. Although the story of the *Ramayana* has been circulating in India for at least two millennia and no one bothered much with the attempt to turn Rama into a real-life historical personage, in recent years some Hindus have felt that their lives as Hindus could not be fulfilled until they were able to demonstrate the historicity of Rama. These are the Hindus who feel that a date must be assigned to Rama. They would like to push the origins of Indian (by which they mean Hindu) civilization to at least as far back as 10,000 B.C. and they have engaged in a search for the precise dates of the war described in the *Mahabharata*.[85] They have now promised, in their language, to "liberate" the *Janmasthan,* or birthplace of Krishna, in Mathura, which is also, they maintain, now occupied by a mosque. Their liberation of Krishna is not unlike the liberation that Bankim desired, who sought to free the historical Krishna from the shackles of the mythical Krishna and so inaugurated the modern phase of Indian nationalism.

History in the Nation-State, Myth in the Civilization

As the most far-reaching critique of the contours of Indian nationalism was to emanate from Gandhi, who is also the initiator of the critique of modernity, it behooves us to consider that no one embodied more the ahistoricity of Indian civilization than Gandhi. In his first and most seminal tract, *Hind Swaraj or Indian Home Rule* (1909), a quasi-Socratic and quasi-Upanishadic exploration of the epistemological evils of modern civilization and the fatal attraction of Indian national-ists to such a civilization, Gandhi sought also to defend the practice of nonviolent resistance. When asked by the imaginary reader whether

---

85. For a perceptive analysis of neo-Hindu history, see Gyanendra Pandey, "Modes of History Writing: New Hindu History of Ayodhya," *Economic and Political Weekly* 29, no. 25 (June 18, 1994), 1523–28; see also Shriram Sathe, *Search for the Year of Bharata War* (Hyderabad: Navabharati Publications, 1983).

there was "any historical evidence as to the [previous] success of . . . soul-force or truth-force," Gandhi replied that insofar as history meant (as it mainly did then) the "doings of kings and emperors," then "no evidence of soul-force or passive resistance was [to be found] in such history." Gandhi certainly was not going to allow the verdict of history to deter him from his chosen path, as he had little use for clichés about the "lessons of history"; and as he matured, his indifference to historical discourses became more pronounced. If Bankim was certain that the *Mahabharata* had a historical core and that Krishna was a real, historical figure, Gandhi was just as certain that no such interpretation was required. "The *Mahabharata*," he wrote in 1924, "is not to me a historical record. It is hopeless as a history. But it deals with eternal verities in an allegorical fashion." As he was to add, Gibbon was only an "inferior edition" of the *Mahabharata*. A year later he affirmed, "My Krishna has nothing to do with any historical Krishna."[86] Although the government of India may not have understood Gandhi's philosophical defense of ahistoricity, apparently they put up numerous banners around railway stations in the centenary year of his birth. One of these banners attributed a saying to Gandhi, "I am not interested in history, I am interested only in getting things done."

It is quite apposite, then, that the most radical and perceptive analysis of the meaning of what transpired at Ayodhya has come from Gandhi's grandson, Ramachandra Gandhi, who has similarly gone far beyond the parameters of historical discourse. He has been less interested in assigning culpability than many others, and he has sought to understand the meaning of Ayodhya in Indian categories. Ramachandra Gandhi has been the first observer to take serious notice of a building, known as Sita-ki-Rasoi or Sita's Kitchen, adjoining what used to be the mosque and standing within the complex. Although India's honor is as important to him as it is to any secular historian, he experienced no moral anguish in recognizing, when he first visited the mosque, that "sacred components of a Hindu temple (or a cognate Buddhist or Jaina shrine) had been used in the construction of the

86. M.K. Gandhi, *Hind Swaraj or Indian Home Rule* (reprint ed., Ahmedabad: Navajivan Publishing House, 1962), 77; idem, "My Jail Experiences—XI," *Young India* (September 4 and 11, 1924), reprinted in Raghavan Iyer, ed., *The Moral and Political Writings of Mahatma Gandhi*, Vol. 1: *Civilization, Politics and Religion* (Oxford: Clarendon Press, 1986), 183, 187; and idem, "Sikhism," *Young India* (October 1, 1925), reprinted in Iyer, ibid., 1:484–85.

mosque in the sixteenth century." Turning his attention to Sita-ki-Rasoi, he ponders its proximity to the Babri Masjid, its origins, and the manner in which it acquired its name. From this musing, Ramachandra Gandhi goes on to spin a radical account of the architectural complex's association with Buddhism, and Sita-ki-Rasoi is itself described as a grove of "aboriginal spirituality" and "sacred fertility" from which Sita fed Rama and his kin and from which, after her severance from Rama, she descended into the bowels of the earth. How is it that the Babri Masjid and Sita-ki-Rasoi stood together, cheek by jowl, for several centuries, and is their severance not like the separation of Rama and Sita, a violent ecological disruption of the order of the world? Is a Hindu or a Muslim complete any longer without the other?[87]

Unless we can entertain some radical skepticism toward the discourses of history, there will surely be other Ayodhyas. The Hindu militants have already identified 2,000 religious edifices that are described as being held in captivity under Muslim jurisdiction, and the terrains of dispute are still more numerous.

The VHP and its friends have designated themselves, for example, as the true inheritors of the legacy of Swami Vivekananda, who came to the United States to represent India and Hinduism at the World Parliament of Religions at Chicago in 1893 and made a profound spiritual impression upon Americans. The government of Rajiv Gandhi, in particular, put Vivekananda before the youth of India as an example of a nationalist devoted to the revival of India who was at the same time an internationalist and a spiritual leader. It is in Vivekananda's life, to follow his hagiographers, that we can witness the mode in which the spiritual and the material, reason and faith, works and devotion all judiciously coexist. Vivekananda had spoken of organizing Hindus, just as he sought to rejuvenate the faith and reinterpret it for the modern age; yet there is nothing in his writings that sustains the view the VHP has promulgated of Vivekananda as a zealous and xenophobic crusader for the faith. Indeed, as Ramachandra Gandhi reminds us, one of the most poignant incidents in Vivekananda's life points to his recognition of the necessity for utter humility in matters of religious faith and the imperative to abjure from violence in every respect. On a trip to Kashmir toward the end of his

---

87. Ramachandra Gandhi, *Sita's Kitchen: A Testimony of Faith and Inquiry* (New Delhi: Penguin Books, 1992), 14–15, 110, passim.

life, Vivekananda felt pained at seeing the ruins of temples and the broken idols of Hinduism's myriad gods and goddesses. Bowing down before the image of the Divine Mother, he asked in anguish, "How could you let this happen, Mother, why did you permit this desecration?" Vivekananda reports that Kali whispered to him, "What is it to you, Vivekananda, if the invader breaks my images. Do you protect me, or do I protect you?"[88]

All contestations in Indian history do not posit Hindus against Muslims, nor is religion the decisive factor in the debates being shaped around Indian history today. It is possible, even, that historical debates about Indian nationhood, partition, and secularism have been shaped by geopolitical considerations as well. Although Indian historians are rightly described as being animated by Nehru's legacy in desiring to keep India secular, it is also pertinent that the one state that was secular in the Middle East, namely Iraq, has been reduced, in the words of one official United Nations report, to preindustrial status. There appears to be every reason to believe, then, that the West would almost not like to see a secular state elsewhere in the world: the East, and particularly a preeminently "religious" country like India, must encourage the self-fulfilling prophecy that secularism will always remain a foreign import.

This may be one reason that Indian historians and scholars are so vociferous in their opposition to communalist interpretations of Indian society: secularism must succeed, if for no other reason than to repudiate commonly held Western views of Indian history. With respect to the thesis that India constitutes the original homeland of the Aryans, it is worthwhile to reflect that, before India's partition in 1947, very few historians subscribed to such a theory. If the idea of the Muslim as foreigner constitutes the true subtext of this theory, then perhaps communalist-minded Indian historians have also been moved to embrace this theory by their recognition of the appalling treatment of minorities in neighboring Pakistan. Whatever the position of Muslims in India may be, Hindus in Pakistan fared much worse, and few remained to offer testimony. Here, too, lies the backdrop, perhaps, to recent attempts to Aryanize Indian history and find execrable "foreigners." Similarly, although Indian historians are perfectly prepared to debate

---

88. Cited in ibid., p. 10; see also Rajni Bakshi, *The Dispute over Swami Vivekananda's Legacy: A Warning and an Opportunity* (Mapusa, Goa: The Other India Press, 1994), although this work is inadequate.

the legacy of partition and the two-nation theory, or to attribute responsibility to one or more parties or individuals, they are increasingly
cognizant of the fact that partition as a strategy of governance has
rarely succeeded anywhere in the world. The problems of Korea,
Northern Ireland, and Israel appear to be quite intractable at present.
That the partition of India cannot, and ought not, to be viewed only
through the lens of religious violence, or via such predictable categories as "responsibility," has become increasingly clear through the
writings of feminist historians, who have alerted us to the common
fate of women—whether Muslim, Hindu, or Sikh—who were abducted and raped.[89]

Tamil antibrahminical histories have a long trajectory, and they, too,
resist the Aryanization of Indian history in their own way, although
here as well, the impulse toward "manifest destiny" has sometimes
been irresistible. How else can one explain the tendency in some
Dravidian histories to insist that the Lanka of the *Ramayana* is modern
Sri Lanka, when the work of many reliable scholars suggests otherwise? *Dalit* histories, which furnish what is conceivably the most radical departure from Indian histories of any political persuasion, are
slowly coming into their own, but the predominant voices in that literature have been those of poets, polemicists, and pamphleteers. Since
history is preeminently the discipline of nation building, an enterprise
from which *dalits* have until very recently been all but excluded, *dalit*
histories will perforce have to be antihistories.[90] Similarly, histories
(and not only in the multicultural mode of consumption) will emerge
from secessionist and insurrectionary movements in Kashmir, Punjab,
Assam, Nagaland, and elsewhere. These developments, and numerous
others, might perhaps help move Indian history away from the Bengali,
Hindu, and modernist strands in which it has been trapped. It is the
congruence of these strands that shaped the minds of Jadunath Sarkar
and his admirer R.C. Majumdar, who between them wrote for 100
years, and of the legion of historians who flourished under their tute-
lage. One shudders to think what the Assamese, for example, must
think of this history, when we consider the dedication that appears in

---

89. See, for example, Ritu Menon and Kamla Bhasin, *Borders and Boundaries: Women in India's Partition* (New Delhi: Kali for Women, 1998).

90. On the *Dalit* interpretation of Indian history, see Gail Omvedt, *Dalit Visions: The Anti-Caste Movement and the Construction of an Indian Identity* (Delhi: Orient Longman, 1995).

one of Majumdar's smaller books on Bengal: "To the Memory of
BENGAL THAT WAS by One who Has the Misfortune to Live in
BENGAL THAT IS While the CROAKING AHOM FROGS Kicked
with Impunity the DYING BENGAL ELEPHANT And the PEOPLE
AND GOVERNMENT OF INDIA Merely Looked On."[91]

The attempt here has not been to enumerate the most significant
developments in the writing of Indian history in the last decade or so,
since one would then perforce have to turn to those areas where some
of the more insightful work has been done, such as women's history
and subaltern history. Rather, the endeavor has been to trace, through
selected chapters and iconic debates, the trajectory of the politics of
history from shortly before the end of colonial rule until the debacle at
Ayodhya, to describe the myriad ways in which history has entered
and informed public debates, and to engage in some further considerations as we contemplate the future of history and knowledge in the
nation-state.[92] While one may be epistemologically indisposed toward
discourses of history, as the spiritual forefathers of Indian civilization
appear to have been, they cannot be disavowed in the late twentieth
century without surrendering what is now unquestionably one of the
tools of citizenship. However, that the destruction of the Babri Masjid
was at all possible, despite overwhelming "evidence" suggesting that
the mosque did not take the place of a temple that was claimed to have
stood on the same spot, points to the fact that historical discourses
largely do not address the world that Indians inhabit. The secular historians remained oblivious to the considerations that many Indians were
not prepared to have the dispute resolved by recourse to some notion
of historical truth, and that the invocation of historical veracity has not
much resonance among a people who have imbibed from the
Mahabharata the notion that *dharma* (right conduct, law, justice) is a
elastic concept.

History is only one way of accessing the past, and in India it is still a
novel way of doing so, since Indians are still more at ease in accessing
the past through nonhistorical modes such as folktales, customary

---

91. R.C. Majumdar, *Glimpses of Bengal in the Nineteenth Century* (Calcutta: Firma
K.L. Mukhopadhyay, 1960). Ahom refers to the Assamese. I am grateful to Dipesh
Chakrabarty for this reference.

92. For an elaboration of directions we might choose to pursue, see Vinay Lal, "Discipline and Authority: Some Notes on Future Histories and Epistemologies of India,"
Futures 29, no. 10 (December 1997), 985–1000.

practices, epic literature, proverbs, and myths. Needless to say, whatever inferences historians might draw from the lives of Aurangzeb, Babur, Tipu Sultan, Shivaji, and other like figures, it can scarcely be argued from their histories that people belonging to various social strata felt their lives to be bounded by oppositional religious feelings. If, on the other hand, Akbar propagated a new syncretistic faith, what do we know about its reception by ordinary Muslims? By what method of transference is it possible to construe that conflicts among the ruling elite are conflicts at the broader social level? Consequently, when historians turn to the intellectual history of the Mughal court under Akbar to find examples of syncretism, or to the *bhakti* poets to understand the nature of anticlerical sentiments, they could also engage themselves with folktales and proverbs. Brahmins, *maulvis* (Muslim priests), and *pandits* (Hindu priests) are the brunt of jokes and abuse in Indian folktales, and these are often more revealing of the ground realities than grand historical treatises.[93] Indian historians should not surrender the use of this huge repository of nonhistorical modes to nationalists and communalists. Rather than berating Indians for their neglect of the past, their indifference to historical truth, their invocation of myths and puranic stories, and their contamination of "authentic" histories by the use of "myths," Indian historians must enter into a more fruitful engagement with Indian myths and other nonhistorical modes. On this matter, as in all others, Gandhi surely did not have the last word, but his endorsement of the saying that "a nation is happy that has no history" should be not only discomforting but arresting.

History has now become universally validated as representing a higher form of cognition than myth, indeed than all other modes of apprehending the past,[94] and it even rivals science as the greatest myth of our times. No people can afford to be without a history, unless they are prepared to be designated as primitive, premodern, or noble savages; and yet, to ignore myth, and transpose it to the Other, is to discard that part of our self that is most capable of resisting dominant discourses and enriching our lives. Perhaps we should mythify history.

---

93. For good examples, see *Folktales from India: A Selection of Oral Tales from Twenty-two Languages*, selected and edited by A.K. Ramanujan (New York: Pantheon Books, 1991), 203–4, 273–74, 319–20.

94. These thoughts are inspired by Ashis Nandy, *The Intimate Enemy: Loss and Recovery of Self under Colonialism* (Delhi: Oxford University Press, 1983), and his more recent essay, "History's Forgotten Doubles," *History and Theory* 34, no. 2 (1995), 44–66.

1995–1997: A Chronology

Shefali Trivedi

January 1995

5   Jitendra Prasad replaces N.D. Tiwari as president of the Uttar Pradesh Congress(I) Committee. Tiwari resigns in late December to protest Prime Minister Rao's refusal to withdraw the party's support from the opposition government of Uttar Pradesh. He accuses the Samajwadi Party–BSP alliance under Mulayam Singh Yadav of favoring lower castes at the expense of other minorities.

7   The chief minister of Karnataka, H.D. Deve Gowda, agrees to hold talks about the Cauvery River with Tamil Nadu Chief Minister Jayalalitha Jayaram. It is hoped that these talks will settle the dispute between the two states over sharing Cauvery waters.

14   The central government, under the Unlawful Activities (Prevention) Act, renews the ban on the Vishwa Hindu Parishad (VHP). The VHP has been under this ban since the demolition of the Babri Masjid in 1992. Rao renews the ban after it expired in December.

17   During the coldest weather the state has experienced in fifteen years, heavy snowfall is followed by two days of avalanches and landslides in

Kashmir. Thousands of people are trapped by the snow in a tunnel on the Jammu-Srinagar highway, and at least 100 people are killed.

19   Activity against Beant Singh, the chief minister of Punjab, escalates. Rebels from the Congress Party call for a "Punjab Congress Bachao" ("Save the Punjab Congress") as well as Beant Singh's ouster and replacement by Buta Singh.

24   Congress(I) suspends Arjun Singh from primary membership in the party. He is accused of engaging in antiparty activities that damage the interests and image of Congress. Rao requests that the party's disciplinary panel frame charges against Singh. For several weeks, Singh has been publicly accusing the party leadership of being soft on corruption and of ignoring its Muslim constituency.

Seven members of the Central Reserve Police Force are killed by Naga guerrillas and several villages are set on fire in Manipur.

26   During Republic Day celebrations, several bombs explode in Jammu and Kashmir.

29   Accusing the government of failure and claiming that they wish to serve as an active opposition, the Congress Working Committee withdraws support from Mulayam Singh Yadav. The Samajwadi Party and BSP alliance Yadav heads has been in power for thirteen months.

February 1995

5   A grenade explodes in the Raj Bhavan compound in Manipur. Authorities suspect that it was set off by members of the People's Liberation Army. There are no casualties reported.

7   Arjun Singh is expelled for a period of six years from primary membership in the Congress(I).

8   **The Mulayam Singh Yadav government in Uttar Pradesh retains its majority in the State Assembly, after being forced to demonstrate its majority when the Congress withdraws support in January.**

9   The first phase of polling in the Maharashtra state elections commences, as the Shiva Sena–BJP combine faces off against Sharad Pawar and the Congress(I). The turnout, at over 50 percent, is average. As the Election Commission does not want the results of this election to affect balloting that will take place over the next month in five other states, counting of votes is scheduled to begin on March 11.

12   In Maharashtra, the second phase of polling proceeds, in 139 constituencies. Turnout, at 70 percent, is heavy and peaceful.

14   In Kerala, K. Karunakaran, the chief minister, defeats a vote of no-trust.

16   The first phase of polling in the Manipur elections takes place, with one-third of the sixty constituencies participating. Turnout is reported to be heavy.

17   In Manipur, in a spate of election violence, two leading political candidates—one the head of the Manipur People's Party, and the other the general secretary of the BJP—are killed in separate incidents.

20   In Gujarat, there is a reported 60 percent turnout during the first phase of polling, with the main contest being between the BJP and the Congress(I).

Five days later, in the second and final phase of polling to the Gujarat State Assembly, 65 percent of registered voters cast ballots.

25   The Congress Legislature Party, under Rishang Keishin, forms the new government in Manipur.

March 1995

1   Citing the poor security situation in the state, Chief Election Commissioner T.N. Seshan postpones elections in Bihar. Seshan delays elections that were scheduled for March 5 to March 11 after Maoist guerrillas kill a leading candidate, bringing to fifty the number of people killed in prepoll violence. He announces that elections will not be held until candidates and party workers are in no danger of being killed.

7   Narasimha Rao renews his pledge that both a Ram temple and a Bari mosque will be built in Ayodhya.

     The first phase of Assembly elections in Orissa takes place; the second phase is two days later.

11   Vote counting begins for elections in Orissa, Gujarat, and Maharashtra, as elections in Bihar and Arunachal Pradesh commence.

14   **In Gujarat, the first BJP-led Ministry is inducted into power. Keshubhai Patel will serve as chief minister. In Maharashtra, the BJP–Shiva Sena combine soundly defeats Sharad Pawar and the Congress(I). Manohar Joshi will serve as the new chief minister.**

15   After being delayed for two weeks, the 1995–96 budget is announced. The presentation of the budget, originally scheduled for February 28, is post-

poned when T.N. Seshan decrees that he does not want voters to be influenced by its content.

16 After being given an ultimatum to leave office by members of his party, K. Karunakaran, chief minister of Kerala, resigns. Five days later, A.K. Antony becomes the chief minister.

20 The Shiv Sena–BJP combine proposes to restrict entry of migrants from other states into Bombay. The government's proposal calls for the issuing of entry permits and the denial of ration cards to non-residents of the city.

28 The five-year rule of the Janata Dal government in Bihar ends as President's Rule is imposed on the state. By asking for central rule, Rao reverses an earlier decision to let Laloo Prasad Yadav serve as a caretaker chief minister for the state. However, in light of the need to pass the budget by March 31, Rao imposes President's Rule.

29 As vote counting begins in Bihar, a Congress(I) candidate and four aides are killed by a car bomb while driving to the site where the votes are being tallied.

31 The 1995–96 Export-Import Policy is announced. Provisions include liberalization of consumer goods imports and selected incentives for producing goods within the country.

April 1995

1 The Tamil Nadu governor gives permission for Subramaniam Swamy, the Janata Dal party president, to prosecute Chief Minister Jayalalitha Jayaram on charges of corruption and criminal misconduct. The decision comes seventeen months after a request for such an action was initially made.

2   **The Janata Dal and its allies are reelected in
       Bihar, after winning 172 of the 285 State Assem-
       bly seats. Laloo Prasad Yadav is reelected chief
       minister, and is sworn in two days later.**

3   Iqbal Mohammed Menon, aka Iqbal Mirchi, is ar-
       rested by Interpol in London at the request of the
       Central Bureau of Investigation (CBI). Menon is
       suspected to have partially funded the Bombay ex-
       plosions of March 1993.

7   The BJP–Shiv Sena government begins a campaign
       to root out "illegals" from Bombay. Nine
       Bangladeshis are deported and twenty-nine others
       arrested on the suspicion of being in the country
       illegally. Advocacy and opposition groups protest
       that harassment of Muslims is the primary goal of
       this campaign.

8   A crowd attacks a group of Ahmadiyas for their
       attempts to proselytize in Malegaon, a primarily
       Muslim town in Nashik district in Maharashtra.

12   Rajan Pillai, the business magnate, arrives in Bom-
       bay. He is fleeing an arrest warrant that has been
       issued against him by the Singapore authorities.
       The next day, he states that while he is willing to be
       put on trial in India, he will fight attempts to extra-
       dite him to Singapore.

14   A bomb explodes in the Madras office of the Hindu
       Munnani, a revivalist organization formed by a
       breakaway faction of the RSS. Two people—the
       suspected bomber, and "Bible Shanmugam," a
       Munnani activist—are killed. The explosion sets off
       a week of communal violence in the city.

21   A trial for several members of the LTTE com-
       mences. The LTTE members stand accused of as-

sassinating Sri Lankan Tamil leader Padmanabha, nine LTTE members, and four bystanders in June 1990.

The seventh test of the surface-to-air, medium-range missile Akash is carried out successfully in Orissa.

24   The AIADMK demands that M. Channa Reddy, the state governor, be recalled.

May 1995

1   Meeting in New Delhi, the foreign ministers of SAARC endorse the formation of a South Asian Free Trade Area. The next day, the eighth SAARC summit commences. Prime Minister Narasimha Rao takes over the chairmanship of the organization. Two days later, the summit concludes with the promulgation of a declaration condemning the spread of terrorism on the subcontinent.

4   Manohar Joshi, chief minister of Maharashtra, announces that Bombay will soon be renamed Mumbai.

5   Taking into consideration the desire of the central government to hold general elections in February 1996, the Election Commission cancels the scheduled by-elections to the Lok Sabha. Nine constituencies in seven states are affected by the measure, which is requested of the Election Commission by the Home Minister.

11   **A shrine in the town of Charar-e-Sharif in Jammu and Kashmir is set ablaze. The five-century-old shrine, dedicated to Sheikh Noorudin Noorani, along with the adjoining Khankah mosque, burns completely to the ground. Fifteen**

hundred homes and businesses are also destroyed in the blaze. Authorities claim that Muslim militants fired on troops and set the shrine and mosque on fire. Militants blame the government, accusing the army of starting the blaze when it stormed the shrine in an effort to flush out rebels occupying the building. An indefinite curfew is imposed on the town and the surrounding area.

12   The Supreme Court blocks prosecution of Jayalalitha by granting the temporary injunction against prosecution asked for by Governor Channa Reddy.

14   In the Kashmir valley, angry crowds burn down school and government buildings as well as Hindu temples in retaliation for the destruction of Charar-e-Sharif.

Prime Minister Narasimha Rao declares that he will let the ten-year-old Terrorist and Disruptive Activities (Prevention) Act (TADA) lapse after May 23. However, some provisions in the Act will be incorporated into the National Securities Act.

15   Narasimha Rao informs the Lok Sabha that scheduled elections in Jammu and Kashmir will go forward despite the crisis that has been precipitated by the destruction of the shrine in Charar-e-Sharif.

17   The central government renews its pledge not to sign the Nuclear Non-Proliferation (NPT) Treaty in its current form.

18   In an effort to replace TADA with less controversial legislation, the Union home minister introduces the Criminal Law (Amendment) Bill in the Rajya Sabha.

Finance Minister Manmohan Singh announces several new tax concessions and modifications to the 1995–96 budget.

19   Citing his "antiparty activities," the Congress(I) expels N.D. Tiwari from the party for a period of six years. The action comes after Tiwari is elected by dissidents in the party, under the leadership of Arjun Singh, to be the leader of the "real Congress."

22   **The breakaway group from the Congress(I), which is led by N.D. Tiwari, announces that a working president, a working committee, and a parliament board have been selected.**

23   The central government announces the creation of a ten-point program to save the Taj Mahal, which is being damaged by air pollution.

      K.K. Tewary resigns from the Working Committee of the newly formed rebel Congress Party. Tewary announces that he is resigning to protest the nomination of new members without the consultation of the senior leadership.

24   United States Secretary of State Warren Christopher tells Pranab Mukherjee, the Indian minister of external affairs, that the dispute over Kashmir can only be solved through bilateral talks between India and Pakistan. Christopher also informs Mukherjee that the United States does not have any plans to attempt to mediate the dispute.

30   T.N. Seshan announces that Assembly elections cannot be held in Jammu and Kashmir. The Rao government, faced with his decree and widespread opposition within Jammu and Kashmir and from other parties, agrees not to hold them at the present time.

31   The Congress(I) expels former Rajasthan Chief Minister Shiv Charan Mathur from primary membership in the party for six years for his "antiparty activities."

June 1995

1   **In Uttar Pradesh, the Bahujan Samaj Party (BSP) withdraws support from the Mulayam Singh Yadav government. The next day, Mayawati, the general secretary of the BSP, is elected the leader of the Legislature Party. She requests that Governor Motilal Vora dismiss the government of Mulayam Singh Yadav and ask her to form the government. On June 3, the governor dismisses the government after the chief minister refuses to resign. Mayawati is sworn in as the new chief minister later that day.**

2   Parliament passes the Constitutional Amendment to continue reservations in job promotions for Scheduled Castes and Scheduled Tribes. Members of Parliament also promise to work to provide similar protection to Other Backward Classes.

3   The central government sends requisitions to the Sri Lankan government requesting the arrest and extradition of three suspects accused of masterminding the assassination of Rajiv Gandhi. The petition for the extradition of V. Prabhakaran, Pottu Amman, and Akila comes after a statement by the foreign minister of Sri Lanka that extradition requests for LTTE members involved in the Rajiv Gandhi assassination will be seriously considered.

4   The U.S. Department of Energy warns India that the future of several private power initiatives in the country will be seriously jeopardized if standing agreements between Enron Corporation and several

Indian states, most notably Maharashtra, are not honored.

19   Three trade union federations of the Central Department of Telecommunications begin a nationwide strike. The action is taken to protest the privatization of the telecom industry.

20   The Unlawful Activities (Prevention) Tribunal removes the ban on the Vishwa Hindu Parishad (VHP) imposed in January by the central government. The Tribunal, under Justice K. Ramamurthy, states that the government failed to provide tangible evidence that the VHP is engaging in illegal activities and needs to be restricted.

The Rao government announces that it will soon ratify the Chemical Weapons Convention (CWC). It also declares that it plans to introduce legislation into parliament that will create a national authority to enforce the provisions of the CWC. The Convention, which was signed by India in Paris in 1993, seeks to destroy the stockpiles of countries that possess chemical weapons and to prevent other nations from acquiring them.

23   Following an agreement with the government, the telecommunications strike is called off.

July 1995

3   **After a review, the $2.8 billion Dabhol power project is cancelled by Manohar Joshi. Joshi tells the State Assembly that the electricity generated will be too expensive for the average person to afford and that the plant will have a detrimental impact on the environment. Since both reasons are against the "interest of the state," Maharashtra will not allow the project to go forward.**

3   In Delhi, the body of a severely burned, unidentified woman is pulled from the tandoor oven of an outdoor restaurant.

4   A group of tourists including two British and two American citizens are abducted in Kashmir. Al-Faran, a separatist organization, claims responsibility for the kidnappings. Three women and a man in the group, as well as their two guides, are released.

5   Authorities identify the body that was found in the tandoor of the Delhi restaurant as that of Naina Sahni, a Congress Party activist and leader of the National Students Union of India. Police begin a search for her husband, Sushil Sharma, who is the primary suspect in the murder investigation. Sharma is one of the owners of the Ashok Yatri Niwas restaurant and former president of the Delhi section of the Youth Congress.

7   Rajan Pillai dies in a Delhi government hospital. The cause of his death is suspected to be cirrhosis of the liver. Pillai was arrested by the CBI three days earlier and was refused permission by a Delhi court to be treated at the Escort Hospital.

8   Dirk Hasert, a German tourist, is kidnapped while on a hiking expedition in the Himalayas. At a nearby location, a Norwegian, Hans Christian Ostro, is also abducted. He is the sixth person to be kidnapped by Al-Faran. The same day, one of the Americans being held hostage escapes. Al-Faran threatens to kill the five hostages unless the Indian government releases several militants being held in custody.

9   Sushil Sharma is expelled from the Congress Party. The murder of Naina Sahni leads to calls for a proper cleansing of the Congress Party's "criminal elements."

10   Sushil Sharma is arrested by police near Bangalore, after arriving by bus from Madras. After protests by women's groups, lawyer's associations, and opposition parties, the Madras High Court revokes the anticipatory bail that had been granted earlier by a lower court.

14   **The Supreme Court rules that the two other members of the Election Commission are equal in rank to the chief election commissioner. The decision states that T.N. Seshan must confer with the two members and that they may overrule him at any time. The review petition filed by Seshan is summarily rejected.**

28   The BJP–Shiv Sena government in Maharashtra renames Bombay "Mumbai."

30   In Manipur, the five-month-old coalition government of Risab Keishing survives a vote of confidence by a single vote.

August 1995

2   The central government sets up a five-member agency that will investigate connections between the mafia, politicians, and bureaucrats. The government's actions are based on the recommendations of the Vohra committee.

9   The government of Gujarat announces that it has discovered a connection between the Bombay explosions and several convicts who had earlier escaped from the Sabarmati Central Jail in Ahmedabad.

13   Hans Christian Ostro, the Norwegian tourist taken hostage by Al-Faran in July, is beheaded by members of the group. In a note left by the body, the

organization threatens to kill the remaining four
hostages if India continues to hold the militants
whose release it earlier demanded.

15   The VHP promises the government of Uttar
Pradesh and the central government that it will not
precipitate a confrontation over the Shahi Idgah
mosque in Mathura. The VHP had earlier threatened to ignore a government order that prevents the
organization from celebrating the birth of Krishna
at the Krishna Janmasthan temple adjoining the
seventeenth-century mosque. After appeals from
Chief Minister Mayawati, the VHP agrees to hold
its ceremonies at a temple three miles away.

20   Both Indian and Chinese troops withdraw from the
Himalayan border, the exact boundaries of which
have been disputed by the two countries for more
than forty years. The withdrawal is considered to be
a demonstration of good faith between the two
countries after several years of confidence-building
measures.

In Firozabad, Uttar Pradesh, the Puru Shottam express train collided into a stationary train. At least
250 people are believed to have been killed in the
accident, and another 300 injured. "Human failure"
is given as an explanation for the accident.

Security forces and members of Al-Faran exchange
fire in Kashmir. Militants claim that two hostages
and one Al-Faran member were injured in the clash.

21   Negotiations between Al-Faran and the government
of Jammu and Kashmir over the fate of the four
remaining hostages end without a resolution.

24   Sonia Gandhi announces that she is distressed that
the investigations into her husband's death have not

been conclusive, and she hints that the Rao government is deliberately slowing down the inquiries. In
her first public speech since Rajiv Gandhi's assassination, she asks the Indian people to help her defend the legacy and values of the Gandhi family,
which she accuses the Congress of abandoning. She
asks the Indian people to join her in demanding that
the government vigorously pursue any leads it has
regarding her husband's assassination.

26 A constitutional amendment on land reforms is
passed by the Lok Sabha. The amendment puts land
reforms in seven states under the Ninth Schedule of
the Constitution. This measure ensures that land reforms cannot have their legality challenged in court.

31 **Chief minister of Punjab Beant Singh and twelve
others are killed and another sixteen are injured
when a bomb explodes outside the Punjab and
Haryana Civil Secretariat. Sikh separatists belonging to the Babbar Khalsa claim responsibility for the attack and state that it was done in
retaliation for Singh's "betrayal" of the Sikh
community.**

September 1995

1 **N.T. Rama Rao resigns as chief minister hours
before he is to face a vote of confidence in the
Andhra Pradesh Assembly. His son-in-law, N.
Chandrababu Naidu, who was elected leader of
the Telugu Desam earlier in the week, is sworn
in as the new chief minister.**

3 Wadhwa Singh, leader of the Babbar Khalsa,
claims that the next target of his organization will
be Narasimha Rao. In an interview with a London
newspaper, Singh states that 1995 will be the year
the Khalistan movement experiences a revival.

4   Hizbul Mujaheddin detonates a car bomb in the center of Srinigar, outside the State Bank of India. At least thirteen people are killed.

5   Lakhvinder Singh, a government driver, and Gurmeet Singh, an engineer, are arrested and charged with the murder of Beant Singh. Police issue two other arrest warrants in connection with the assassination and report that a former police officer served as the suicide bomber.

6   India ratifies the Chemical Weapons Convention.

8   The Punjab Congress Legislature unanimously elects Harcharan Singh Brar to lead the party. He is then sworn in as the new chief minister of the state.

12   A total of Rs.850 crore is set aside by the central government for the purpose of eliminating child labor by the year 2000.

13   Narasimha Rao reshuffles his cabinet. Several ministers resign and thirteen new members are inducted. The prime minister assigns various remaining members to different positions.

14   Home Minister Rajesh Pilot requests the CBI to take the politically well-connected "god-man" Chandraswami into custody. Chandraswami, an enterprising spiritual leader, is suspected of having links to Dawood Ibrahim, who is alleged to have orchestrated the Bombay explosions of March 1993. Chandraswami has also been mentioned in connection with various other scandals, including the St. Kitts forgery case and the assassination of Rajiv Gandhi.

15   Rao transfers Pilot from the Home Ministry to the Ministry of Environment and Forests.

21   In villages, towns, and cities throughout the country, there are reports that idols of Ganesh have been drinking offerings of milk.

October 1995

1   Expelled BJP rebel leader Shankarsinh Waghela claims that he has the loyalty and support of half the party caucus. In response to these assertions, the governor of Gujarat gives Keshubhai Patel one week to prove his majority.

7   Shankarsinh Waghela decides that the factions he leads will support the current BJP government. The about-face comes after national-level BJP leaders mediate a truce between the squabbling factions. Later that day, the government of Keshubhai Patel wins a vote of confidence, with all 120 BJP members voting for the chief minister. The next day, the BJP revokes the expulsion of Shankarsinh Waghela and asks Keshubhai Patel to step down as chief minister.

17   After the CBI concludes that Sanjay Dutt is a "deserving candidate," the Supreme Court orders the government to release the film star on bail. Dutt has been charged with weapons possession and facilitating terrorist activities in connection with the Bombay bombings of March 1993. He has been jailed under TADA for fifteen months.

In Uttar Pradesh, after corruption charges mount against Mayawati, and upper castes begin to angrily complain against perceived favoritism toward *dalits* by the BSP, the BJP removes its support from Mayawati's two-month-old government. Two days later, President's Rule is imposed on the state.

22   Former Industries Minister Suresh Mehta is sworn
            in as the chief minister of Gujarat.

25   Narasimha Rao travels to New York for a United
            Nations conference. While there, he speaks with Sri
            Lankan President Chandrika Kumaratunga about
            the possibility of extraditing Prabhakaran, the
            leader of the LTTE, who is wanted in India in con-
            nection with the assassination of Rajiv Gandhi.

29   The central government dissolves the Uttar Pradesh
            Assembly.

November 1995

1   The Indian government protests the sale of French
            Mirage fighter jets to Pakistan. The French govern-
            ment is informed that further trade of this nature
            with Pakistan could lead to problems in relations
            with India.

4   The cabinet, under the recommendation of the
            prime minister, decides on a mid-December date for
            holding elections in Jammu and Kashmir, where poll-
            ing for the legislative assembly last took place in
            1987. Rao also hints that the government is willing to
            consider a form of limited autonomy for the state.

10   After its members travel to Jammu and Kashmir to
            assess the polity climate in the state, the Election
            Commission disagrees with the government over
            holding Assembly elections. It rejects earlier state-
            ments made by Rao that elections can be held in the
            state in mid-December, stating categorically that
            free and fair balloting cannot take place there at the
            present time.

22   Narasimha Rao rejects the recommendation of the
            Finance Ministry to raise the price of petroleum.

The ministry had projected that a hike in prices would raise more than $159 million for the current financial year.

24   The government is informed by the IMF that it needs to reduce the country's public sector deficit, which has not decreased since 1991. The lending organization warns that if India does not take steps to lower its debt, its current structural reform policy will be seriously hindered.

28   BJP parliament members walk out of the Lok Sabha after Speaker Shivraj Patil denies their request for a debate on Kashmir that would have forced a vote on Rao's decision to hold elections there.

December 1995

4   A Kentucky Fried Chicken restaurant in New Delhi reopens after a court overturns a November 15 decision by the Municipal Corporation of Delhi, under the orders of BJP chief minister Madan Lal Khurana, to shut down the fast-food restaurant for alleged health code violations.

7   The opposition in the Rajya Sabha demands the resignation of Telecommunications Minister Sukh Ram. Members charge that he changed the bidding rules for telecommunications licenses to benefit Himachal Futuristic Communications, Ltd. (HFCL), a consortium of Thai, Indian, and Israeli companies. Opposition parties on both the left and the right threaten to halt the proceedings of the Upper House for the entire winter session if a committee to investigate the matter is not immediately created.

9   After the Lok Sabha is disrupted for the second day, the government offers to show opposition leaders all documents related to the telecom incident.

11   **A three-member Supreme Court panel upholds the law that prohibits politicians from using religious appeals to gain votes. The law had been challenged by Bal Thackeray and the BJP in response to a previous ruling that prevents Thackeray from running in the April/May 1996 elections. However, in a separate decision, the court overturns a lower court decision that would have kept Manohar Joshi from holding office for the next six years. The ruling states that Joshi's pledge to make Maharashtra a Hindu state is not in violation of the 1951 law.**

14   The opposition continues to ask for an investigation into the telecom license case. It is not satisfied with the earlier decision of the Speaker of the Lok Sabha that the problem should be dealt with by the Supreme Court, not Parliament.

15   The Rajya Sabha passes a resolution approving the government decision to impose President's Rule in Jammu and Kashmir. A six-month extension of President's Rule in Jammu and Kashmir is also approved by the Rajya Sabha.

17   In West Bengal, three parachutes holding a large number of arms are dropped from an AN-26 aircraft over Purulia district. The next day, several members of the Ananda Marg Hindu sect are arrested in connection with the arms drop. However, authorities find no connection between the suspects and the weapons, and they are almost immediately released.

22   Police arrest two more people in connection with the August assassination of Beant Singh. The suspects, Jagtar Singh and Balwant Singh, are taken into custody by police in Rajpura. Their arrests bring the number of people detained in connection

with the chief minister's death to eight. The two, along with a third person, are also accused of conspiring to assassinate Narasimha Rao and Bhajan Lal, the chief minister of Haryana. Police report seizing explosives from the three suspects.

An AN-26 transport plane lands in Bombay. It is seized by authorities, and its five-member Latvian crew, along with a British arms dealer, are arrested in connection with the arms drop over Purulia on December 17.

23   During a function at the Dayanand Anglo-Vedic school in Mandi Dabwali, Haryana, a fire breaks out, killing more than 400 people. The blaze occurs when a *shamiana* (marquee) in the marriage hall catches fire and collapses, trapping hundreds of people beneath it; 500 of the 1,200 people present escape unharmed. The lack of emergency exits in the hall is blamed for the high death toll. The state government promises to implement stricter safety regulations for buildings and to provide remuneration for the injured and next of kin.

January 1996

1   India and Pakistan exchange lists of atomic installations and each side pledges not to attack. The action is part of a confidence-building agreement between the two states.

10   **The Supreme Court reprimands T.N. Seshan for overstepping the mandate of his office by using the commission as the sole mechanism for scheduling general elections.**

16   **The CBI files numerous charge sheets in connection with the Jain Hawala case. In addition to three Jain brothers, several national politicians**

are named, including L.K. Advani, Arjun Singh, and Devi Lal. The charge sheets are under Section 7 and Section 12 of the Prevention of Corruption Act, 1988. They state that Advani, Singh, Lal, and four others provided political favors for the Jain brothers in exchange for large monetary payoffs. Advani declares that he will resign from his position in the Lok Sabha. Moreover, he states that he will not run in the upcoming elections unless he is cleared of all charges.

17   Madhavrao Scindia, V.C. Shukla, and Balram Jakhar resign from the Narasimha Rao government. Their resignation follows CBI disclosure that it has sought permission to charge-sheet the three cabinet ministers in connection with the Jain Hawala case and it appears that Rao will agree to the request.

18   N.T. Rama Rao dies at the age of 73, leaving his son-in-law, Chandrababu Naidu, and his widow, Lakshmi Parvati, to fight for control of the Andhra Pradesh government. Two days later, Lakshmi Parvati is elected president of the Telugu Desam.

21   In Allahabad, the Bajrang Dal, the militant youth wing of the VHP, brings together 100,000 supporters to protest cow slaughter.

22   Sharad Yadav, leader of the Janata Dal parliamentary party, resigns from the Lok Sabha.

23   In Maharashtra, the government refuses to renew the mandate of the Srikrishna Commission. The commission had been probing the Bombay riots of January 1993, in which more than 1,000 people were killed and Rs.1,200 crore of property was

damaged. Critics argue that the government has dis-
banded the commission because Shiv Sena activists
were involved in the riots.

23   **Atal Behari Vajpayee, the leader of the opposition in the Lok Sabha, releases a statement made
to the CBI by S.K. Jain. In it, Jain alleges that
Narasimha Rao received Rs.3 crore as payment
from him in 1991. Vajpayee demands that Rao
immediately resign.**

24   **Former Union Minister H.K.L. Bhagat is arrested in connection with the Delhi anti-Sikh
riots that followed the assassination of Indira
Gandhi in 1984.**

30   In Bangalore, members of the Karnataka Rajya
Raitha Sangha, a farmers' association, attack a
newly opened Kentucky Fried Chicken restaurant.

February 1996

4   In response to a U.S. request that it cease firing
missiles, India declares that it will not stop test
launches of Prithvi.

5   The rupee falls to Rs.38.30 against the U.S. dollar,
following a dollar-buying binge led by the State
Bank of India in the Bombay foreign exchange
market.

9   The Allahabad High Court awards substantial com-
pensations in connection with police brutality that
occurred during the October 1994 campaign for the
creation of a separate hill state of Uttarakhand.
These include Rs.10 lakh to the dependents of those
killed and to the seven rape victims, and Rs.5 lakh
to each woman who was subject to physical abuse.
The court holds the "state machinery" responsible

for the deaths of Uttarakhand activists and other incidents of police brutality.

12   Kalpanath Rai is sent to jail by a Delhi Court after being charged with hiding members of Dawood Ibrahim's gang.

15   The Supreme Court orders the closure of five chemical plants in Rajasthan. It tells Hindustan Agro-Chemicals and its sister companies, which own the plants, to compensate the villagers of Bichri for the environmental damage caused. The National Environmental Engineering and Research Institute estimates the damage at Rs.37 crore.

16   In Uttar Pradesh, there are reports that those on a fast for a separate state of Uttarakhand are becoming extremely weak. The government refuses to consider the issue of a separate state.

17   Delhi police stop a vehicle and discover a large cache of weapons and ammunition. Mohammed Hasan Pador, an Iranian living in Lahore, and Christoph Martin Zellweger, a Swiss national, are arrested. The authorities have no information on who was to receive the shipment.

20   Two more ministers, Buta Singh and Arvind Netam, resign from the Narasimha Rao government in connection with the Jain Hawala case.

      Four members of the Hizbul Mujahideen are arrested by the Delhi police in connection with the January explosion in Sadar Bazaar.

26   **MP Shailendra Mahato, who recently joined the BJP, announces at a press conference that in 1993, he and three other members of the Jharkhand Mukti Morcha received Rs.40 lakh each**

from Narasimha Rao. They claim that Rao bribed them to vote in favor of the minority Congress government, allowing it to overcome a no-confidence motion.

March 1996

4   Members of the People's War Group attack a police station in the Karimnagar district in Andhra Pradesh. A policeman is killed, and a large supply of weapons is looted from the building.

9   BJP President L.K. Advani sets out on a *rath yatra.* It is the second one he has undertaken in six years.

Lakshmi Parvathi begins her electoral campaign for the Lok Sabha from Tirupathi.

14   The CBI is directed by the Madras High Court to investigate allegations that the AIADMK-controlled government in Tamil Nadu misused central government funds that were allocated for the poor.

15   Members of the Indian Union Muslim League (IUML) and the breakaway Indian National League (INL) agree to contest the Kerala parliamentary and Assembly elections together.

19   Shankar Dayal Sharma returns two ordinances to the central government without signing them. He argues that the ordinances, which seek to extend reservations to *dalit* Christians and to abbreviate the electoral campaigning period, may not be mandated by the Constitution.

21   The Supreme Court upholds an earlier decision that suicide and assisting suicide are punishable under law. The decision states that the guarantee of an individual's right to life, which can be found in

Article 21 of the Constitution, does not refer to a right to die.

24   At the Hazratbal shrine near Srinigar, members of the Jammu and Kashmir Liberation Front (Siddiqi) and the police clash. Two people are killed and five injured in the shooting. Two days later, the Jammu and Kashmir police take control of the shrine. The central government states that elections will proceed as scheduled.

26   The Supreme Court issues an initial reprimand against the CBI. The judges accuse the organization of investigating the various criminal allegations against Chandraswami far too slowly.

April 1996

1   The A.K. Antony government closes all country-liquor stores in Kerala. The move is estimated to reduce total revenue in the state by 10 percent, or Rs.350 crore. The move follows a substantial hike in the price of foreign-made Indian liquor.

4   A ruling of a two-member Supreme Court bench states that as long as a political party is able to account for every penny spent, there are no ceilings on the amount it can spend in support of a candidate. However, if it cannot provide a full account, then the expenditure will be considered the candidate's own. Furthermore, if it is deemed to be the candidate's responsibility and it exceeds the 4.5 lakh ceiling set for candidate spending, the candidate's election can be nullified.

21   **Sheila Kaul, governor of Himachal Pradesh, resigns. The action comes following disclosure of a CBI report stating that she acted improperly while in the position of minister for Urban De-**

velopment. **She is accused of improperly distrib-**
uting permits for stalls and shops in Delhi.

27   The first phase of polling for the Lok Sabha and
state assemblies begins. One hundred and forty million people in fourteen states and the Union Territories are expected to vote.

May 1996

2   The second phase of polling for the Lok Sabha and
state assemblies commences. Several constituencies
report incidents of sporadic violence.

7   The third phase of polling for the Lok Sabha and
state assemblies begins, and further violence is
reported.

The first phase of three-stage polling begins in
Jammu and Kashmir. As the National Conference is
boycotting the election, the main contest in the state
is between the Congress(I) and the BJP.

9   **As election returns come in, it is clear that the**
Congress(I) has suffered severe electoral losses
in several states, including Kerala, Assam, Hary-
ana, and Tamil Nadu. A few days later, the BJP
emerges as the single largest party in the Lok
Sabha, with 155 seats. The Congress comes in
second with 133 seats.

Jayalalitha is defeated by the DMK candidate in
her home district of Bargur, and resigns as
Tamil Nadu chief minister. The AIADMK-Con-
gress alliance proves a complete failure, as the
DMK wins the vast majority of open seats in
both the Lok Sabha and State Assembly.

10   **Narasimha Rao submits the resignation of his**

Council of Ministers to President Shankar Dayal
Sharma.

13   M. Karunanidhi, leader of the DMK, becomes chief
minister of Tamil Nadu.

15   The Asom Gana Parishad, led by Prafulla Kumar
Mohanta, comes to power in Assam amid worsening ethnic conflict in the southern districts of the
state.

**The president appoints as prime minister the
leader of the largest party, Atal Behari Vajpayee
of the BJP, even though his party does not have
a majority in the Lok Sabha.**

22   The opposition United Front, headed by Karnataka
Chief Minister H.D. Deve Gowda, calls for a vote
of no-confidence against the BJP coalition government of Atal Behari Vajpayee.

28   **The BJP government resigns before a vote of confidence can take place. Congress refuses an opportunity to try to form a government, leaving Deve
Gowda and a thirteen-member United Front coalition to take control of the central government.**

June 1996

1   H.D. Deve Gowda is sworn in as prime minister.

2   The Congress wins four of the six open Lok Sabha
seats in Jammu and Kashmir amid allegations that
security forces coerced people to vote.

4   Pakistani Prime Minister Benazir Bhutto suggests
to H.D. Deve Gowda that India and Pakistan renew
bilateral talks that have been suspended for more
than two years.

8   The CBI announces that it is now "actively" investigating the Rs.133 crore urea import case. The new interest in the case follows allegations made by one of the accused, N. Sambasiva Rao, that payoffs were made to Narasimha Rao's son, Prabhakar Rao and Sanjeeva Rao, a family friend.

9   The prime minister suggests that the foreign secretaries of Pakistan and India meet. The meeting is suggested as part of a longer-term revival of dialogue between the two countries.

12   Deve Gowda wins a parliamentary vote of confidence with the support of the Congress Party.

18   India declares that it is opposed to the idea that the Comprehensive Test Ban Treaty (CTBT) should only come into force if India, along with Israel and Pakistan, become signatories. The three countries are considered by other nuclear weapon states, including the United States, to be essential to the success of the treaty.

20   The Congress(I) announces that it will ally with the Bahujan Samaj Party in Uttar Pradesh assembly elections.

July 1996

1   I.K. Gujral, minister of External Affairs, reiterates his position that India will not sign the CTBT.

3   Deve Gowda raises fuel prices, bringing criticism from his allies in the Communist party and from the Congress.

6   The United Front is forced to lower the price increase in petroleum products to 15 percent. The ac-

tion comes after widespread protests over the severity of the increase.

6   Deve Gowda tours Kashmir, the first prime minister to do so in more than a decade.

9   A court in Delhi informs former Prime Minister Narasimha Rao that he is to stand trial in the Lakhubhai Patel case.

23   **P. Chidambaram presents the 1996–97 Union Budget. In it, he offers fiscal concessions and incentives to both international and domestic investors. In addition, he promises that infrastructure development will be a priority. Other highlights include reforms of the tax system, removal of several state controls on agriculture and industry, and increased funds made available to farmers in the form of rural credit and irrigation plans. Food subsidies are increased by $110 million a year, bringing the total to $1.68 billion a year.**

August 1996

4   The wives of two of the four tourists held hostage by Al-Faran in Kashmir ask the people of Kashmir to help them locate their husbands, who have been in captivity for one year.

8   Telugu Desam Party (TDP) criticizes the United Front for allowing the height of the Alamatti Dam in Karnataka to be raised. The party claims that this construction has affected the water supply in Andhra Pradesh, and it accuses Deve Gowda of displaying favoritism toward his home state. The TDP threatens to withdraw support from the United Front and warns that there will be "serious consequences" if the two billion rupees grant to

Karnataka from a federal irrigation plant is not withdrawn.

10   Talks on the Alamatti dam between Karnataka, Maharashtra, and Andhra Pradesh fail. Prime Minister Deve Gowda had brought together the chief ministers of the three states to discuss ways to share the water equitably.

15   In an Independence Day speech, the prime minister commits the central government to facilitating the creation of a separate Uttarakhand state.

25   Continued snowfall and slow rescue measures lead to the death of 39 more Amarnath *yatra* pilgrims, bringing the death toll to 110.

27   Jayalalitha announces that she is breaking off her association with Sasikala, her close friend, and Sudhakaran, her foster son. Her decision comes amid growing speculation that the three were deeply involved in several illegal activities while Jayalalitha was serving as Tamil Nadu chief minister.

A Delhi court sentences 89 people to five years of "rigorous imprisonment." All were charged with participating in the 1984 anti-Sikh riots that followed the assassination of Indira Gandhi. In a ninety-two-page ruling Judge S.N. Dhingra notes that "those who engineered the riots and who made the above poor persons their tools for the riots are still at large."

29   In a meeting between I.K. Gujral and Malcolm Rifkind, the British foreign secretary, Gujral reiterates India's position that it will not sign the Comprehensive Test Ban Treaty (CTBT).

September 1996

7   Voters in Jammu and Kashmir vote in the first local elections since insurgency broke out in 1990. The four-stage polls will end on September 30.

11   The CTBT is approved by the U.N. General Assembly. However, India votes against the CTBT and declares that it has no intention of signing it in the future.

12   In Pulwana district in Kashmir, a grenade is thrown at Farooq Abdullah, the Congress Party's top politician in the state. The explosion leaves four policemen and two civilians injured. Abdullah escapes unharmed and the attacker is arrested.

17   **The CBI arrests Sukh Ram, the former Minister of State for Communications for conspiring with an official in the ministry to give a telecom license to the HFCL, a move which caused the government a loss of Rs.16.8 million. The CBI also wishes to discuss Rs.1 million discovered in Ram's residence when the organization raided his home in August. Ram claims that the money belongs to the Congress Party and is meant to fund the campaign for the upcoming elections in Uttar Pradesh.**

21   **Narasimha Rao resigns as Congress president amid numerous allegations of corruption, all of which he denies any involvement in. Two days later, Sitaram Kesri becomes president of the Congress(I).**

26   Narasimha Rao and Chandraswami are chargesheeted by the CBI in connection with the St. Kitts forgery case.

October 1996

2   **The pro-India National Conference party wins an absolute majority in the Jammu and Kashmir State Assembly elections. Farooq Abdullah, leader of the National Conference, is sworn in as chief minister.**

8   The Samajwadi Party threatens to leave the United Front government if Deve Gowda supports the efforts of the Congress Party to form a government in Uttar Pradesh with the BSP.

The Bombay police file charges against M.F. Husain. The artist is charged with obscenity and offending the sensibilities of religious groups for paintings of his that depict a naked Saraswati and Drapaudi. Police file charges against him after Maharashtra Minister of Culture Pramod Navalkar brings the paintings to the attention of the Shiv Sena.

10   In Ahmedabad, Bajrang Dal activists storm a gallery and destroy sixteen works of M.F. Husain.

11   **Assembly elections in Uttar Pradesh produce a hung assembly, with no single party winning a majority. The BJP has the largest number of votes and states that it will try to form a government.**

15   At a meeting of the National Inter-State Council in Bangalore, Deve Gowda agrees to create a standing committee to examine various center-state issues, including a repeal of Article 356. The committee will look at ways to prevent the abuse of President's Rule and the governor's power in state affairs.

17   President's Rule is imposed in Uttar Pradesh.

23   About one million postal and telephone workers go on strike to protest the government decision to impose a ceiling of Rs.3,500 on annual bonuses as an austerity measure. Workers argue that such a restriction is unfair, as the bonus ceiling has already been lifted for railway workers.

The Mahagujarat Janata Party (MJP) forms a government in Gujarat, ending a five-day spell of President's Rule. Shankarsinh Waghela is sworn in as the chief minister. Congress extends its unconditional support to the MJP and the governor asks Waghela to prove his majority within fifteen days.

27   H.D. Deve Gowda announces a Rs.6,100 crore aid package for the northeastern states.

29   Postal and telephone workers call off their week-long strike after the government agrees to lift the ceiling on bonus payments. The State Telecommunications Department will assume the additional financial burden of the bonus payments, which is expected to be Rs.1.2 billion for 1995 and 1996.

29   The CBI files a charge sheet against Narasimha Rao in connection with the Jharkhand Mukti Morcha case.

November 1996

7   A cyclone strikes Andhra Pradesh, killing hundreds and leaving thousands homeless.

8   Sheila Kaul, the former governor of Himachal Pradesh, is ordered by the Supreme Court to pay a fine of Rs.60 lakh to the State Exchequer within the next nine months. The money is in payment of damages for her provision of 52 government stalls

to various relatives when she served as Minister for Urban Development.

21   Rajinder Kaur Bhattal of the Congress(I) becomes the chief minister of Punjab after the resignation of Harcharan Singh Brar, who had come under pressure from the Congress Punjab Legislature Party. Bhattal is the first woman to serve as chief minister of the state.

23   Miss Greece, Irene Skliva, wins the Miss World beauty pageant in Bangalore. The pageant takes place after weeks of angry demonstrations by women's groups and Hindu organizations. Hundreds of police were deployed during the event, as several individuals threatened to set themselves on fire if the beauty pageant took place.

26   H.D. Deve Gowda declares that he will not repeal the Illegal Migrants Determination Tribunal Act.

29   **During a visit by Chinese President Jiang Zemin, India and China take steps to stabilize the Himalayan border region and to prevent a military escalation. They agree to bring armed forces along the border to a minimum, and to inform each other about military moves taken along the Line of Actual Control. They also sign agreements to not attack each other and to work together to fight terrorism and drug trafficking. Finally, China promises that it will not transfer nuclear technology or M-11 missiles to Pakistan.**

ULFA militants blow up three crude oil pipelines in Nalgari district in Assam. The lines are part of the Oil India Ltd. Trunk pipeline. As a result of the explosions, Bongaigaon Refineries and Petrochemicals Ltd., which owns the pipelines, shuts down its main crude processing plant.

December 1996

3   The Bombay High Court rejects a suit that wants to block the continued construction of the $2.8 billion Dabhol power project.

3   Two days after he is arrested by the CBI on additional charges, Sukh Ram is expelled from Congress.

7   Former Chief Minister Jayalalitha is arrested in Madras and charged with heading a kickback scheme in which public funds were used to purchase televisions. She is accused of spending $2.4 million to purchase televisions for village *panchayats*. The next day, more than 5,000 of her supporters are detained in Madras after protests against her arrest become violent; one man even sets himself on fire. Thousands more are arrested throughout the state in scattered incidents.

11 M.S. Gill becomes the new chief election commissioner, replacing the retiring T.N. Seshan.

The Supreme Court issues a directive to the government to implement measures to end child labor. It orders the government to ban children from working in 12 industries deemed to be hazardous. In addition, it tells the government to ensure that children in nonhazardous industries work only six hours a day and receive at least two hours a day of schooling.

12 **India and Bangladesh sign a treaty in which they agree to share the Ganges waters for the next three decades.**

The government of Jammu and Kashmir offers a reward of up to 10 lakh rupees for anyone providing information on the four tourists that have been held hostage by Al-Faran for a year and a half. The action comes after the U.S. State Department offers a $2 million reward for information on Donald Hutchings, the American being held hostage.

13   In a raid on the home of Jayalalitha, police seize 10,500 saris, 750 pairs of shoes, nearly a ton of silver, and 60 pounds of gold. So far, Jayalalitha has been charged in seven corruption cases.

29   Trishul, a surface-to-air-missile, is test-fired successfully in Orissa.

30   The Delhi-bound Brahamaputra mail train is bombed near the Sisapani station in Kokrajhar District, Assam. More than forty people are killed. Authorities suspect that Bodo militants placed an explosive on the track and triggered it by remote control.

January 1997

1   A thirty-year treaty between India and Bangladesh, in which they agree to share the waters of the Ganges, takes effect.

9   Prime Minister Deve Gowda announces that a series of steps to liberalize the economy will be taken over the next two weeks. One of the measures to be implemented will be a complete elimination of intermediaries in government transactions.

15   Datta Samant, the militant trade union leader, is shot and killed by two unknown men near his residence at Pawai in Bombay. News of his death is followed by a spontaneous strike by industrial workers in the north and central parts of the city. Many schools, restaurants, and stores close for the day in deference to the strike.

21   The first group of bank documents relating to the Bofors case are turned over to the Indian government by the Swiss government.

22   The former Haryana Chief Minister Bhajan Lal, former union ministers Ajit Singh and Ram Lakhan Singh Yadav, and five others are charge-sheeted by the Central Bureau of Investigation in connection with the Jharkhand Mukti Morcha bribery case.

31   Prime Minister Deve Gowda travels to Davos, Switzerland, to participate in the second session of the World Economic Forum.

February 1997

7   Elections to the 117-member Punjab Assembly are held. Polling is peaceful, and turnout is estimated at 65 percent.

11   **On the basis of documents received in January by the Indian government, the CBI reveals five names connected to the Bofors incident. They include Ottavio and Maria Quattrocchi, Win and Kanta Chadha, and their son W.H. Chadha. However, the Hinduja brothers and Rajiv Gandhi, who are widely considered to have received payments, are not listed in the documents provided by the Swiss government.**

12   **The Akali Dal and BJP alliance wins a landslide victory in the Punjab assembly polls. Parkash Singh Badal, leader of the Shiromani Akali Dal (Badal) is sworn in as the chief minister. The Congress(I) is soundly defeated, and the results are seen as a vote against central intervention in the state over the last fifteen years.**

12   Fresh ethnic violence breaks out between Nagas and Kukis in Senapati district in Manipur.

13   The Gujarat government suspends nine constables in response to reports that seven people were blinded while being held in police custody. In addition, the government orders a magisterial inquiry into the incident and appoints a commission to investigate.

14   India and Bangladesh agree to continue to consolidate their special ties.

15   The Congress(I) renounces the unconditional support that it previously gave to Deve Gowda's thirteen-party coalition. It announces that from now on, its support to the United Front government will be based solely on "issues."

23   At least 175 people are killed and more than 500 are injured during a fire in Baripada, Orissa.

28   P. Chidambaram, the finance minister, presents the 1997–98 Union Budget.

March 1997

1   **Finance Minister Chidambaram announces that the general aim of the 1997–98 budget is to catalyze a relatively stagnant domestic economy. The measures include the elimination of double taxation of dividends; simplification of excise duties; reduction of the corporate tax rate; and an increase in the limit of foreign aggregate investment in domestic companies. Critics hail the budget as being "pro-reform" and the Bombay stock market jumps almost two hundred points in response.**

6   A BJP-sponsored motion against Romesh Bhandari, the Uttar Pradesh governor, is admitted by the

speaker of the Lok Sabha. The BJP motion con-
demns Bhandari for publicly disagreeing with
Home Minister Indrajit Gupta. The home minister
had earlier stated that Uttar Pradesh was headed for
"anarchy, chaos and destruction."

10   Union Home Minister Indrajit Gupta asks that all
political parties in India think of ways to resolve the
current political crisis in Uttar Pradesh.

After several days of erratic power supply in districts in and around Hyderabad, groups from several villages clash. Villagers complain that their
supply is inadequate compared to other villages.

12   In the Delhi High Court, N. Natrajan, the prosecu-
tor for the CBI, argues that both BJP President L.K.
Advani and V.C. Shukla, the former union minister
received bribes from the Jain brothers. He argues
that entries in the diaries of the Jains for Rs.3.5
million (35 lakhs) and Rs.3.8 million (38 lakhs),
show conclusively that Advani and Shukla received
these payments.

The central government agrees, in principle, to the
proposal that the Andaman and Nicobar Islands be
given a greater measure of self-rule. While it is
currently a Union Territory, a legislative assembly
may be created there in the near future.

13   In Calcutta, the senior nuns of the Order in the Mis-
sionaries of Charity choose Sister Nirmala to succeed Mother Theresa.

P.A. Sangma, speaker of the Lok Sabha, decrees
that the central government may continue
President's Rule in Uttar Pradesh for another six
months. His decision quashes an attempt by the BJP
to block any extension of President's Rule.

18   Sukh Ram, former Minister of State for Communications, along with two others are charge-sheeted by the CBI.

19   **The BJP and the BSP finalize an agreement to form a coalition government in Uttar Pradesh. The decision is expected to bring an end to President's Rule, which has been in force for a year. Mayawati is to serve as chief minister for the first six months, after which she will step down and transfer power to the BJP. The coalition agreement is for one year, after which alliance between the two parties will be reevaluated.**

29   A week after seven Hindu families are killed by separatists, 3,000 additional police are deployed in Kashmir. The government directs the soldiers to keep panic-stricken Hindus from fleeing the valley.

April 1997

8   **The Delhi High Court rules against the charges of corruption and criminal conspiracy leveled by the CBI against L.K. Advani and V.C. Shukla in the Jain Hawala case.**

9   In Delhi, Minister of External Affairs I.K. Gujral and Gohar Ayub Khan, the Pakistani foreign minister, hold an "ice breaking" meeting. The purpose of the 90-minute meeting is to create an atmosphere conducive to future dialogue, particularly on Jammu and Kashmir. A future meeting is promised between the two in Islamabad.

10   The United Front and the Congress(I) resume talks after a meeting held on the previous day fails to produce a consensus.

11   **Prime Minister Deve Gowda loses a vote of confidence in the Lok Sabha, and submits his resig-**

nation, as well as those of his Council of Ministers, to President Shankar Dayal Sharma. Deve Gowda agrees to remain as caretaker prime minister and recommends that the Lok Sabha not be dissolved.

Parties agree to take up the budget during a three-day session beginning on April 21. The budget must be approved by May 15.

19   **The United Front chooses Minister of External Affairs I.K. Gujral to form the new government. Three days later, he wins a vote of confidence in the Lok Sabha.**

27   **The CBI decides that it will pursue the prosecution of Laloo Prasad Yadav, the chief minister of Bihar. He is accused of being involved in a Rs.950 crore fodder scam, in which money from the Bihar animal husbandry department was used to purchase fodder and medicine for cattle in nonexistent "animal cooperatives." The embezzlement, which was first discovered in 1994, had been going on for more than a decade.**

29   Citing its concern for the country's political stability, the Tamil Maanila Congress agrees to join the United Front.

May 1997

1   The United States charges India with failure to implement its obligations under the trade-related intellectual property agreement, and places it on a "priority-watch" list.

6   **A court in Delhi orders that charges be brought against former prime minister P.V. Narasimha Rao, along with nineteen others, in**

the Jharkhand Mukti Morcha bribery case. The twenty are charged with corruption and criminal conspiracy.

7   In Sivakasi, in southern Tamil Nadu, the police open fire on a crowd of 10,000 people who have gathered to protest caste discrimination. Three people are killed and two are injured.

8   Sonia Gandhi enrolls as a primary member of the Congress(I).

12   During a SAARC summit in the Maldives, I.K. Gujral and Nawaz Sharif hold a meeting. It is the first time in four years that Indian and Pakistani prime ministers have held talks. The two agree to create joint working groups, which will work on a range of issues agreed upon by the Foreign Ministers of the two countries.

16   In the Lok Sabha, argument ensues over the fate of a bill to reserve one-third of the seats in the Lok Sabha and state assemblies for women. Opponents of the bill, including the Janata Dal and the Samajwadi Party, argue that the bill needs provisions for Muslims and OBCs. The Speaker of the Lok Sabha, P.A. Sangma, moves the bill for consideration, but defers it to the next session.

Violence ensues in Madurai during protests against the defacing of a statue of Ambedkar in Valliyoor. An attempt by the Tamil Nadu government to end the recent caste violence in the southern districts fails when its offer to divide the Veeran Sundaralingam Transport Corporation is rejected.

29   M. Karunanidhi, Tamil Nadu chief minister, visits several districts in the southern part of the state. He promises an additional 1 million rupees (10 lakh) in

relief aid to those affected by the recent caste violence. A total of Rs.2.8. million (28 lakh) have already been distributed.

29   Prime Minister Gujral announces that due to the high price of oil the cost of various petroleum products will soon increase.

June 1997

5   Prime Minister Gujral and Nepali Prime Minister Lokendra Bahadur Chand hold a series of meetings in Kathmandu. Five agreements are signed, including a Memorandum of Understanding on civil aviation and an agreement that will facilitate the activities of companies in the development of hydropower projects in Nepal.

10   In Patna, Ranchi, and Calcutta, the CBI raids eight buildings in connection with the Laloo Prasad Yadav fodder scam. The owners of the buildings are present at the raids and are taken into custody to be interrogated.

12   **Sitaram Kesri is elected president of the Congress(I), soundly defeating Sharad Pawar and Rajesh Pilot, the two other candidates.**

13   In a fire in the Uphaar Grand Cinema in New Delhi, at least sixty people are killed.

20   Two explosions, one in Sadar Bazaar and the other in Chandni Chowk, occur in North Delhi.

23   After four days of talks in Islamabad, the foreign secretaries of India and Pakistan issue a joint statement. In it they agree to discuss the issues that currently stand between the two countries, including economic and commercial cooperation, terrorism, and Jammu and Kashmir. The decision to discuss Jammu

and Kashmir is the first formal renewal of dialogue on the subject since the Simla Agreement of 1972.

Laloo Prasad Yadav refuses to resign as chief minister of Bihar, despite the leveling of charges brought against him by the CBI in connection with the fodder scam case. The charges come two days after the CBI raids the home of the Bihari chief minister, as well as the residences of his two brothers-in-law. Fifty-five others are charged with involvement in the case.

24   Paramilitary troops are sent into Bihar in reaction to the filing of charges against Laloo Prasad Yadav, and his refusal to resign as chief minister.

26   Laloo Prasad Yadav reiterates that he will not resign, claiming that the fodder-scam charges are an attempt by politicians, in conjunction with the CBI, to destabilize his government.

India declares its chemical stockpiles and production facilities, fulfilling its obligations under the CWC.

29   M.V. Bhaskara Rao, former director general of police, launches a "third front" in Andhra Pradesh. He announces that his new party, Andhra Nadu, will work for the backward classes, SCs, STs, and other minorities.

30   Joginder Singh is removed as director of the CBI and is posted as special secretary in the Union Home Ministry. He is succeeded by Special Director R.C. Sharma.

July 1997

2   India and Pakistan renew their agreement to exchange advance information on flooding rivers.

Until October 10, India will supply Pakistan with news on the state of five rivers that flow into the country.

3   The pro–Laloo Prasad Yadav faction in the Janata Dal boycotts internal elections to select the party's next president. Yadav calls the party elections a "farce." In Karnataka, several Janata Dal members abstain from voting, despite threats from J.H. Patel that he will call for disciplinary action against those who boycott the elections. Sharad Yadav appeals to party members not to precipitate a split in the Janata Dal.

4   The families of the tourists taken hostage by Al-Faran in 1995 travel to Srinagar on the anniversary of the kidnappings. They appeal to Al-Faran to give them information on the four remaining hostages.

One million bank employees go on a one-day strike to protest the creation of Local Area Banks.

6   **Laloo Prasad Yadav splits the Janata Dal when he announces the formation of a new party, the Rashtriya Janata Dal. The BJP asks President Shankar Dayal Sharma to dismiss Yadav's government.**

11   Following the vandalism of a statue of Ambedkar in Bombay, crowds protest violently. Police respond with gunfire, killing 10 people and injuring another 34. Chief Minister Manohar Joshi announces that an inquiry into the incident will be conducted. The next day, a *bandh* is called by opposition parties to protest the police actions. In fresh violence and police firings, at least 7 people are injured and 1 person is killed.

13   In Bombay, a mass funeral is held for the 10 people

killed by police during protests by *dalits*. Several *dalit* politicians are attacked by their membership for not providing adequate leadership to their supporters.

15   With the help of the JMM(M) and the JMM(S), as well as several independents, Laloo Prasad Yadav demonstrates his majority in the Bihar State Assembly. The Janata Dal, as well as several Left parties in the United Front, announce that they will continue to seek the resignation of the chief minister.

17   **Vice-President K.R. Narayan wins the election for president, defeating T.N. Seshan, his only rival for the position. Narayan receives the largest number of votes in a presidential election in more than forty years.**

24   The Patna High Court rejects the anticipatory bail petition of Laloo Prasad Yadav.

25   **Hours after a court issues an arrest warrant against him, Laloo Prasad Yadav resigns as chief minister. Rabri Devi, Yadav's wife, is immediately sworn in as the new chief minister.**

August 1997

1   Lieutenant General Ved Prakash Malik becomes the new chief of the army staff. He replaces General Shankar Roychowdhury, who retires from the army on September 30.

A New Delhi court orders framing of charges against Sharad Yadav, president of the Janata Dal, for his participation in the Jain Hawala case. The decision comes a day before commencement of the Janata Dal's two-day national convention. Sharad Yadav announces that he intends to retain his position as party president. This is acceptable, despite the charges pending, because he holds only a party position, and no other public office.

6   Prime Minister I.K. Gujral is forced to withdraw the Insurance Regulatory Authority Bill from the Lok Sabha due to strong opposition from the BJP and the Left parties. The bill seeks to regulate the insurance industry. It is opposed by both the BJP and the Left because it is seen as a privatization initiative: the BJP opposes the entry of foreign companies into the sector, and the Left opposes private companies being included.

10   **Elections to the Congress Working Committee (CWC) are held in Calcutta. Sonia Gandhi attends the events and addresses the crowd, fueling speculation that she may be ready to actively participate in the party. Those elected to leadership positions include Jitendra Prasad, Rajesh Pilot, and Madhavrao Scindia. No women, SCs, or STs are elected to the organization. However, Sitaram Kesri, the Congress(I) president, nominates ten members from these groups in order to make the CWC more representative of the population as a whole.**

Three states experience bomb blasts. In Tamil Nadu, at least 12 people are injured in four separate explosions. In Assam, an explosion derails a train on a section of the Northwest Frontier Railway. In Andhra Pradesh, a blast injures 14 policemen.

17   **Krishna Kant, governor of Andhra Pradesh, wins the election for vice president.**

I.K. Gujral suggests that during her visit to India in October, Queen Elizabeth should not travel to Amritsar, the site of both the Golden Temple and Jallianwalla Bagh.

21   It appears that a consensus has been reached among various members of the government vis-à-vis a rise in the price of petroleum products after a meeting of the United Front Core Committee members at the residence of Prime Minister Gujral. However, a decision will be made only after the special session of Parliament ends on August 29.

26   A four-day special session of Parliament commences to create an agenda for the next millenium. The various challenges facing the country, including the criminalization of politics, are to be discussed.

September 1997

1   The central government announces price increases of diesel fuel, petrol, and cooking gas that range from 20 to 50 percent. The increase is expected to generate more than Rs.9,000 crore in the next year. The price hikes come after a six-month political debate, in which the opposition and the allies of the United Front, and the Communist Party in particular, disagree with the need for any increase.

6   Mother Theresa dies in Calcutta.

In Bihar, members of the banned Maoist Communist Centre (MCC) kill 15 CPI(M-L) activists.

Security forces in Nagaland extend a unilateral cease-fire to all insurgent groups in the state by another 60 days.

9   **A Lucknow court files charges against 49 people in connection with the 1992 destruction of the Babri Masjid. Those charged include Bal Thackeray and several senior BJP leaders, including L.K. Advani and Kalyan Singh.**

15 Police in Assam arrest S.S. Dogra, general manager of Northern Indian Plantations, which belongs to the Tata Tea Company. He is charged with aiding and abetting ULFA members.

16 The third round of India and Pakistan foreign secretary-level talks begins in New Delhi.

20 **Mayawati resigns as the chief minister of Uttar Pradesh. The next day, Kalyan Singh is sworn in as the new chief minister. Under a BJP-BSP coalition agreement, Singh's government will be in power for the next six months.**

25 In Delhi, former prime minister Narasimha Rao and 19 others are formally charged in connection with the JMM bribery case; they plead their innocence in court.

 The Assam government denies press reports that several of its ministers have connections to ULFA. The government promises action against anyone linked to the banned organization.

30 At least 20 civilians are killed and 30 injured in firing between Indian and Pakistani troops in Kashmir.

October 1997

7 The British High Commissioner in India announces that Queen Elizabeth will not apologize for the 1919 Jallianwalla Bagh massacre. However, during her visit to Amritsar, she will lay a wreath at the site as a gesture of respect.

14 Queen Elizabeth and Prince Philip visit Amritsar.

19 **Condemning his "anti-*dalit*" policies, the**

Bahujan Samaj Party withdraws its support from Kalyan Singh. Singh asserts that he will seek a vote of confidence in the State Assembly. Two days later, with the help of several United Front members who defect to the BJP, Kalyan Singh wins a majority for his government in the Uttar Pradesh Assembly.

21   Citing the need to increase investments, catalyze the economy, and maintain price stability, the Reserve Bank of India ceased controls on interest and deposit rates.

22   **After President K.R. Narayan refuses to implement the cabinet's recommendation to impose President's Rule in Uttar Pradesh, the United Front government reverses its decision on the need for central control of the state.**

24   Prime Minister Gujral attends the Commonwealth Summit in Edinburgh, Scotland.

27   The governor of Gujarat invites Dilip Parikh, leader of the Rashtriya Janata Party, to form a new state government after Congress withdraws its support from Shankarsinh Waghela.

29   Assam closes all routes leading to its border with Bhutan, citing its need to keep insurgents from entering the state.

November 1997

4   **The trial of the twenty suspects accused in the Jharkhand Mukti Morcha bribery case begins. Shailendra Mahato, who has been granted a pardon, serves as the main prosecution witness.**

5   The Steering Committee meeting of the United Front begins: one of the main issues on the agenda

is tightening the antidefection laws of the various parties. It is suggested that defectors from political parties be forced to demonstrate that they can be elected under the banner of the party they have joined.

6   The central government grants several chosen public sector banks greater administrative autonomy, particularly with regard to hiring and posting job vacancies in management positions. Banks that meet various liquidity and stability criteria are affected by the decision.

8   The weekly newsmagazine *India Today* publishes excerpts from the Jain Commission report implicating the DMK in the assassination of Rajiv Gandhi. In the report, the DMK is accused of collaborating with the LTTE to assassinate the former prime minister. The DMK denies any allegations of involvement with the LTTE, and Congress claims that it is "totally united" behind the present leadership.

10   Kashmiri Chief Minister Farooq Abdullah reiterates his position that he will not hold talks with any separatist organizations in the state.

13   The Rashtriya Janata Party and Dilip Parikh survive a vote of confidence in the Gujarat Assembly with the help of the Congress(I).

19   India and the United States enter into an Investment and Incentive Agreement. The purpose of the Agreement is to better protect U.S. investments in India.

20   **The interim report of the Jain Commission is tabled in both the Rajya and Lok Sabha. The Congress(I) announces that its continued support for the United Front hinges entirely on the**

immediate removal of the DMK ministers from the government. Tamil Nadu Chief Minister Karunanidhi asserts that the Jain Commission report is "politically motivated." He continues to deny both the truth of the allegations and the need that he and his ministers leave the government. I.K. Gujral is reluctant to demand ousting of the DMK. In retaliation, the Congress parliamentary ministers prevent any other issues from being discussed in either the Upper or the Lower House.

28   After Congress(I) withdraws support from the United Front, Prime Minister Gujral submits his resignation, as well as his cabinet's, to President Narayanan. Soon after, the various parties that made up the ruling coalition approach the president to announce that they will not support a Congress or BJP-led government.

December 1997

1   At least 60 people in Bihar are killed by members of the Ranbir Sena, a private army of landowners. The killings occur when more than 300 Sena members enter the village of Lakshmanpur-Bate, drag from their homes people who they suspect of being supporters of the CPI(M-L), and shoot them.

4   President Narayanan dissolves the Lok Sabha and calls for fresh elections. He orders that a new house be constituted by March 15, 1998.

The World Bank earmarks a loan for Haryana worth Rs.2,350 crore.

11   The World Bank approves more than two billion rupees in aid for a forestry project in Uttar Pradesh,

as well as another four hundred million rupees for an environmental protection initiative in Gujarat.

17   The BJP and the AIADMK agree to contest together Lok Sabha elections from Tamil Nadu and Pondicherry.

The fight over the Shiv Sena between Chief Election Commissioner M.S. Gill and Election Commissioner G.V.G. Krishnamurthy ends, with the latter returning from his leave to resume his job.

22   Congress rebel Mamata Banerjee is expelled from the party in West Bengal after she announces that she will contest the upcoming Lok Sabha elections under the banner of a different party, the Trinamul Congress.

25   Governor Krishna Pal Singh dissolves the Gujarat Assembly. The Congress(I) asks for President's Rule to be imposed, while the BJP requests that it be allowed to attempt to form a government.

29   **Sonia Gandhi decides to campaign for the Congress Party in the upcoming Lok Sabha elections.**

Glossary

Some Common Abbreviations

AIADMK: All-India Anna Dravida Munnetra Kazhagam
AGP: Asom Gana Parishad [Assam People's Party]
BJP: Bharatiya Janata Party
BSP: Bahujan Samaj Party
CBI: Central Bureau of Investigation
CPI: Communist Party of India
DMK: Dravida Munnetra Kazhagam
JKLF: Jammu and Kashmir Liberation Front
JPC: Joint Parliamentary Committee
LTTE: Liberation Tigers of Tamil Eelam
NRI: Nonresident Indian
OBC: Other Backward Classes
PWG: People's War Group
RBI: Reserve Bank of India
RSS: Rashtriya Swayamsevak Sangh
SAARC: South Asian Association for Regional Cooperation
SC/ST: Scheduled Castes/Scheduled Tribes
SJP: Samajwadi Janata Party
SP: Samajwadi [Socialist] Party
TADA: Terrorist and Disruptive Activities (Prevention) Act
VHP: Vishwa Hindu Parishad

Akali Dal. The major party of the Sikhs, it has governed the state of Punjab on a number of occasions, most recently since February 1997. In 1998, it joined the BJP-led coalition government in Delhi.

All-India Anna Dravida Munnetra Kazhagam (AIADMK). Tamil nationalist party in the state of Tamil Nadu led by Jayalalitha, one of the most powerful women in Indian politics. In alliance with the BJP, it won a sweeping victory in the 1998 parliamentary election in Tamil Nadu and joined the BJP-led coalition government.

Arya Samaj. Literally, "society of the Aryans"; a movement of "protestant" Hinduism founded by Dayanand Saraswati in 1875. Rejecting, among other things, the "accretions" to the Vedas of caste, idol-worship, and ritual, it campaigned also for the "re-conversion" of Muslims and others to Hinduism. Its greatest strength has been in the Punjab.

Ascriptive hierarchy. One that is assigned to groups on the basis of "birth" as opposed to one that results from the actions of the groups.

Ayodhya. A small city in east-central Uttar Pradesh believed to be the birthplace of Ram (or Rama, the god-king who is the hero of the *Ramayana*) and site of the disputed Babri mosque/Ram temple shrine. The mosque was demolished on December 6, 1992, provoking widespread rioting and a major political crisis.

Babri mosque/Ram temple (Babri Masjid/Ramjanmabhoomi). Literally, "Mosque of Babur/Birthground of Ram." Ram (or Rama), an avatar of the god Vishnu and the hero of the Ramayana, is believed to have been born in Ayodhya on a particular spot of ground on which a mosque was believed to have been built by the Mughal emperor Babur (r. 1526–30). The mosque was demolished on December 6, 1992, and a shrine to Ram was installed on the site.

Bajrang Dal. Militant youth organization associated with the Rashtriya Swayamsevak Sangh.

Bhadralok. Literally, the "respectable people" in Bengal; the superior social elite, distinguished by their "refined" culture, drawn from— but not the same as—the upper castes of Bengal.

Bhakti. The devotional tradition of Hinduism, originating as a movement in southern India in the 6th century and proceeding northward and lasting in full force until the 16th century. In contrast to Vedic-origin, Sanskritic Hinduism, the poet-saints of this tradition emphasize personal devotion to God.

Bharatiya Janata Party (BJP). Party formed from the Janata Party by elements of the Jana Sangh, with support mainly in northern India. It favors a Hindu nationalist ideology, but its appeal has also been derived from a reputation for discipline and integrity of its core leaders. At present the largest single party in Parliament, and the core party of the governing coalition, it received 25 percent of the vote in the 1998 election. Its strength is greatest in the western and northern states of Delhi, Gujarat, Himachal Pradesh, Madhya Pradesh, Maharashtra, Rajasthan, and Uttar Pradesh.

Congress Party. The dominant Indian national party since independence, it formed the government after the 1991 elections. In the parliamentary elections of 1996 and 1998, it lost strength both in terms of seats and vote share—in 1998, its vote share (25 percent) equaled that of the BJP. Also known as the Congress(I), the name of the faction created by a party split in 1977 and initially led by Indira Gandhi (the "I" stands for Indira).

Congress(I). See Congress Party.

Crore. Ten million (10,000,000).

Dalit. Literally, "oppressed" or "ground down," the term for people of the Scheduled Caste preferred by militant and educated ex-untouchables and by many of those who sympathize with their aspirations.

Dharamkosa. Literally, "dictionary of [the Hindu] religion"

Dharmashastras. Sacred texts of legal and moral materials, the best known being the "Laws of Manu."

Dravida Munnetra Kazhagam (DMK). Tamil nationalist party led by M. Karunanidhi, who served as chief minister of Tamil Nadu from 1969 to 1976, 1989–90, and 1996–.

Dwija. Literally "twice born," it refers to the rite of passage of admission to study of the Veda; the *brahmin, kshatriya,* and *vaishya varnas.*

Emergency. Declared by the Indira Gandhi government in June 1975, it lasted 21 months; opposition leaders were jailed, press censorship imposed, and the constitution amended to restrict the judiciary. It ended with the defeat of Indira Gandhi in the 1977 election.

Five-Year Plans. Formulated by the Planning Commission and approved by parliament, these plans analyzed the economic situation of the country and set broad goals and specific guidelines for investment and other economic policy, for both public and private sectors.

Gandhi, Indira. Daughter of Jawaharlal Nehru and prime minister from 1966 to 1977 and from 1980 to 1984, when she was assassinated by her own Sikh bodyguards.

Gandhi, Mohandas K. The preeminent leader of India's fight against British colonial rule from 1919 until independence. He was assassinated in January 1948 by a Hindu nationalist fanatic. Also known as Mahatma Gandhi and Gandhiji.

Gandhi, Rajiv. Son of Indira Gandhi and prime minister from 1984 to 1989 when the Congress Party lost the parliamentary election. He was assassinated on May 21, 1991, while campaigning in Tamil Nadu.

Garibi hatao. Literally, "remove poverty"; the slogan Indira Gandhi adopted in the 1971 election she won in a landslide, as the counter to the opposition's slogan, "Remove Indira."

Godmen. People who make a profession of being religious leaders (with the definite flavor of "insincere").

Green Revolution. The transformation of agriculture beginning in the mid-1960s based on the development of high-yielding varieties of wheat and rice, the adoption of necessary modern practices of irrigation, and of fertilizer and pesticide use.

Guru-sishya parampara. The traditional system (*parampara*) of education in which the teacher (*guru*) takes on a disciple-student (*sishya*).

Harijan. Literally, "people of God," the name Mohandas K. Gandhi used for the Scheduled Castes. See also *dalit*.

Hindutva. Literally, "Hindu-ness," the term was used as the title of a book written in 1922 by Hindu nationalist leader V.D. Savarkar to argue that Hindus were a nation. It is now used as the equivalent of "Hindu nationalism."

Jajmani. A formalized patron-client system in which serving families performed certain duties (e.g., barbering) for patron families, typically in return for a guaranteed amount from the patron's harvest plus other goods, such as clothing.

Jammu and Kashmir Liberation Front (JKLF). Militant group fighting for the independence of Kashmir.

Jana Sangh. Properly the "Bharatiya [Indian] Jana [People's] Sangh [Party]," founded in 1951 with an ideology of Hindu nationalism, it developed strength in west and north India. It reemerged as the present-day BJP (Bharatiya Janata Party) after merging with other parties to form the Janata Party in the crucible of the 1977 elections that ended the Emergency rule of Indira Gandhi.

Janata Dal. A party formed from the Jan Morcha, the Janata Party, factions of the Lok Dal, and a Congress splinter known as the Congress(S). It had 141 of the 144 seats held by the National Front in the Lok Sabha elected in 1989 that formed the government led by V.P. Singh. The party split in November 1990, but defeated an incumbent Congress government in Karnataka in November 1994. Led by Chief Minister Laloo Prasad Yadav, it won reelection in Bihar in March 1995. The Janata Dal Orissa government was defeated in the March 1995 election.

Jati. Caste or subcaste that defines acceptable interactions in marriage, dining, and other caste-related practices.

Jharkhand. The region of east-central India (covering parts of the states of Madhya Pradesh, Andhra Pradesh, Orissa, and West Bengal, but mainly the southern segment of Bihar) in which various tribal people live. Name given to the state or autonomous region sought by those people.

Kanyakumari. The southern tip of India (formerly Cape Comorin).

Khadi. Hand-spun, hand-woven cloth (mainly cotton). Popularized by Gandhi during the nationalist movement as a direct statement of self-reliance, and a badge of membership in the Congress movement, its production has been subsidized by the government after independence (and it is still worn by Congress politicians and Gandhian movement workers).

Lakh. One hundred thousand (100,000).

Liberation Tigers of Tamil Eelam. Sri Lankan Tamil militant group, which is urging a guerrilla war for a separate state for Sri Lankan Tamils in the northern and eastern sections of the island.

Linguistic states. Most of India's states had their boundaries fixed on a linguistic basis in 1956, with the overwhelming majority of the people of each state—and subsequent ones as well—speaking one language. In the larger states, with the exception of Hindi-speakers, who reside in six major states, almost all the speakers of a given language are resident in the state associated with that language.

Lok Sabha. Lower house of India's bicameral parliament. Equivalent to the British House of Commons, all but 3 of its 545 members are directly elected from district constituencies for a five-year maximum term.

Mahabharata. One of two major epics of India, it describes the internecine warfare that results from the a feud of succession involving descendants of the legendary king Bharata.

Mandal Commission. The common name—from its chairman, B.P. Mandal—of the Backward Classes Commission. The Mandal Commission report published in 1980 proposed far-reaching governmental regulations to increase the employment of "backward" classes.

National Front. An electoral alliance composed of the Janata Dal, DMK, Telugu Desam, and AGP, it formed the government headed by V.P. Singh after the 1989 election.

Naxalite. A revolutionary or radical activist ready to adopt violent means. The name comes from participants in a rebellion in Naxalbari, West Bengal, in 1967.

Nehru, Jawaharlal. Nationalist leader who served as prime minister from 1947 until his death in 1964.

Other Backward Classes (OBCs). "Backward" classes other than the Scheduled Castes and Scheduled Tribes. Typically defined in caste terms, to mean the non-elite, non-untouchable *jatis.*

Panchayat. Literally, a council of five. A village or *jati* council. The Panchayati raj system of rural local self-government introduced in 1959 was entrenched in the constitution as the 73rd amendment in 1993, with institutions at village, block, and district levels now exercising significantly enhanced political and financial powers.

Pandava. The five brothers who are the heroes of the *Mahabharata* epic.

Planning Commission. Government body that prepares five-year plans, which provide a broad framework for public and private economic goals.

President. In India, the equivalent of a constitutional monarch, who gives formal assent to bills but whose powers are severely restricted. Elected by members of parliament and the state legislatures for a five-year term.

President's Rule. Suspension of a state's assembly and direct rule of the state by the central government through the centrally appointed governor, typically when the state government loses its majority or is deemed unable to govern due to a "disturbed" political situation. It has sometimes been used by the center to topple opposition-controlled state governments.

Rajya Sabha. Upper House of India's bicameral parliament. All but 6 of its 256 members are elected by the legislatures of the states for staggered six-year terms. Roughly equivalent in power to Britain's House of Lords.

Ramayana. One of two major epics in India, it described the adventures of Rama, a warrior-king and the incarnation of the god Vishnu.

Rashtriya Swayamsevak Sangh (RSS). Literally, "National Volunteer Association"; militant Hindu organization founded in 1925 and associated with the Bharatiya Janata Party, the Vishwa Hindu Parishad, and the Bajrang Dal—the members of the "Sangh parivar" (RSS family). The RSS draws its membership mainly from urban and lower-middle class and seeks the consolidation of a Hindu nation.

Reservation. The provision for quotas in legislative bodies, civil services, educational institutions, and other public institutions, typically in proportion to the percentage in the population, for qualified members of Scheduled Castes and Scheduled Tribes, and, in some places, for Other Backward Classes.

Sabha. Literally an "assembly," it also is extended to mean "association."

Samiti. Literally a "committee," it usually refers to an organization, typically a voluntary organization.

Sanskritization. A term coined by the eminent social anthropologist M.N. Srinivas to describe the process of upward social mobility in which a *jati* gives up certain practices considered to be polluting, and adopts other practices usually associated with upper castes, such as vegetarianism.

Saurashtra. The western part of the state of Gujarat.

Savarnas. Literally, "of the same *varna* (caste-cluster)."

Scheduled Castes and Scheduled Tribes (SCs/STs). The "schedule" refers to a list of untouchable, or Harijan, castes and tribes drawn up under the 1935 Government of India Act and subsequently revised. Legislative seats as well as government posts and places in educational institutions are reserved for members of these castes and tribes.

Shiv Sena. Militant nativist communal organization, it was founded in Bombay in 1966 to agitate against South Indian immigrants to the state of Maharashtra. Alleged to have played a major part in the riots in December 1992 and January 1993 in Bombay, following the demolition of the Babri mosque. In alliance with the BJP, it won the March 1995 elections in Maharashtra.

Sikh, Sikhism. The religion of Sikhism was founded in the 16th century by the first guru, Nanak, drawing on Hindu devotionalism and Islam. Persecuted by the later Mughal emperors, Sikhs developed into a martial community, led by the tenth and last guru, Gobind Singh. A Sikh kingdom in central Punjab was defeated by the British in the mid-19th century.

Shramanic. Having to with the (traditional) four stages of life for the "twice born."

South Asian Association for Regional Cooperation (SAARC). Organization formed in 1985 to enhance regional cooperation in social, economic, and cultural development. The SAARC members are Bangladesh, Bhutan, India, the Maldives, Nepal, Pakistan, and Sri Lanka.

Swadeshi. Literally, "[one's] own country." A nationalist slogan in the early 20th century that asked Indians to boycott foreign goods, especially cloth, in favor of Indian manufactures. More recently used to indicate an ideology of economic self-reliance.

Tantric. Possibly as old as Hinduism itself, but also a strand of Buddhist belief and practice, tantrism is a significant system of belief. However, it is popularly associated with "dark" practices, particularly erotic ones, confined to certain sects.

Terrorism and Disruptive Activities (Prevention) Act (TADA). Intended for use in Punjab in the mid-1980s and allowed to lapse in May 1995, this law permitted extended preventive detention and secret testimony (to protect witnesses under threat from terrorists) and required those charged of certain crimes to prove their innocence, among other provisions. Extended to almost all states, it was widely abused by police and state governments and strongly criticized by both Indian and foreign human rights organizations, including the chair of the Indian Human Rights Commission.

Ustad. A "master" or "teacher" in the Muslim tradition; the most common title of a Muslim musician.

Vale of Kashmir. Also the Kashmir Valley. The spectacularly beautiful valley of the river Jhelum, a part of the Indian state of Jammu and Kashmir (the other major regions being Buddhist-dominated Ladakh and Hindu-dominated Jammu, with other areas claimed by India now controlled by Pakistan and China), which is populated almost entirely by Muslims. The political heartland of the state.

Varnas. The four "castes" of textual Hinduism—*brahmin* (priests), *kshatriya* (warriors), *vaishya* (merchants, farmers), and *shudras* (workers serving the families of the other *varnas*). At present, a categorization into which various *jatis* are placed; thus "caste clusters."

Vishwa Hindu Parishad (VHP). A movement seeking to reinvigorate Hinduism. Leader of Hindu sentiment and organizer of actions regarding the Babri mosque/Ram temple controversy, although precisely what its responsibility was for the demolition of the mosque is not clear.

Vote-banks. In early postindependence analysis of politics, a body of citizens of a particular caste or community whose votes a leader could reliably deliver. Now in more popular usage, castes, caste groupings, or religious communities that tend to vote similarly, for one party or the other.

Washington consensus. Arrived at by the Washington-based international institutions, the World Bank, and the International Monetary Fund. It advocates free trade, balanced budget, and privatization for efficiency and growth, and also argues that growth will help the poor.

Yadav. An agrarian (cowherd) caste of the Gangetic plain, it forms a substantial bloc within the "backward" castes; leaders of the community have governed as chief ministers of Uttar Pradesh and Bihar.

Suggestions for Further Readings and Websites

Readings

Politics

Khilnani, Sunil. *The Idea of India*. New York: Farrar, Strauss, Giroux, 1998.

Kaviraj, Sudipta, ed. *Politics in India*. Oxford in India Readings in Sociology and Social Anthropology. Delhi: Oxford University Press, 1997.

Chatterjee, Partha, ed. *State and Politics in India*. Delhi: Oxford University Press, 1997.

Kothari, Rajni. *Politics in India*. Boston, MA: Little Brown, 1970.

Economy

Chakravarty, S. *Development Planning: The Indian Experience*. Oxford: Clarendon Press, 1987.

Jalan, Bimal, ed. *The Indian Economy: Problems and Prospects*. New Delhi: Penguin Books India (P) Ltd., Viking, 1992.

Parikh, Kirit S., ed. *Indira Gandhi Institute of Development Research, Mumbai, India Development Report—1997*. New Delhi: Oxford University Press, 1997.

Srinivasan, T.N., ed. *Agriculture and Trade in China and India: Policies and Performance since 1950*. San Francisco, CA: San Francisco International Center for Economic Growth, 1994.

Society

Ambedkar, B.R. *Who Were the Shudras?* Bombay: Thacker & Co. Ltd., 1946.

Beteille, Andre. *Caste, Class, and Power: Changing Patterns of Stratification in a Tanjore Village*. Bombay: Oxford University Press, and Berkeley, CA: University of California Press, 1966.

Gould, Harold A. *Politics and Caste: The Hindu Caste System*, Vol. 3. New Delhi: Chanakya Publications, 1990.

Jayaraman, R. *Caste and Class: Dynamics of Inequality in Indian Society*. New Delhi: Hindustan Publishing Corporation (India), 1981.

Khare, R.S. *The Untouchable As Himself: Ideology, Identity, and Pragmatism among the Lucknow Chamars*. Cambridge, MA: Cambridge University Press, 1984.

Kolenda, Pauline. *Caste in Contemporary India: Beyond Organic Solidarity*. Jaipur: Rawat Publications, 1984.

Lohia, Rammanohar. *The Caste System*. Hyderabad: Rammanohar Lohia Samata Vidyalaya Nyas, 1964.

Malik, S.C., ed. *Determinants of Social Status in India*. Shimla: Indian Institute of Advanced Study, and Delhi: Motilal Banarsidass, 1986.

Ram, Jagjivan. *Caste Challenge in India*. New Delhi: Vision Books (P) Ltd., 1980.

Sinha, Sachchidanand. *Caste System: Myths, Reality, Challenge*. New Delhi: Intellectual Publishing House, 1982.

Foreign Relations

Barnds, William J. *India, Pakistan and the Great Powers*. New York: Praeger, 1972.

Gopal, S. *Jawaharlal Nehru*. Cambridge, MA: Harvard University Press, 1979.

Gould, Harold A. and Sumit Ganguly, eds. *The Hope and the Reality: U.S.-Indian Relations from Roosevelt to Reagan*. Boulder: Westview Press, 1992.

Heimsath, Charles H. and Surjit Mansingh. *A Diplomatic History of Modern India*. Bombay: Allied Publishers, 1971.

Kux, Dennis. *Estranged Democracies: India and the United States, 1941–1991.* Washington: National Defense University, 1993.

Lamb, Alastair. *Kashmir: A Disputed Legacy.* Hertingfordbury, Hertfordshire, England: Roxford Books, 1991.

Mansingh, Surjit. *India's Search for Power.* New Delhi: Sage Publications, 1984.

Maxwell, Neville. *India's China War.* New York: Pantheon Books, 1970.

McMahon, Robert J. *The Cold War on the Periphery.* New York: Columbia University Press, 1994.

Nanda, B.R., ed. *Indian Foreign Policy: The Nehru Years.* Honolulu: University Press of Hawaii, 1976.

Nehru, Jawaharlal. *India's Foreign Policy.* New Delhi: Government of India Ministry of Information and Broadcasting, 1961.

Schaffer, Howard B. *Chester Bowles: New Dealer in the Cold War.* Cambridge, MA: Harvard University Press, 1993.

Wirsing, Robert. *India, Pakistan. and the Kashmir Dispute.* New York: St. Martin's Press, 1994.

Culture

Banga, Indu, and Jaidev, eds. *Cultural Reorientation in Modern India.* Shimla: Indian Institute of Advanced Studies, 1996.

Joshi, P.C. *Culture, Communication and Social Change.* Delhi: Vikash Publishing House, 1989.

Singh, B.P. *India's Culture: The State, the Arts and Beyond.* Delhi: Oxford University Press, 1998.

Sundar, Pushpa. *Patrons and Philistines: Arts and the State in British India.* Delhi: Oxford University Press, 1995.

Vatsyayan, Kapila. *Some Aspects of Cultural Policies in India.* Paris: UNESCO, 1971.

History and Politics

Dutta, Madhusree, Agnes Flavia, and Adarkar Neera, eds. *The Nation, the State and Indian Identity.* Delhi: Samya Publishers, 1996.

Gopal, Sarvepalli, ed. *Anatomy of a Confrontation*: *The Babri Masjid-Ram Janmabhumi Issue.* Delhi: Penguin Books, 1991.

Habib, Irfan. *Interpreting Indian History.* Shillong: North-Eastern Hill University Publications, 1988.

Lal, Vinay. "The Discourse of History and the Crisis at Ayodhya: Reflections on the Production of Knowledge, Freedom, and the Future of India." *Emergences*, nos. 5–6, 1993–94, pp. 4–44.

Nandy, Ashis. *The Intimate Enemy*: *Loss and Recovery of Self under Colonialism.* Delhi: Oxford University Press, 1983.

————, et al. *Creating a Nationality*: *The Ramjanmabhumi Movement and Fear of the Self.* Delhi: Oxford University Press, 1995.

Pandey, Gyanendra. *The Construction of Communalism in Colonial North India.* Delhi: Oxford University Press, 1990.

Thapar, Romila, Mukhia Romilar, and Chandra Bipan. *Communalism and the Writing of Indian History.* Delhi: People's Publishing House, 1969.

Websites

Comprehensive Gateways

SARAI: South Asian Resources Available on the Internet
http://www.columbia.edu/cu/libraries/indiv/area/sarai/

India Resources
http://www.clas.ufl.edu/users/gthursby/ind/index.htm

University of Texas Gateway
http://asnic.utexas.edu/asnic/countries/india/

CyberIndian Homepage
http://www.CyberIndian.com/index.htm

Government of India: Discover India
http://www.indiagov.org

Other Important Government of India Sites

National Informatics Centre
http://www.nic.in/

Census of India
http://www.censusindia.net/

Ministry of Finance
http://www.nic.in/finmin/

Specialized Sites

International Relations and Security Network
http://www.isn.ethz.ch/lase/

Journalists' Stylebook on South Asia (SAJA)
http://www.saja.org/stylebook.html

About the Contributors

Marshall M. Bouton is Executive Vice President of the Asia Society. He has spoken and consulted widely on Indian and South Asian affairs to companies, associations, and public groups. He is a frequent commentator on Indian and other Asian developments for the media, and he has been a regular guest on CNN's Business Asia. In 1996, he received the award of the Indo-American Society, Bombay, for his contributions to understanding and improving relations between the two countries. Bouton has coedited three editions of *India Briefing,* and is the author of *Agrarian Radicalism in South India* (Princeton University Press). His article "India's Problem Is Not Politics" appeared in the May/June 1998 edition of *Foreign Affairs.*

Vinay Lal is assistant professor of history at the University of California Los Angeles. He has published articles in three dozen periodicals on a wide variety of subjects, including Indian history, colonialism, popular cinema, the political culture of India, the Indian diaspora, and the politics of knowledge systems. He recently edited a special double issue of the journal *Emergences*, titled "Multiple Selves, Plural Worlds: Ashis Nandy and the Post-Columbian Future," and an old ethnographic classic, *The History of Railway Thieves.*

Philip Oldenburg is Associate Director of the Southern Asian Institute at Columbia University. He has published on topics of domestic and foreign policy in South Asia, including work on Indian electoral politics, rural development, and municipal government. His current research project is on the grass-roots foundations of state legitimacy in India.

Kirit S. Parikh is Founder Director and Vice Chancellor of Indira Gandhi Institute of Development Research (IGIDR), Bombay. He has been professor of economics since 1967, and is a member of the Economic Advisory Council of the Prime Minister of India. Parikh has published works on planning, water resource management, appropriate technology for housing, optimum requirement for fertilizers, energy systems, national and international policies for poverty reduction, trade policies, economic reforms, sustainable human development and environmental accounting, and general equilibrium modeling.

Howard B. Schaffer is a retired American Foreign Service Officer who spent much of his 36-year career with the State Department in dealing with U.S. relations with South Asia. He served as political counselor in India (1977–79) and Pakistan (1974–77), and as ambassador to Bangladesh (1984–87). He was twice Deputy Assistant Secretary of State responsible for South Asia. Ambassador Schaffer is presently Director of Studies at the Institute for the Study of Diplomacy, part of the School of Foreign Service at Georgetown University in Washington. He is the author of a biography of an American politician-diplomat, *Chester Bowles: New Dealer in the Cold War* (1993), which was issued in an Indian edition in 1994.

D.L. Sheth is Senior Fellow and former director of the Centre for the Study of Developing Societies (CSDS), Delhi. He was appointed Member (Social Scientist) to the National Commission for Backward Classes (1993–96). A political sociologist, Sheth has made important contributions to the study of society and politics in India, the politics of social issues and grass-roots movements. He is editor of *Citizens and Parties* (1975) and (with Ashis Nandy) *Multiverse of Democracy* (1996). Sheth is editor of the journal *Alternatives: Social Transformation and Humane Governance* and a founder member of Lokayan (Dialogue of the People). His current research is on changing social and cultural identities and the making of the middle class in India.

Shefali Trivedi is a Ph.D. candidate in the Department of Political Science at Columbia University.

Kapila Vatsyayan is Academic Director of the Indira Gandhi National Centre for the Arts (IGNCA). Among her publications, *The Square and the Circle of Indian Arts* is considered a new conceptual theoretical model for the study of Indian arts. Her works include *Classical Indian Dance in Literature and the Arts* (1968), *Ramayana and the Arts of Asia* (1975), and *Bharata—The Natyasastra* (1996). She has published numerous articles and papers on the various genres of dance in India and Indian dance scholarship, cultural policies in India, and various topics on art. In November 1998, she was given the 1998 Congress of Research on Dance award.

Yogendra Yadav is a fellow at the Centre for the Study of Developing Societies (CSDS), Delhi, and also the director of Lokniti: Institute for Comparative Democracy, a research program of the CSDS. He has written papers on political theory and Indian politics published in the *Economic and Political Weekly* and *Seminar*. He has directed a number of election related academic surveys undertaken by the CSDS in the last two years. These include the National Election Study, 1996 and 1998, which are among the largest academic surveys of election in the world. His special interests include psephology and politics of socialism. He is currently involved in running *Samayik Varta*, a non-commercial monthly political journal in Hindi.

Index